With a Diamond in My Shoe

SUNY series in Latin American and Iberian Thought and Culture
───────────
Jorge J. E. Gracia and Rosemary G. Feal, editors

With a Diamond in My Shoe

A Philosopher's Search for Identity in America

Jorge J. E. Gracia

On the cover: *Isla en crisis*, by Humberto Calzada, courtesy of the artist

Published by State University of New York Press, Albany

© 2019 State University of New York Press

All rights reserved

No part of this book may be used or reproduced in any manner whatsoever without written permission. No part of this book may be stored in a retrieval system or transmitted in any form or by any means including electronic, electrostatic, magnetic tape, mechanical, photocopying, recording, or otherwise without the prior permission in writing of the publisher.

For information, contact State University of New York Press, Albany, NY
www.sunypress.edu

Library of Congress Cataloging-in-Publication Data

Names: Gracia, Jorge J. E., author.
Title: With a diamond in my shoe : a philosopher's search for identity in
    America / Jorge J. E. Gracia.
Description: Albany : State University of New York Press, [2019] | Series:
    SUNY series in Latin American and Iberian thought and culture
Identifiers: LCCN 2019018550 | ISBN 9781438477275 (hardcover : alk. paper)
|
    ISBN 9781438477282 (pbk. : alk. paper) | ISBN 9781438477299 (ebk.)
Subjects: LCSH: Gracia, Jorge J. E. | Philosophers—United States—Biography. |
    Philosophy, Latin American. | Hispanic Americans—Ethnic identity.
Classification: LCC B945.G7274 A3 2019 | DDC 191 [B]—dc23
LC record available at https://lccn.loc.gov/2019018550

10 9 8 7 6 5 4 3 2 1

*For the United States and Canada,
the countries that gave me refuge in a moment of need,
and for Cuba,
where I was born and raised.*

Contents

List of Illustrations		ix
Prologue (2018)		xi
1	Farewell to Cuba (1961)	1
2	Good Morning, America (1961–1962)	15
3	Hungry in Miami (1961)	23
4	A Gate to the Real America (1962)	33
5	Foreigner in a Foreign Land (1962–1965)	45
6	Surviving Evangelical Fundamentalism (1962–1965)	57
7	Knowing Myself (1962–1965)	69
8	Make Love, Not War (1965–1966)	79
9	Becoming a Medievalist (1966–1969)	91
10	Pilgrimage to Europe (1969–1971)	103
11	Landing a Job, with Verve (1971)	115
12	Buffalo Department of Philosophy (1971–1973)	123
13	The Vocation and Profession of Philosophy (1975)	137
14	Two Alternative Research Programs (1971–1974)	151
15	Medieval Philosophy (1975–1985)	157

16	Latin American Philosophy in the United States (1939–1985)	165
17	From Rookie to Chair (1980–1986)	183
18	Beyond Medieval and Latin American Philosophy (1990–2000)	201
19	The Call of Ethnic, Racial, and National Identities (2000–present)	213
20	A Place for Literature and the Arts (2005–present)	225
21	From Hispanic to Latino and Latinx Philosophy (2000–present)	237
22	Return to Philosophy through Its History (1990–2000)	245
23	A Paradigm of Courage (1971–1976)	257
Epilogue: With a Diamond in My Mind		265
Acknowledgments		269

Illustrations

With my family in Cuba	xii
The diamond in my shoe	8
Appropriated Memories: Havana Harbor, Cuba (view of El Morro), by Alberto Rey	14
My Cuban passport photo, age eighteen	16
Wheaton College, in my room	36
Wedding day, reception at International House	88
Wearing the Pontifical Institute of Mediaeval Studies academic regalia	90
Spain, Salamanca, university, front view, 1905	104
On my sixth birthday with the beautiful mare Yegüita	112
Finally settled in Buffalo	125
Risieri Frondizi	171
With UB president William R. Greiner at the SUNY Distinguished Professors award ceremony	198
High school graduation day, with my mother, Leonila Gracia (Cuba 1960)	256
With Norma and grandchildren James Griffin, Clarisa Griffin, Sofia Taberski, and Eva Taberski	268

Prologue (2018)

This is the story of the American Dream becoming a reality, the story of a Cuban refugee who entered the United States on the day he turned nineteen, alone, without a supporting family, and with no knowledge of the English language or American culture. It is a story about identity, about a Cuban who, without forgetting his roots, became Canadian, American, Hispanic, Latino, and Latinx in order to survive and thrive. More concretely, it is an individual's search for identity and the place of philosophy and its history within it. Nowhere else in the world could this story be duplicated. Only in a country that seeks to be a land of opportunity, of unfettered freedom, where merit can take precedence over lineage, position, money, and influence, a land that aims to reward talent, hard work, and honesty, promising the opportunity of free and open discussion, would this be. And it is, of course, my story.

It was on 9/11, while watching the burning towers of the World Trade Center, that I first fully understood how much I owed to the United States. Yes, I am one of the most fierce and unrelenting critics of our faults as Americans, of a past tainted by racial and ethnic discrimination against some of our own people that still survives, and too often thrives, in the present, of a country daringly capable of electing as president a black man in a society with racist overtones. But my criticisms are meant to be constructive in that they arise from a desire to make better what is already good in many ways. I have never cast doubt on the love and gratitude that is at its roots.

My grieving for the victims of this unpardonable act of violence inflicted on innocent people made me recognize the significance of America for me. My grieving lasted for weeks. Its object was not just the group of those who had died, but also the nation as a whole that had been wounded, and even those of us who were immigrants, in the country that had generously opened its doors to me, thus making possible the uniquely rewarding life of the philosopher.

With my family in Cuba. My parents (*seated*) Ignacio and Leonila, and (*standing from left*) my sister, Nena, Aunt Rosario, and myself. Photograph courtesy of the author.

1

Farewell to Cuba (1961)

Most of those who left Cuba in the first few years after the triumph of Castro's Revolution on January 1, 1959, traveled by air, and their departure was anything but memorable. I am told that at the airport they were placed in a room, separated from relatives and friends, together with people they didn't know, strangers for whom, under the circumstances, they did not care, and of whom they were afraid. They could be informants, waiting for them to let down their guard and say something that might be used against them as a way of instilling terror in their victims, and most likely as an excuse for an arrest, thwarting their only chance to escape the nightmare that the revolution, which had promised so much, had become.

So they waited, frightened, nervous, over long hours that seemed interminable, eventually boarding a plane with small windows that allowed a view as limited as it was significant. They needed to see those on the ground, the family and friends of whom they hoped to have at least a glimpse before the plane departed. This was perhaps the last opportunity for them to do so, maybe for the last time in their lives. They had to work hard to get some tears going under these pedestrian circumstances and to feel appropriately sad rather than merely frustrated, afraid, and exhausted.

My departure, in contrast, was intensely dramatic and very different, except for the fear that gripped me, allowing plenty of opportunity for regret, suffering, tears, and even guilt for leaving my loved ones behind. I left by sea, on the last ferry that sailed from Havana to West Palm

Beach—a ship formerly used by wealthy vacationers who went to the beach to play and that had now become a way to escape from Cuba. The farewell was prolonged and emotional, extending for a whole day, and symbolically ending at dusk, just before night enveloped us in its indecipherable intent.

Passengers had to report to the ferry terminal early in the morning and thus spent the entire day there, ill prepared to face the reality of their state of mind after a sleepless night. Preparations for my trip had taken some time and considerable effort. Although I was not a seminarian and had no visa to enter the United States, ecclesiastic or otherwise, I was included in a group of seminarians who were leaving for Miami to join their associates. Shortly after, Castro placed the foreign-born priests and members of religious orders onto a ship and sent them to Spain. Only Cuban-born clergy and members of religious orders were allowed to remain in Cuba, at least for the moment.

Some Cuban-born seminarians also remained, but even before I left, rumors circulated about the imminent closing of the Seminary El Buen Pastor, where most of them were studying for a religious life. The exodus of members of the Catholic establishment had begun, and only increased as time went by. Not enough teachers were available to train seminarians and the Archdiocese of Havana was looking for ways to send them to other countries to continue their training, graduate, and eventually return to Cuba when conditions permitted it.

The situation was increasingly pressing, and the Catholic hierarchy was particularly intent on sending seminarians to the United States because of its proximity to Cuba and the support, particularly financial, on which they could count from the Church hierarchy in Florida. The program, known as Operación Pedro Pan (Operation Peter Pan), had been in effect since 1960 and would last until 1962. Overall, it was able to send more than fourteen thousand Cuban children to the United States with the help of the Archdiocese of Miami. The program began after rumors circulated to the effect that the Cuban government was planning to take children away from their parents and put them under government control, as had happened in the Soviet Union. Unfortunately for me, this program applied only to children, excluding young adults such as myself. I was eighteen years old.

Leaving the country was not easy. The revolutionary authorities had to be persuaded that those departing had what they considered legitimate reasons to leave, and that they were not needed in the island. Those whose profession or trade was considered essential to the well-being of the nation also encountered difficulties in trying to leave Cuba.

In the first two years of the revolution (1959 and 1960) a very large number of professionals had left, and this resulted in critical needs in practically every professional and scientific field, especially in medicine and technology. In addition, the authorities required evidence that those intending to leave had not engaged in antirevolutionary activities and would not join counterrevolutionaries in Miami. In the summer of 1961, the government's success at the Bay of Pigs was still quite fresh in everyone's mind.

One of the most difficult hurdles for those who wanted to leave the island was the cost of the fare, which had to be paid in dollars originating from outside Cuba. One could not buy tickets to travel overseas with Cuban pesos, nor could one use dollars that had been stashed away and hidden under mattresses before the revolution. This posed a problem for almost everyone who wanted to leave Cuba, and particularly for the archdiocese, which did not have the needed resources to pay for the fare of so many seminarians. The trip to the United States or Spain, the two primary destinations available, was expensive, and other countries were not generally willing to accept Cubans. Some, like Mexico, because they had good relations with the Cuban revolutionary government, and others, like Argentina, because they did not want the added burden of refugees. Paradoxically, this created an unexpected opportunity for me. Indeed, "No hay mal que por bien no venga," as we say in Spanish, or, "Every cloud has a silver lining," as we say in English.

I had friends outside Cuba who had sent me money to buy a ticket to leave Cuba through Spain. And I had friends at the Seminary El Buen Pastor, in Havana, who had been schoolmates of mine at the Colegio Champagnat in La Víbora, commonly known as Los Maristas, which I had attended for the last year of primary school and the first three years of prep school. The seminarians who wanted to leave Cuba and I hatched a plan that would help us all to leave. We would visit Monsignor Eduardo Boza Masvidal, explain our situation, and hope that he would give me a letter similar to the one he had been giving to seminarians so that they could travel to the United States.

The monsignor was a rising star in the Cuban Catholic hierarchy and a known opponent of Castro's intention to turn Cuba into a Marxist state. Cardinal Arteaga was old and feeble, and Boza Masvidal had been named assistant bishop of Havana after the Universidad de Villanueva, of which he was rector, had been closed by the government. With his letter I could go to the Cuban authorities and get a permit to join the seminarians in their exodus, a relatively easy matter because the government was anxious to get rid of as many members of the clergy as possible.

The letter would also serve to secure entrance to the United States. The payback to the seminarians for this favor to me was that I would buy the ferry tickets of several seminarians who otherwise might not be able to leave the island for lack of funds. This was possible for me to do because the cost of the ferry fare was a fraction of that for the airplane to Madrid, the only other way to escape that was open to me, insofar as some of my Spanish friends had secured visas for me.

That's what we did. Together with one of the seminarians who knew Boza Masvidal well and was a leader of the group, we went to his office on Calle Reina—coincidentally the street where my paternal grandparents had resided, and where the birth of my father was registered. (In fact, my father was born in the Canary Islands, where my grandparents were spending a year away from Cuba, hoping the change of air would help one of my great-aunts recover her failing health.)

My first impression of the bishop's office was that it was rather shabby. With the political crisis of the Church in Cuba, the hierarchy had more important things to worry about than keeping up physical appearances in an important colonial street. The building had been an impressive structure, but at the time it was, like most areas of downtown Havana, dirty and in disrepair. The office was furnished with dark mahogany pieces, heavy, old, and badly maintained, although at some point they had been carefully and elaborately carved. Bookcases lined some walls, filled with dusty volumes written in Latin that appeared not to have been picked up and opened for decades and whose originally gilded decorations on the bindings had lost their light. A sour smell of mildew permeated the air, and the windows suffocated the minimal light that entered the room. The gloom was overpowering and I had to work hard not to read it as a bad omen.

When we entered the bishop's office, he was sitting at his desk. He was a relatively young man for the exalted office he held and for the cardinal's hat he was supposed eventually to receive. He seemed out of place in this decadent environment, although he had already adopted the ecclesiastical manner so common among clerics: a kind, gentle attitude that inspired confidence.

I had been terrified of the visit, well aware that my future hung on the success of this interview, and that if I failed I had very little hope of leaving Cuba for the foreseeable future, if ever. If circulating rumors were true, fairly soon I might be drafted to serve in the military and once that happened it would be years before I could apply to leave, let alone be granted permission to emigrate. These rumors turned out to be true; compulsory military service was instituted, beginning at seventeen years of age, in 1963.

Other hurdles remained. Indeed, it took my sister, Nena, and her family nine long years, years of frustration and pain to finally be allowed to leave the island, and it took my mother fifteen. If I had to wait that long I would be much older, perhaps with a family of my own and corresponding obligations, and the future would be even more uncertain than if I left now, when I was young, unattached, and full of energy.

Besides, what could I do in Cuba if I stayed? Private property had been abolished in the country, all jobs were government jobs, and they were apportioned according to the level of enthusiasm for the revolution demonstrated by candidates. A university education was also out of the question, for a tight ideological filter let pass only those committed to the revolutionary ideals that had been put in place after the Bay of Pigs fiasco.

Getting into the ferry appeared to be my last chance for a future, which at this moment depended on this man. My hands were sweaty and I felt a storm brewing in the pit of my stomach, but the bishop's manner soothed me and I was able to present my case with a reasonable degree of equanimity. Still, *la procesión iba por dentro*. It was essential that I say the right things, that I did not lie, and yet it was also essential that I did not tell the crude truth: that I was desperate to leave Cuba, I was willing to pose as a seminarian when I was not and never had been one, and I was willing to pay to get some others out in exchange for my freedom. That would not do. The church was not for sale. My task was nearly impossible. Only a fine use of casuistry would ensure success.

After presenting my case, the bishop looked thoughtful, and for a moment I thought I was doomed and he was going to tell me that he regretted not being able to help me. What could I do if he did? What would I say? I had no alternative plan of action. His rejection would crush me. I could not go back and pick up my life at the point I had left it. The doors of the university were closed to me after the Bay of

Pigs invasion, and so was every other door in Cuba. Of course I would kneel and beg him for my life, but what would that do? It might be counterproductive, and, in fact, it seemed to me to be in bad taste.

To my surprise and without further ado, however, Boza Masvidal asked me whether I had brought a document that he could sign. Fortunately, we had drafted a letter and translated it into English so that it could also be presented to the American authorities when I arrived in the United States. The bishop took the letter and after reading it he opened a drawer in his desk and took out a letterhead that he passed on to his secretary, asking him to type on his stationery a copy of the text of the letter we had brought in.

He had decided in my favor! I could hardly contain myself when I realized the significance of what had happened, but I remained silent and so did the bishop and my friend. It was also possible that he would edit the text, making it useless. We heard typing in the adjacent room and then the secretary came back into the office and handed the letter to the bishop, who read it, signed it, and gave it to me to read. My seminarian friend and I were silent, aware of the significance of the moment.

On reflection, however, what else could he do, considering the circumstances? He was trapped as I was, and he knew it. And, after all, he was not doing it for me, I am sure, but for the church. The situation of seminarians had become critical and time was of the essence since the ferry to West Palm Beach was scheduled to make only one more trip. Indeed, in the fall of 1961, just shortly after this interview, the bishop and many others were forced to leave the island.

And although I was not a seminarian, and I had said nothing about being or becoming one, how would he know how I would end up? After all, I had come to his office with a letter signed by seminarians whom he trusted and wanted to protect. Who knew God's plans for me? Only I was aware of my intentions, but even I could not fathom God's intentions, which were the only ones that mattered in the cleric's mind. The only thing I was sure of was that the only necessary condition of my future well-being was to leave Cuba. And the bishop was a generous man familiar with human nature.

Having signed the letter, the bishop exchanged some pleasantries with me. He inquired where I went to school and when I said that I had been going to the University of Havana until the Bay of Pigs catastrophe, but had graduated a year earlier from St. Thomas Military Academy, he inquired whether I had known a young relative of his, who it turns out was one of my classmates and friends at the school, and whose family had already left Cuba. This bit of pleasantry made all the difference to me. I took it as a sign of things to come.

All of a sudden, the gloomy building looked beautiful, the sun was shining outside, and I felt as if my life were beginning. Hope was transforming itself into reality! It surely became a thing with feathers, ready to fly. I wanted to run, in case the bishop changed his mind, but controlled myself. My friend was as happy as I was, for he was one of the seminarians who would benefit from our arrangement. My emotions were so strong and mixed that my eyes became moist and I had difficulty controlling myself. I could not speak, but I managed to receive the bishop's blessing and kiss his ring.

With the letter in hand I got my permit from the Cuban authorities and bought my ferry ticket and those of as many seminarians as possible. To make matters appear authentic in the eyes of the Cuban authorities, my friends got me a soutane to wear on the day of departure, July 17, 1961. I still have it. It is a memento I shall keep while I live, just in case I should need it again. You never know when you have to leave a country in a hurry and in disguise. It hangs in a coat closet in my daughter Leticia's home in Toronto.

Many other preparations were required. I needed winter clothes, but where could they be bought? Because of the Cuban climate, it was difficult under normal circumstances to buy warm clothes, but after 1959 the exodus to the north had been steady and the stock of warm clothing had been exhausted. Eventually, Mother and I were able to find some appropriate material in Calle Zanja, and a tailor made me an overcoat that I wore throughout my college years in the United States. To make it serve its purpose, it had three layers: an outer layer for looks, a middle layer for warmth, and an interior layer for comfort. It did the trick beautifully. When I wore the coat with an astrakhan hat and a cashmere scarf I bought in Chicago, it looked quite sharp, and it disguised my current poverty.

More difficult still than winter clothing was the matter of money. But there was not much we could do about it. The Cuban government allowed each traveler to take only five dollars out of Cuba. No jewelry or valuables of any kind, except for personal clothing, were permitted. One could wear a watch provided it did not have a gold band, so I left my own watch with my family and took instead what had been Father's because it was gold but had a leather band. To leave one's country with only five dollars in one's pocket, going into the unknown, was frightening. What would I find when I got to my destination? Five dollars would not last long, even for sidewalk food. And what about transportation? How would I get from the ferry terminal in West Palm Beach to Jacksonville, where the friends lived who had sent me the ticket money and where I intended to go?

I tried not to dwell on these thoughts. Providence would provide. But I did take one minor precaution apart from taking Father's watch. I made a hole in the heel of one of my shoes and put in it a diamond ring that belonged to Mother, then nailed and glued the shoe heel back on. The watch and the ring were meant as insurance. I could sell them in case of extreme need. It turns out that I sold neither, although I did inquire once about the cash value of the ring at a pawn shop when I was strapped for funds and hungry. My daughter Leticia has the watch and I gave the ring to my wife, Norma, when we became engaged in 1966, which will go to our other daughter, Clarisa, when my wife passes.

Of course, I would never sell or pawn the diamond, for its significance grew with the future. At first it had represented some financial security, but it soon began to develop a different, deeper character, becoming a symbol of Cuba, my family, friends, and what they meant to

The diamond in my shoe. Photograph courtesy of the author.

me. It became a talisman that I always kept near as a source of strength in moments of doubts and fear. It was always there, quietly speaking to me about my past. And it was an object of beauty, something I needed after all the ugliness that the prior three years in Cuba had meant. And there would be more beauty as my life developed in the United States.

The wait at the ferry terminal seemed endless; it was exhausting and worrisome. And my anxiety grew with the passage of time. The discovery of the ring would be fatal. It would result not only in its confiscation but in serious charges and penalties. I certainly would not have been permitted to leave Cuba and likely would end up in jail, in the company of the prisoners from the Bay of Pigs, who were kept in the ubiquitous El Morro, the fortress that guards Havana's harbor and is visible from every vantage point of the Cuban capital.

When I reached my turn on the luggage inspection line I tried to keep a steady demeanor, but I was so nervous that at certain moments I feared I would unintentionally reveal the location of the ring with the diamond. During the process, which seemed to take an eternity, I never dared look at my feet while trying to appear concerned with the contents of my two duffel bags. That helped me, for the inspectors paid detailed attention to the bags, asking many questions while ignoring the shoes and soutane I was wearing.

Choosing what to pack in the two duffel bags had been difficult. What would be necessary or useful? What would I need? What mementos should I take to remind me of my dear ones? My family and I tried to think about possibilities, but we had no guidance. I did not know where I would live or the kind of climate I would face. Who would be my friends, and what kind of clothing would be appropriate for me to wear? But these were not the more agonizing moments. Those had to do with photographs of my family, and of course, the diamond that was intended to be sold but which I vowed to keep, come what may. And there were the books that had been my friends throughout my life, as I returned to them again and again. It seemed clear that I should take my credentials, records from prep school, and samples of my work at the University of Havana, where I had been studying architecture.

I should also take copies of the prizes I had received in school. I was planning to get back to my studies as soon as possible, so I thought hard about anything that I might need to apply to schools. But I had no guidance about what I needed at the moment of departure. I was worried about some of the things I took, which might be compromising. There were all kinds of stories circulating about the authorities confiscating all sorts of odds and ends. And I kept thinking about the things I would forget to include and need afterward.

The wait and the bureaucratic procedures, the checking of documents and permits, appeared to go on and on. The process continued for hours in a suffocating small space full of people who shared the anxiety and fear I felt. In fact, some were prevented from leaving because they were trying to smuggle something forbidden out of Cuba or because their papers were not in order. A woman in a corner was so distraught that she vomited before she could get to the ladies' room. Some people were crying, others prayed, and still others begged. And there were some who quarreled with the officers. The smart ones kept quiet and were obliging, although they did not humiliate themselves by being servile. It was a question of pride and honor even in extreme circumstances. I stuck closely to the seminarians, wearing my soutane and looking pious, while my stomach churned and felt weak and tight.

To repeat, it was the last day of my eighteenth year and I was embarking all alone on a life-shattering adventure for the first time in my life, in a country where I did not know the language or customs, without money or family support. The greatest fear I had was that something would prevent my departure. Those who have never lived in a country where it is not the law that rules, but rather the whims of those in power, cannot understand the fear of those who have. Indeed, what they experience is not fear but terror. A terror that goes down to the gut and knees. At certain moments you think you are going to die, that you are facing a firing squad, as many Cubans had in fact faced since the revolution had won. You can imagine the pain of the bullets tearing up part of your chest, your belly, and your face. At certain moments you anticipate humiliations, insults, while you feel the hatred of those who have power over you and who blame you for crimes you have not committed.

What can compare with being at the mercy of others, of people who detest you and mean you ill? After all, we are social beings who prize and value company and fellowship. There is no recourse in such circumstances. The rulers decide, their passions are the last word, so there is nothing anyone can do to overcome their will. After the infamous Bay of Pigs invasion, the situation in Cuba had deteriorated considerably. The government had complete control of the country and challenged anyone to disagree with its plans for the island. Indeed, in the eyes of the government, disagreement meant treason. It was that understanding that had convinced me that the only thing to do was to get out of Cuba, at whatever cost.

Finally, after what seemed endless hours of bureaucratic harassment at the terminal—what seemed to be an infinite number of documents to fill out, irrelevant questions to answer, fruitless luggage searches, and hateful treatment (after all, we were what the Cuban government would come to call "worms" (*gusanos*), a term used by revolutionaries to refer to those leaving Cuba because of the kind of duffel bags we took with us, but which had a much more deprecatory connotation)—we boarded the ferry. Still, it took two more hours for the boat to begin its slow passage out of Havana harbor. The ferry terminal was set quite a bit back into the bay, and the family and friends of those departing lined the promenade extending along the bay. They continued to accompany the slow-moving ship until it entered open sea. The passengers were gathered on the deck, looking at them, waving and crying. This was to be a day of tears.

The significance of the moment became evident when the ferry started moving. There had been rumblings coming from within its belly, and all of a sudden, at about six, subsequent to a general tremor, it began to inch ahead. This was the instant when I realized the full impact of what was happening. Until then I had focused only on the goal of departing, forgetting what departure meant.

Now I realized it was a unique circumstance that I would never encounter again, a moment that would change my life forever and define my future for better or worse. It was the end of my life as I had known it—of my life as I had lived it and of my very identity—and the beginning of something else, a new existence about which I knew nothing. Until this moment I had lived in my native land, but soon I would arrive at a country that would consider me a refugee, the lowest legal status in the country. Refugees have limited rights; they can be deported or confined to areas or camps. They are not citizens or legal immigrants; they are accepted under strict conditions. Often they are accepted but not sought. And in many cases, they are hated. Being a refugee is a temporary status granted as an act of kindness. But refugees not only feel, but are, at a disadvantage in the societies in which they live.

For me, becoming a refugee meant that I had escaped the Castro regime, that I had been granted a reprieve, a temporary break, but the status was unstable and those who have it feel vulnerable. Traveling outside the receiving country is difficult if not impossible. To leave the country without permission is considered a surrender of the status, making it impossible to return. It is a status that responds to charity and not to the will of all the citizens of the receiving country. Fortunately for me and other Cubans, the United States is, at least on paper, a country of laws in which everyone has basic protections regardless of their status. Nonetheless, there is always a fear associated with it, for to be a refugee is very different than being a citizen or a permanent resident. Refugees lack the confidence of residents and citizens.

At any moment the winds of politics can change and refugees may find themselves in camps, isolated and semi-abandoned if not exactly jailed, although that has also happened in the best of countries. We need only remember what happened to the Japanese in the United States during World War II, even to those Japanese who were citizens. Xenophobia is never very far and does not discriminate by country. Then it was the Japanese; now it is so-called undocumented Mexicans. Demagogues have always used scapegoats to excite fear in a population that is ignorant of the facts, and unscrupulous politicians exploit those fears for political profit.

On the one hand, the movement of the ferry indicated a liberation from and negation of all that had happened in Cuba since the triumph of the revolution, the abuses of the government and its bureaucracy, the fear that had increasingly permeated my life. In a few moments I would be free of block committees and informers, of being at the mercy of those who ruled by ideology, self-interest, or both. On the other hand, it meant a drastic change from the known to the unknown, a change of life and future. Indeed, a change of identity. What would happen to me? Where would I end up? Who would I become? Surely I would change, but what I would become was a mystery. After all, most likely I had a long life ahead of me and the possibilities appeared to be many.

While these thoughts repeated themselves in my mind, the ground seemed to be giving way under my feet and I thought I was going to faint. Was I doing the right thing? Maybe I should jump into the dirty waters of the bay, embrace the Cuban revolutionary ideology and join its agenda. After all, others had done it. But the temptation lasted only a moment, and it fell away when I looked at the members of my family.

My mother, sister, nephews, maternal grandmother, and dear Aunt Maruca were all perched on the pier, walking its length as the boat moved slowly, deliberately, as if unsure it wanted to go, making groans that suggested it felt a pain similar to that experienced by its passengers. When would I see my relatives again?

Perhaps never. Now they were waving, and I was waving back, drowning in agony. Thoughts crowded my mind as I fought to get a hold of the instant, to grasp its sense and relevance. I wanted to fix the moment in some way so its image would survive and endure. I could not afford to forget this moment; it was the last link to my previous life.

Tears flowed freely as I gazed upon a slowly disappearing Havana, its monuments and promenades, El Prado, El Malecón. How many times had I walked these parks and avenues, how many times had I admired the monuments? When would I see any of them again? As we went along, the sun was setting. By the time we reached the mouth of the bay it was growing dark, and as we entered the strait that separates Cuba from Florida, I could still see the fortress of El Morro, forbidding, imposing in its various shades of gray at dusk, moving away in the distance. As a symbol of Cuba it was both comforting and painful. Comforting because it seemed to defy change, and painful because inside it were the Cuban prisoners who had fought the revolutionary forces at the Bay of Pigs.

One part of my life was over and another lay ahead. I looked ahead and saw only a vague horizon of shadows. An ominous night was closing on me. All of a sudden it was cold and I shivered. It felt like death, a passing on to another world. The month before I'd had a dream that I feared was a premonition. A very heavy weight was crushing my chest, just like the one that accidentally had crushed and killed my older brother, Ignacito, when he was twenty-two years old at our sugarcane plantation. I was sure it was the moment of my death. I tried to speak, to appeal to others for help, but no sound came out of my mouth and no one helped, no one responded to my plight. Death was inevitable and I had to face it alone. I now relived that dread, but a new hope sprung from it. Because it had only been a dream, a nightmare that passed when I awoke, so I hoped this also would pass.

At that moment I remembered the diamond, with its beauty, light, and strength. Yes, this could be a light to guide me, the link between the old me and the new me. The diamond was a symbol of what I brought with me and what the revolutionary government could not take away—memories of the past, what I had learned from my family, the values that I carried with me everywhere, and a love of justice, beauty, and rationality. Slowly, I caressed the shoe where I had hidden it. Yes, it was there, and the hard consistency associated with diamonds suddenly seemed to give me strength. Yes, I would do the best I could and I would succeed, in spite of the many obstacles that I would surely face.

Years later, I met a Cuban artist, Alberto Rey, who had painted exactly the last image I had of Cuba, a portrait of El Morro seen from the ocean, in grays, at dusk. That painting now hangs above the fireplace of my daughter Leticia's living room in Toronto, and whenever I look at it, it brings me back to that moment of departure and the two years packed with events that had led me to it.

Appropriated Memories: Havana Harbor, Cuba (view from behind El Morro), by Alberto Rey, oils on plaster. Photograph courtesy of the author.

2

Good Morning, America
(1961–1962)

I woke up upon hearing other ferry passengers stirring. I had spent the night on a lounge chair on the deck of the ferry, where I had fallen asleep like a dead weight after the vivid emotions of the departure from Havana. Now I felt cold and stiff, but it did not take much effort for me to get up, as I was curious to see what was happening. I had no idea what awaited us, but I was both relieved and apprehensive. I had succeeded in escaping Cuba, but ignorance about the future gnawed at me. An ambiguous excitement impacted my emotions.

Still wearing the soutane, I joined my group of friends, the seminarians, to look at the land that lay ahead. It appeared to be slowly moving in our direction, becoming more defined by the light of the new day. The ferry groaned, like a cat complaining about being forced to do something it did not want to do. Finally the ferry touched the pier, ropes were thrown out and picked up by the land crew waiting for us. Movement stopped and the engine became silent, resigned to the immobility and captivity of land. Everybody was eager to disembark. People and luggage were everywhere. My two duffel bags weighed a ton and made movement difficult. My feet got tangled in the soutane, as I was unused to wearing ecclesiastical clothes, but eventually I managed to join the line of passengers exiting the boat.

The seminarians and I slowly made our way to the gangplank that was used to cross onto land, where we met immigration authorities. Some of the passengers had visas to enter the United States, but most of us did not, so we were accepted as refugees, thanks to the rule that President

Kennedy had established after the Bay of Pigs debacle. This regulation, which was unfortunately rescinded by President Obama in his last days in office, is known as the "wet foot, dry foot" policy. According to this policy, Cubans who reach dry land in the United States are allowed to stay in the country as political refugees. This status was made clear on a blue card we received, which I have kept as a memento of a significant event in my life.

I had worried about my entrance to the United States, but none of the seminarians had any document other than what I had, namely the letter from the auxiliary bishop of Havana stating that we were coming to the United States to continue our studies—the soutane did the rest. American immigration authorities were polite and efficient.

I had not known what to expect, and after the cold and hostile treatment by Cuban authorities at the terminal in Havana, I did not know whether something similar would happen in West Palm Beach.

My Cuban passport photo, age eighteen. Photograph courtesy of the author.

I had not yet learned that the United States is a land of immigrants, where everyone has some ancestor who came from elsewhere, and therefore, notwithstanding the xenophobia that periodically animates some Americans, many others tend to sympathize with those of us who have come here in pursuit of the "American Dream," an expression I had yet to hear or understand.

Someone was waiting for the group of seminarians to pick us up and take us to the seminary in Miami, and I tagged along. At the seminary we were settled in a dormitory and fed. The true seminarians stayed there, but the seminary administration contacted my friends, the Inclans, in Jacksonville. Alberto Inclan had been my classmate in St. Thomas Military Academy, where I had done my last two years of prep school, and he, his sister, and his mother, Mary, who were American citizens, had left Cuba a year earlier. They lived on a farm belonging to her parents in the countryside, close to Jacksonville. She worked as a nurse in a hospital and also supervised a group of Cuban children who had participated in the Peter Pan program and had no relatives in the United States. Alberto had a clerk's job in town and was taking courses in business school. They stayed in a comfortable apartment on top of the farm garages.

I traveled by train to Jacksonville, where Mary, Alberto, and his sister were at the station to take me to the farm. Everything was new to me—the pine forests, the Spanish moss, and the peculiar smell in the air that I could not quite identify but which I later found out came from a pulp and kraft paper mill. On the train to Jacksonville, my main concern was to make sure I would get off at the right station, for my English was de facto nonexistent. Indeed, I could not even understand when the conductor called out the names of the various stations we were passing.

As a precaution, I had written down "Jacksonville" on a piece of paper and showed it to him when I boarded the train. He responded with what I hoped was a reassurance that he would let me know when we reached my destination, for I could not make out a word of what he said. Still, we managed to communicate through signs, and fortunately my friends were waiting for me at the station. When we arrived at their home, Mary asked me whether I had tried to talk with my mother by phone. Since I had not, she phoned our home in Havana and, surprisingly, was lucky enough to get through. I spoke with my mother, who was naturally quite anxious about my situation. Telephone communication with Cuba was unreliable, so I could very seldom succeed in talking to my family after that first lucky call. Besides, I was concerned about the expense, so I rarely initiated a conversation about it.

Life at the farm was slow and pleasant. It was there that I was first introduced to the enormous barbecued chuck steaks the family regularly ate. Normally in Cuba we ate small, rather thin steaks, fried and thoroughly cooked, which, with the exception of filet mignon, were as tough as leather. Here, I was presented with what looked like a largely raw piece of meat of such enormous proportions that I was not sure how to deal with it. Its size was intimidating and I did not think I could handle it. I had never faced such a large, raw piece of meat before. My mother came from a vegetarian family and my father was concerned with his health. Indeed, only my brother was a true carnivore.

But when I stepped off the ferry I had made clear to myself that my future was in the United States; I was here to stay and I should do everything I could to adapt myself to the customs of the country. So not only did I eat the giant steak with which I was presented, I liked it! And from then on I ate my portion and more. This was a major feat, because I had always been a finicky eater. Mary's parents loved to see the recently arrived Cuban refugee gorging himself on steak, potato salad, and Jell-O for dessert. I still love all three—even Jell-O, a fact that is nearly scandalous to my daughters and grandchildren. Keep in mind that by the time I left Havana, the first batch of ration cards had been circulated.

Mary and Alberto went to work every morning and came back late in the afternoon, except for Saturdays and Sundays. I stayed in the apartment trying to learn some English. Sometimes Mary would take me with her to visit the camp that had been set out for Cuban children participating in the Peter Pan program so I could meet some of my fellow Cubans. On the weekends we visited the areas surrounding Jacksonville, including the beach.

During the week I would spend the time watching TV to learn how to pronounce English words and working on English grammar. I was quite disciplined and did all I was supposed to do to advance my language skills, but it was a slow process and I spent most of the day by myself, and when Mary and Alberto arrived home, that was the end of English. So I made no serious progress. Alberto was happy because he had a friend from Cuba, and Mary was a wonderful person who adopted a motherly attitude toward me, so there was no pressure for me to do anything in particular.

But I was anxious. I was not happy staying at the home of my friends and living off their friendship and generosity. Besides, I wanted to repay Mary for the money she had sent me to make the journey from Cuba. I needed to find a job to earn some income. Mary agreed that I should look for a job, so she took me to Jacksonville several times to fill out job applications at various places. At the time, Jacksonville was a relatively small, conservative town, with very traditional Southern values.

The greatest shock I received when I first went downtown was the open discrimination against blacks. Most obvious was that blacks had to sit at the back of public buses. Prominent signs indicated that that was the only place where they could sit down. I wondered what would happen if the only seat available was designated for whites and no whites were on the bus or vice versa, if the only available seat was designated for blacks and no blacks were on the bus. Would blacks or whites sit in the wrong seat, or would the black person have to stand if the seat remained empty? I wondered what would happen if a white person were subjected to the same indignities that were endured by black people.

There was segregation of blacks and mulattos in Cuba. But segregation was only permitted in private places and institutions, such as clubs and associations, and the places that belonged to them. Segregation was not permitted in public places and institutions. This was bad enough, but there was an important difference between this and the sort of segregation I was witnessing in Jacksonville. I could not believe that this kind of segregation was practiced in the United States.

My job searches failed, but that failure was not due to racial discrimination. Although I was Cuban I was regarded as white because of my appearance. My failure to get a job was due to my inability to speak and understand English. Indeed, who would give a job to someone who could not even understand directions? A kind soul offered me a job as a dishwasher, but Mary did not think that was appropriate and the pay was miserly—psychologically, she was still living in Cuba, where such a job would have been considered demeaning for me.

After three weeks of this routine, I raised the matter of my future with Mary. I pointed out that I could not continue as I was. I loved living with her family and was grateful for her help, but I could not see any future ahead. Most importantly, my linguistic skills were not improving, and there was no way to reverse this situation unless I went to school and had contact with the general population, which would never happen if I continued to live on Mary's family farm. I had started corresponding with some Cubans who lived in Miami and they had mentioned that there the government offered free English classes, financial help to refugees, and a placement service that supposedly helped them find jobs. So I told Mary that I wanted to go back to Miami and see what I could do on my own.

With some regret, Mary agreed that this was the only good long-term solution to my predicament. I then wrote to Kathleen Belknap, who managed a refugee center for Cubans in Miami, and asked her whether she could help me get settled there. Apart from directing a refugee center for Cubans in Miami, Kathleen had two other qualifications that would be key in her ability to help me, although I did not know anything about them at the outset. First, she was an alumna of Wheaton College, and more important, she was a personal friend of the longtime president of the college. Kathleen, who had adopted the name "Karlin" in Cuba because Cubans could not pronounce her English name to her satisfaction (she was tough as nails), had been a missionary and pastor at my mother's church. She replied enthusiastically in the affirmative to my request. Indeed, she was thrilled that I was in the United States and had contacted her, for she had always hoped she could convert me to her evangelical brand of Christianity.

So the date was set. Mary bought me a one-way train ticket to Miami, gave me some money to tide me over for the first month, and put me on the train. I had no idea what was waiting for me in Miami, where I was ultimately going to go, or how I would get there. But Karlin was at the station in Miami waiting for me with a big smile on her face. Was this the reception I should expect of others? Not quite! The time of living comfortably with friends and eating two-pound steaks had come to a sudden end. Now, for the first time in my life, I was going to be largely on my own; although Karlin was willing to help me in some ways, she would not provide money, food, or lodging. Nevertheless, I was grateful for her conditional help, for, although I needed money, food, and lodging, I did not want to drift into a situation where I became financially dependent on her, or anybody else. Still, I was afraid of the future, but as my mother always said, "Del cobarde no se ha escrito nada" ("Nothing has ever been written about a coward"). The time I spent in Miami taught me self-reliance, independence, and the value of economy and hard work, qualities that had never been expected of me before.

The sheltered life I had lived until then in Cuba, where my main concerns had to do with which school I should attend, what kind of car to drive, the color of the suit I would wear to a party, the girl I would invite to it, and whether I would spend time at our club (the Casino Español) or go with my friend to the Miramar Yacht Club for a swim. My future had been smoothly paved, but now things were different. Security was over and my future depended on what I alone would do. The future looked rough, but I did not dwell on the difficulties ahead. After all, I had surmounted the greatest difficulty in getting out of the prison that was Cuba, and I was free! I looked upon my situation as a challenge and an opportunity to prove myself rather than as an insurmountable set of obstacles. And if matters went sour, there was the diamond in my shoe. Still, I did have some apprehensions in the back of my mind and experienced some hard times in Miami.

3

Hungry in Miami
(1961)

The reality of my new situation became apparent rather quickly. Its messenger was hunger. Hunger is a terrible thing. I mean hunger in the sense that one does not have food available to eat or money to buy it. I never before had the feeling I had in Miami, and I never thought I would be hungry in the United States, presumably the land of milk and honey. To say that feeling hungry is not a good feeling is a major understatement. It is characterize by an emptiness that weakens you. Walking streets filled with restaurants, take-out eateries, bakeries, and the scents that envelop the passerby are torture if you are hungry.

Your empty belly cries out for attention, for something to fill it: some *chicharrones, una malanga hervida, arroz con pollo, costillitas de lechón asado* dripping fat onto your fingers that you cannot wait to lick with gusto. I have never been a dessert person (except for *dulce de guayaba con queso crema*), but savory dishes drive me crazy. And going to bed with an empty stomach, or one just filled with a few crackers and a slice of bread, was no consolation. Keep in mind that I was eighteen years old. My body wanted, indeed demanded, real, filling food, and I remembered with longing the two-pound steaks I used to eat in Jacksonville. I don't recommend being hungry, if one can at all help it. The condition sours life, weakens the body, and drives one crazy.

Karlin put me up at her apartment for a couple of days while she got a place for me in a rooming house that catered to starved-for-cash Cuban refugees. The lady that ran the place, named Felina, was warm and sympathetic with an occasional sharp edge. She understood what being a refugee entailed. Her husband, who had run away with a younger woman and abandoned her, had been an important officer in the Cuban army during Batista's regime. They had lived well, but when the revolution came, they had to leave Cuba in a hurry and landed in Miami with no resources to speak of. The wayward husband took with him whatever money he was able to take out of Cuba and left Felina to fend for herself. Someone of a lesser character would have thrown her arms up into the air, waiting for God to help her.

But Felina was a tough woman who did not consider giving up and thought that appealing to God under these circumstances was useless since He was probably responsible for her situation in first place, at least by permitting her present predicament. In any case, she believed in the Cuban adage that says, "Orando y con el mazo dando." She had never held a job other than that entailed by being the wife of a high-ranking member of Cuba's military. But that had only prepared her for running the home of a well-to-do man. Now, being by herself after her husband abandoned her, what could she do?

In telling her story, she said that the first day she understood the reality of her situation, she cried bitterly. But the next day she figured out a way of making ends meet: she would rent rooms to Cubans recently arrived from the island. The first step was to rent a large apartment to accommodate her tenants. She soon found one on top of a rather dilapidated former store on Flagler Street and near one of the few refugee centers that were set up to help new Cuban arrivals.

I do not know how she did it, since her funds were very thin, her English nonexistent, and her knowledge of how things work in America was anecdotal and often wrong. But she did, which is unbelievable when one takes into account that she had never done anything remotely like this before. This was a woman who had enjoyed a leisurely life. But she was made of steel, and thinking about the alternatives strengthened her resolve.

She had some help, however. Her nephew, who lived with her and worked as a bartender at night, moved into one of the rooms of the house, and he not only paid rent for it but also helped her keep the house. Not that she ever sat and waited for someone to do it. She worked constantly but never complained, except for occasionally cursing Fidel along with her former husband, two people she said belong to the same kind of human trash.

Still, there were problems, such as how to acquire furniture for someone who did not have any cash to spend. But the solution was easily found in the garbage, for the residents of Miami discarded what she regarded as *tesoros increíbles*. Every garbage pickup day, she, her nephew, and some friends, including some of her tenants, went throughout Miami's streets collecting discarded furniture. Felina's business was to rent rooms to recently arrived Cubans to Miami, and everyone who landed in the place was considered part of the family and treated as such. The system of picking up discarded items from the sidewalk on garbage pickup days did not always work. I remember one day she came home with her nephew crowing because of the two mattresses they had picked up, only to find out later in the evening that they were infested with *pulgas*. Some of us were scratching ourselves for weeks.

Of course, Felina had her favorites in her menagerie, and I was lucky enough to qualify, which meant that I was given some special treats. Indeed, she used to save goodies for me, behind the backs of her other tenants, except for her nephew, who was also partial to me. And some of those days in which she knew that I did not have any money to cover the meal to which I was not entitled by my rent, she tried to save me a bit of *arroz amarillo* and a piece of stale bread.

She was generally happy, although she complained bitterly and constantly about Castro and his "maldita revolución." But she also worked very hard, cooking, cleaning, washing, and she had the good sense of humor of most Cubans. It was a hard existence for a woman who was no longer young and had been used to a different lifestyle, but it was not very different from that of other Cuban refugees living in Miami. Just imagine what it means to be deprived of everything you own at a time when you are thinking about enjoying the things you have worked for all your life. Would you not be frustrated, angry, and depressed? And would you not be tempted to jump off a ten-story building to end this nightmare?

Angry and frustrated yes, but suicidal? No! She had too much to do and too many people to help to end it all in a meaningless and narcissistic gesture. Indeed, given the unexpected tragedy Cubans were suffering, one would have expected a high number of suicides among them. But Cubans did not respond in this way. They accepted their situation and made plans to make it better. Felina was no different. She functioned as a kind of mother figure to all of us, feeding and caring for all. Her tough courage was limitless, as was the case with that of my mother.

One night a thief came into the house (it is inaccurate to say that he broke into it since we slept with all doors and windows open because we had no air-conditioning, not even fans) and threatened her with a gun. Instead of raising her hands, begging for mercy, and telling him where the money was (the pittance she had in her purse), she got up from bed, yelled at him, and followed him out of the house beating him with a broom. The guy had a loaded gun with him, a bullet from which we found the following morning on the floor of the bedroom where my roommate and I slept. But he could not cope with Felina, whose name fit her perfectly. She was a wild cat.

That kind of indomitable spirit and uncompromising courage exemplified by Felina explains to a great extent why Cubans have done so well in this country. The Cubans who left the island in the early sixties generally belonged to the professional class, and were not used to manual labor. But that did not stop them from doing whatever they needed to do to earn a living and get ahead. Although there was a small group of members of the army and the Batista regime who took plenty of money out of the island, most Cubans who landed in Miami came with few, if any, resources. Although they belonged to a rather substantial middle class, they could not practice their professions in the United States, in part because they did not know English well enough and in part because they lacked proper certification. Physicians became employed as floor cleaners, lawyers washed dishes, dentists drove taxis, businessmen turned into bartenders or waiters, and so on with the rest of them.

In Felina's house I found plenty of support. Everyone knew everything that I needed to do after arriving as a refugee. First was to register with the United States government in order to receive the stipend that was given to refugees. These differed depending on a variety of factors; I got seventy-five dollars a month plus a box of powdered milk and a jar of peanut butter each week—the peanut butter remained uneaten because Cubans did not know how to eat it properly, and I was no different. (Indeed, years later, after I had discovered how well jam goes with it, I became an addict, but that was long after I had left Miami.)

My roommate, Pepe, who had arrived a few months earlier, only received sixty-five dollars in addition to the milk and peanut butter. Of the seventy-five dollars I received, sixty-five dollars went to pay for my room and part of my board, that is, a breakfast of bread and café con leche, and a midday dinner—usually a plate of rice and black beans.

For those who received less than seventy-five dollars, Felina charged only sixty dollars for room and board, but they had to keep it a secret, which revealed the measure of Felina's sensitivity and generosity. That left me with ten dollars for all other expenses—transportation and food for one meal a day. Obviously, that was not enough to cover even a hamburger per day (fifteen cents at McDonald's). I was hungry most of the time in Miami for the first time in my life and I lost weight. Since I was already thin, I began to look skeletal.

It was urgent for me to get a job, any job, to survive. But jobs that Cubans could do were very rare in a place crawling with refugees with no resources or skills and seeking employment. A problem for me that others did not have was my age: I was nineteen, which meant that I could not work in restaurants and bars where alcohol was served. Indeed, Felina's nephew got me a job as a busboy in the restaurant where he worked as bartender, but when I told the owner my age he said he could not hire me. So my roommate, who was several years older than me, got the job originally intended for me.

It was at times like these, when I was hungry and alone, that I would take the ring with the diamond out and play with it in my hands. It was like having a talisman that could bring me luck. Its power and beauty mesmerized me and I remembered happy times, particularly our family vacations at the beach. But it was also at these times, especially when I had not had sufficient food to eat, that I was tempted to pawn the ring. Indeed, one time when I felt particularly desperate I went to a pawnshop to see how much I could get for it. And it turned out the amount I could get would last me for quite a while. So I turned the ring over and over, looking at the diamond and its faceted surface. Eventually I thanked the owner of the shop and walked out. That night I went to bed very hungry, but I felt good that I had resisted the temptation to sell what had become a constant companion since I left Cuba.

Fortunately, once in a while I did get a job. Among the many for which I applied was washing cars. This turned out quite well, because when I filled out the application in my fancy handwriting (I had been an architecture student in Cuba and had developed an unusual hand), the guy must have felt sorry for me, so instead of washing cars he gave me the job of inspecting them. Unfortunately, the job lasted for only two weeks. I was anxious to do a good job and prove myself so I could keep the job, but the result was that I finished my task too early—there is a lesson to be learned somewhere in this story! Still, my earnings were enough for me to eat well for those two weeks and save some money for emergencies.

The worst job I had was selling ice cream, an experience that proved beyond a reasonable doubt that I am really not a good salesman. The pay was based on commissions; you got some money for each ice cream you sold. I spent the first, and only, day on the job in the unbearable heat of Miami summer, running around with my cart trying to sell ice cream. I will never forget the experience. I sold only one ice cream in the entire day, and that was to myself! That convinced me that I should never try to be a salesman again. Indeed, for a while I even hated ice cream.

A more pleasant way of earning some money was playing cards. At the rooming house where I lived there was always a game of canasta, which I had learned to play in Cuba, going on in the evening. Poker and other games were not played; we only played games that lasted a long time so that we would be entertained without risking much money. We did not play for much—a quarter a game. So I took my chances, and I was lucky; most of the time I won enough in a night to buy a hamburger. The card games usually went on until about eleven thirty at night, after which I ran to the corner McDonald's before it closed and got my hamburger.

Oh, how I loved those hamburgers! They were divine! I'd never tasted anything so good. Indeed, I was so hungry that those midnight hamburgers tasted better to me than the large steaks I had eaten in Jacksonville or some of the fancy meals I had at the Casino Parisien in Havana. The experience also taught me something about people who do not have enough food to eat. Apart from the taste of hamburgers, I learned that my future might lay in gambling, not sales.

Unlike many Cubans recently arrived from Cuba who surrender to the understandable temptation to stay in Miami and make a go of their lives there, or at least stay there until what they believed to be the imminent collapse of Castro's regime happened, my expectations were different. I never intended to stay in Miami. I looked at Miami as a stepping stone, a place to learn some English, become independent, and save some money. Of those three goals, I was misguided about the first and the last. Living among Cubans who did not speak English was certainly not the way to learn the language, and it was impossible to make money in a place where there were no jobs and a large population of unemployed people willing to do anything for a buck. Of course, for those Cubans who were able to establish themselves, the temptation to stay in Miami was overwhelming, for, after all, they would have most of the things Cubans had in Cuba. But I did become independent, and I was able to take the first steps on the way to acquiring an education and realizing the American Dream.

My plan all along was to go to college, of course. But how? Without money, without American credentials, and not knowing English? Still, I was not deterred. I daily remembered my mother's saying about cowards. Not that I was anxious to become famous, but I did want to study and fulfill the American Dream, that is, having a good job that I liked and a family I could support. In fact, even in Jacksonville I had written to schools I had heard about, such as Harvard and the Catholic University of America, to ask for application forms.

When I got to Miami I began the process of filling out these forms, which, with my faulty English, required a lot of work. For this I needed help and Karlin once again came to my rescue. But she did something better, in part because she liked me and wanted to help me, and in part because, as I said earlier, she had been the pastor of my mother's church in Cuba and that church owed much to my mother. evangelical churches in Cuba were generally poor because they appealed to people with limited means. For them, a person like my mother, who had the means to help, was a godsend.

Karlin also hoped that at some point I would convert from Catholicism to evangelical Christianity. She knew that I had a sterling academic record in Cuba, transcripts of which I had brought with me, and had gone to excellent schools, so she was sure I would get accepted to the college from which she had graduated, Wheaton College in Illinois. But just in case, she contacted the president of the college, a man she knew personally.

One of the complications I faced was that I wanted to leave Miami and enter college as soon as possible, which was in the spring rather than the fall of 1962. Accepting students for the spring semester was unusual for most colleges, as they accept most students for the fall semester. Would Wheaton consider me for the spring semester? With Karlin's help I filled out the application forms and sent them to Wheaton. I also sent applications to Harvard and the Catholic University of America, the only American universities I had ever heard of. Everyone in the world seemed to have heard of Harvard, while every Catholic appeared to have heard of the Catholic University of America.

The replies from the latter two were encouraging but noted that I would have to wait until the fall semester of 1962 for them to consider me. In all cases I was eligible for a tuition assistance program that the Kennedy administration had put in place after the Bay of Pigs fiasco. But that, of course, would not enough. Even at that time college was expensive. I needed some help from the college itself and a job where I could earn some money to pay for my personal expenses.

Wheaton came back with a very generous package that I could not refuse. They would apply to get the federal government tuition assistance for me, they would add some scholarship funds for room and board, and they would give me a part-time job for sixteen hours a week at a rate of $1.25 an hour to take care of my other expenses. Moreover, the American government would pay for my relocation expenses, namely the trip from Miami to Chicago.

This is how I ended up going to Wheaton College—thanks to Karlin, the extraordinary generosity of Wheaton College, my excellent school record, and my personal initiative in trying to make something of myself rather than stay put in either Jacksonville or Miami. Karlin got her wish that I go to Wheaton, and I got mine that I go to college.

Obviously I was lucky, but luck is not the entire story. It is true that luck constitutes a great part of what leads to success. Everybody can cite examples that show luck to be probably the most important factor in success. Nothing is more important than being in the right place at the right time and having someone to lend you a hand when you need it. But it is also important to be on the lookout and alert for opportunities and to have a goal, a plan that will allow you to help materialize opportunities along the way.

It is not so much that we have the power to realize opportunities; it is that we need to be actively searching for them and telling others what we are looking for. Indeed, in Miami I met many Cubans who had arrived months before me and were still looking for a job, but felt discouraged by the lack of success in finding work. We need to be like Felina, continually looking for opportunities and never giving up, because one never knows what the future will bring and when.

My case, and that of Cubans generally, should refute the all-too-common view that immigrants come here to live on handouts, that they do not want to work, that they have no initiative, that they do not want to learn English, and that they do not contribute to the country. The Cuban experience is proof that these beliefs are unsubstantiated assumptions based on biases and false generalizations that have scant basis in reality. I did all I could to learn English, to go to college, and get ahead. But as immigrants or refugees we need a bit of help. President Kennedy's program for Cubans was a first step on a ladder that would make it possible for Cubans to find a place in the American social order.

The proof is everywhere in Miami and elsewhere. My generation and subsequent ones prove critics of immigration wrong. Most immigrants work hard and assimilate into the larger population. When they do not, it is often because they are prevented by others or by social structures that stand in their way. True, many Cubans that came here belonged to a professional class and had a set of values that helped them flourish. But even those that did not have tried very hard to become faithful citizens of the United States and to contribute to American society. It is only a small minority that has failed in this endeavor.

This applies to immigrants throughout American history. Think of the Jews, the Poles, the Italians, the Swedes, the Germans, and so many others. Those immigrants were not different from immigrants today such as Mexicans, Central Americans, Colombians, Peruvians, Vietnamese, Haitians, Syrians, Chinese, Jamaicans, and so on. We all want the same thing, namely, the so-called American Dream. Moreover, when the newcomers become Americans, as most Cubans have become, they contribute to the rich social fabric of this country, because they are hungry for things American. Their arrival fueled the kind of energy that helped make this country a land of immigrants, and it is the immigrants who have made it what it is.

4

A Gate to the Real America (1962)

Up until the moment I reached Wheaton College in January of 1962, I had not really been confronted with the real America. My experience of it had been filtered through a Cuban environment in Miami, and my exposure to Americans and American culture had been superficial and tangential in spite of the fact that I had been living in the United States for several months. On the ferry, my thoughts had been about my recent personal history in Cuba and the events that had led me to leave my native land.

The details of my arrival had kept me largely insulated from anything not Cuban. During my stay in Jacksonville I lived with a Cuban family. Alberto and his sister were Cuban and Mary was not, but she had married a Cuban and had lived in Cuba for many years. Once I went to Miami I hardly had anything to do with Americans or American culture. I lived in what was a de facto Cuban ghetto. It was nice and comfortable, but culturally isolated from the American mainstream.

This was the reason why, unlike many other Cubans of my age who welcomed the opportunity to stay in a Cuban environment, I thought I needed to move away from Miami as soon as possible and go to college. My English did not allow me to communicate even at the most rudimentary level. Was I dreaming? I began to understand why Miami was full of Cubans who had ventured outside this bubble and had returned, and others who had never tried. They feared the unknown, and what was foreign to them. And pretty soon I started feeling the same fears that other Cubans felt. Rather than succumb to what appeared inevitable, my fears and doubts made me even more desperate to leave and anxious to join the real America. That dream, I am sure, convinced others, particularly Karlin, that I was ready to leave Miami and go to college.

At Wheaton I entered an environment that had not one connection Cuba, with one exception. Thanks to Karlin, my roommate in Miami, Pepe, had also been accepted at Wheaton, but he was the only Cuban at the college other than me. Indeed, except for one faculty member, none of the faculty or students had ever been to Cuba, had anything to do with Cubans, or knew anything to speak of about Cuba. The shock of encountering the real America would affect me deeply and on various levels.

The plane ride to Chicago from Miami was itself a new experience. I had never traveled by plane before (this was 1962, when plane travel was still a novelty), and had a completely wrong idea of what it entailed. Moreover, as a Cuban I had never experienced extremely cold weather, nor did I have any sense of how to dress for it, and I had no idea how buildings, planes, and cars were heated. I had only heard the terribly exaggerated stories Cubans told about how cold the North was.

The place sounded to me like the Hell of Dante's *Divine Comedy*, a frozen ring where those condemned spent eternity. Accordingly, I proceeded to dress for the trip as if I were going to be traveling in the North Pole: warm undergarments, wool sweaters, coats, overcoats, socks, and gloves. I was ready to face the elements! Or so I thought. But a few minutes after entering the plane I realized I had made a terrible mistake, because the plane was heated and I was boiling. I had to take off most of what I had put on, but unfortunately I could not take off my wool undergarments. The heat was unbearable. When we got to Chicago I felt as if I had been properly roasted; even for a tropical Cuban this was too much. But then once I went outside the cold forced me to put back on some of my attire. Then it was too hot again in the car from the airport, and then too cold. This rapid zigzagging of temperature led me to conclude that the Miami Cubans had it right: This was a Dante's Hell.

Two Wheaton students were waiting for Pepe and me at the airport. They were very friendly and attentive, and introduced themselves to us as our "big brothers." Brothers? What did they mean? They certainly were big, particularly my future roommate, who was a football player and built like a machine. After many attempts at communication, Pepe and I concluded that they were students who were there to take us to the college. In any case, time would tell, and indeed it did. We learned that the college had a system of senior students to help freshmen acclimate to the new environment.

Our big brothers tried to be as helpful as possible. Unfortunately, our English, particularly mine, was of no use. Pepe had been in Miami for several months and had learned some English, but my knowledge of the language was nonexistent and thus did not match their expectations. They talked to us, but I understood nothing. The situation was embarrassing, worrisome, and painful. How could I function in such a foreign environment? I felt like a two-year-old attempting to converse with a nuclear physicist. I did not understand a word of what was said to me, and I could not make myself understood. In short, I smiled and nodded at everything. I must have appeared to be deaf or a complete idiot. I can only surmise the nonsense I uttered in conversation, if it could be called that.

Upon exiting the airport I saw snow for the first time, and it was nothing like the snow I had seen portrayed on Christmas cards. What a disappointment! It wasn't fluffy, pretty, or white. It had become dirty and parts of it were partly frozen and melting fast. Was this even snow? One thing I expected was confirmed: it was indeed cold, in contrast to the warm welcome of our big brothers.

The college itself was another surprise. Most Wheaton buildings are in the style of Georgian architecture. Coming from Cuba, where architects had sought to be avant-garde and different, and particularly having been a student of architecture for a year, to me this architectural style looked awful. I was unimpressed with the simple decorative details, the fake Greek facades and columns that had nothing to do with American culture or history, the traditional brass fixtures, and the red brick exterior walls. Indeed, it has taken me many years to learn to appreciate good Georgian architecture.

Not that I have ever compared it favorably with Gothic, Greek, or the contemporary avant-garde. But it is certainly clean, pleasant, and rather cheerful if compared with the centuries old, gray stone Gothic favored by many educational and religious institutions in particular. I could understand why Greek-like motifs appealed to academics, since it was the Greeks who invented science, philosophy, and the academy. But it was ironic that Christian evangelicals, opposed as they are to ancient Greek values, would choose to build their churches in a neo-Greek style. Of course, this was only one of the very many contradictions that characterized life at Wheaton.

Wheaton College, in my room. Photograph courtesy of the author.

Next Pepe and I were taken by our assigned roommates to the rooms we shared at the dorm with American students. Eventually I had to learn to wrestle with my American roommate. Remember that he was a football player and strong as an ox. Other students on the same dormitory floor came to greet the Cubans, attracted by the novelty and the genuine desire to be friendly. I could say very little, but they were kind and understanding. They took us to do all the required paperwork and to show us the campus, including the chapel, which looked as Georgian as everything else on campus and had no indications of being a place of worship. To me, accustomed as I was to baroque and Gothic Catholic churches, it looked like a large barn to which Greek columns and decorative motifs had been added.

This was the time when I learned to say "nice" in order to disguise my ignorance and get out of difficult situations. "Oh, how nice!" This was a most useful expression that avoided serious judgment and was not rude. That night I went to bed exhausted, not so much from the trip but from the effort to appear intelligent when I was deaf and mute. Next morning my arms ached terribly from the repeated action of putting on and taking off my overcoat. And it was cold, colder than I had ever experienced in my life. The idea that someone would choose to live in a place so cold mystified me.

One thing that was particularly welcome was the food. Not that I liked it much at first, but I had been chronically hungry in Miami, and the fact that the dining hall was "all you can eat" meant that I could eat all I wanted for the first time since I had been in Jacksonville. And I drank milk by the buckets. In time some of my American friends and I had competitions to see who could put away the most glasses of milk in one sitting, and often I won. A few months after my arrival my weight had reached 155 pounds, which is close to the most I have ever weighed in my life.

The college population was almost entirely Anglo-American and from the Midwest, with the exception of literally a handful of students from Latin America. They were as nice as the other students, and it was a relief to find that there were some people in the college who spoke Spanish. The Spanish-speaking students wanted to get together with us to help in any way they could, and I was grateful for their attention. However, at that moment I realized that if I hung out with them, I would never become integrated into the student population, and, worse still, I would not learn English.

I resolved, then, generally to keep apart from Spanish-speaking students until I felt that I had mastered the language sufficiently to cope with my studies. Besides, I did not want to be a foreign pariah; I wanted to be part of the student body. Not that I wanted to avoid my Spanish-speaking colleagues completely and forever. I had in mind controlled access and a limited moratorium.

Because we had arrived at Wheaton in the middle of the winter break in early January, the students had arranged and paid for us to go with them to a ski resort in Indiana for a couple of days. This was the first time I came in contact with abundant snow. It was fluffy and white and as beautiful as I had originally expected. Still, I must say that although in time I learned to ski, ice skate, and enjoy snow and winter, at that time my Cuban self objected to the cold in spite of the coats, sweaters, hats, scarfs, and gloves.

Then classes began and so did the regular college routine. The first important decision was to choose a major. A major, what is that? This was another entirely new experience for me. In Cuba, as in most other countries in the world, a university education begins with a choice of a professional career, such as medicine, engineering, or law. In each case, the courses are carefully tailored to produce a narrow expert in the field. Indeed, in most cases there are no courses in general education. Even students who want to pursue careers in the sciences, the humanities, or the arts specialize from the very beginning. They are required to take courses that are focused on the main discipline they intend to pursue. This was certainly me experience in my first year of studying architecture in Cuba.

By contrast, the American system of education begins by giving college students a taste of most basic disciplines through a variety of general education courses in science, the humanities, the social sciences, and the arts, while allowing some introduction to the main fields students intend to pursue in their professional lives through the choice of a major and sometimes a minor.

The notion of a liberal arts education is perhaps the most important contribution of American education to world education, and I am sad to see that it is being increasingly eroded because of financial pressures among other things. College gives students the opportunity to sample many disciplines, to discover if one has a natural talent for and inclination toward them.

Thinking that I would be pursuing architecture, the career I had chosen in Cuba and to which I had devoted my first year of university, I declared mathematics as a major, and expected the narrow focus I had experienced in Cuba, but the reality turned out to be something quite different. Wheaton was a college of liberal arts with a religious evangelical bent that required students to satisfy various requirements throughout the curriculum, including courses on the Bible. In addition, there were elective courses on subjects ranging from music appreciation to creative writing and geology. For me, this was like being a sugar junkie. Could anyone dream of a better system? I felt that I had come to a place where dreams become reality, where I could satisfy all my intellectual cravings.

Most students complained about what they considered distractions from their narrow, career-minded goals. But for someone like me, the system seemed ideal because one of the greatest problems I had was deciding on and narrowing the field that I should pursue for life. I had wavered from natural sciences, such as physics and biology, to the social sciences, such as psychology and history, the humanities, such as philosophy, and the arts. After much thought, I had chosen architecture because it incorporated natural sciences, social sciences, and the arts.

Although I had been happy in Cuba as an architecture student, and I think I would have been a happy architect if I chose it as my profession, I felt I had missed out on some of the other fields that I had previously considered and that were now open to me.

At Wheaton I could postpone my final career decision and thus have the opportunity to delve into other fields that had intrigued me in such a way that it would surely make clear whether they were the right choices for me. Little did I know that I was not going to choose one of the fields I had considered in earnest in Cuba, and instead choose one that I had never considered seriously, although I had liked it when I was introduced to it in the last year of prep school.

From what I have said it should not been inferred that Wheaton was all work and no play, making all of us dull. For the men, there were plenty of gorgeous women to romance, and I had no great difficulty attracting the attention of some of them. Indeed, shortly after my arrival, I noticed a dark-haired beauty with a lovely fair complexion and stunning blue eyes that changed intensity and even tone with the light.

I first saw her at the cafeteria. She and her friends were surveying the territory, and I could not take my eyes off her. I was sitting with a group of guys, including my roommate, who immediately started joking and saying that I should go and introduce myself to her. I felt timid, but those blue eyes lit a fire that I could not resist. So I got up my courage and in my cryptic English introduced myself to her.

That was the beginning of a romantic interlude that lasted the entire semester. We were together constantly, and in the evenings sat on the grass in front of Blanchard Hall to kiss. There was very little else we could do because I could not express myself in English, but those kisses told everything. I was still writing to the girl I had left in Miami, but my letters were less and less frequent and enthusiastic. Suspecting a change of heart in me, she got in touch with Pepe, but we had no future together. As I had told her when it was clear that I was leaving for Wheaton, we should have broken up the relationship before I left. So I wrote to her again, telling her the truth, which she did not take well.

In spite of the intensity of the romance with the Wheaton student, we also broke off our relationship. Once she left for summer vacation we both realized that romance was not what we had come to college to pursue, and agreed it would be better to put things on ice until she returned from vacation. Of course, the distance cooled our passion. As the Spanish saying makes clear, "distancia quiere decir olvido."

So when she came back, we met, had a nice talk, and parted from each other. She was beautiful and I was good-looking, and we made a lovely couple, but we were too young and there were obstacles that separated us, including religion. The truth was that I could never think about her wearing the diamond that had belonged to my mother and that I carried with me wherever I went. It was an unbreakable tie to my Cuban identity. The diamond, set on strong, unbreakable platinum, was waiting for the right love.

One of the many things I learned to love while at Wheaton was opera. Prior to my third semester, I moved out of the dormitory and into the home of a lady who rented rooms to students. She was an opera fan. I remember that first day I went to talk to her about the room, she was playing a favorite of hers, Wagner's *Tristan and Isolde*, on her record player. We could hardly hear each other because the music was so loud, but the experience was explosive.

Wagner's exploration of the theme of love in this opera is surely one of the greatest musical achievements of all times. This is not only because of the novelty or the sheer musical power that overwhelms the listener, but because, in my view, it is the most accurate musical rendition of the act of love. It begins slowly and playfully, builds up to a crescendo, and ends in a climax. Who can forget this sublime moment upon listening to it?

I am no fan of Wagner. My favorite opera composer is Verdi, for no one can capture themes of love, hate, life, death, jealousy, anger, and treason like an Italian. Verdi, in my opinion, is the Italian version of Shakespeare, speaking to all human beings on a fundamental level and capturing humanity in a way no one else has been able to do since. But this should not devalue the sublimity that Wagner frequently achieves, although at a cost, often too high. For whereas Verdi's operas contain not a single note that could be dispensed with, Wagner's operas are full of boring, unnecessary moments.

I rented the room and instantly became a favorite of the landlady, Mrs. Blanche Way. She was a widow who had courageously taken over her husband's insurance business after he died, and had managed to do well in his absence. As an opera fanatic she had a subscription to the Lyric Opera of Chicago, and when she saw that I had been impressed by what I had heard, she encouraged me to subscribe as well. At first I was hesitant—both because of the time commitment it would involve and the cost. It meant going to the opera in downtown Chicago several times a year, and I was busy with my studies and poor as a mouse. Besides, in

Cuba I had only been to *zarzuelas* and operettas at the Teatro Martí in Havana and thought that perhaps full opera was a little too much for a young man. But I took the plunge and bought season tickets in the last row up next to the ceiling. I have never regretted it.

Prior to this, I had thought that opera was an imperfect aesthetic medium because, unlike orchestral music, chamber music, comedy, drama, ballet, poetry, painting, and sculpture, which may be regarded as purer forms of art, this is a composite medium, a kind of Frankenstein's monster that tends to prevent the appreciation of the contribution made by its components.

In many ways I still agree with this judgment to some extent. But some composers are so gifted that they can overcome the difficulties of the medium and create well-integrated works of art. This is a feat achieved by very few composers, and not always with every piece they create. The two most successful in my mind are Verdi, who achieved it in most of his operas, and Wagner, who achieved it in several of them.

Despite the strict evangelical rules of conduct imposed at the college, there were still plenty of fun activities allowed at Wheaton. And there were plenty of female students who paid attention to what they probably thought was an interesting young man recently arrived from Cuba. My three and a half years at Wheaton were not dull, and I managed to survive them without becoming too attached to anyone in particular. I felt I was too young for a serious romantic relationship, and besides, I had other plans for myself. I was alone in the United States with no financial resources to back me up. How could I, then, make a serious romantic commitment? I had already faced this issue in Miami, and was not about to make the same mistake again.

Still, temptations abounded. Two in particular were significant. One was a beautiful blonde who wrote love poems to me under the pen name of Butterfly. And in the last year of college I enjoyed a relationship with a fantastically smart and funny coed with whom I had much in common. With both young women I was honest in telling them that I was not ready to make a commitment. The second woman had another admirer who was deeply in love with her and serious about their future together. I could not, in good conscience, encourage her to have hopes with me when she had a secure future with someone else. Understanding the situation, we parted company but remained friends.

It spite of all I have said, it should not be inferred that I spent most of my time on opera and women. There was also hard schoolwork and my job. During the school year my job was an unpleasant chore.

For sixteen hours a week after 6:00 p.m., I swept, mopped, and waxed floors, threw out garbage, put classroom chairs in proper order, wiped blackboards, made sure there was an ample supply of crayons in class, and did all the maintenance required.

The routine was exasperating because I could think of a thousand other things I could be doing rather than cleaning floors. To make matters worse, my boss was a rather idiotic man whose idea of work was to do it as slowly as possible while always looking busy so that no more work was assigned to him—so perhaps he wasn't that stupid after all! His favorite topic of conversation was complaining about how hard he had to work. Of course, my idea of the job was to do my chores as quickly as possible, so I could have some free time to read and do my school assignments. We would fight over this, and eventually he became worried that I might complain to some higher-up at the college, so he left me alone.

I also worked during the summers, in this case every day from mid-afternoon until one or two in the morning. This was fun because I worked with other students who, like me, wanted to make some money. The work was harder. It consisted mostly of stripping floors and waxing them. Fortunately, the waxing took little time and since the wax had to dry between coats, it gave us an opportunity to talk and, for those of us in summer school, even do some homework. While we worked we discussed everything under the sun. I made great friends among the working students, and in some cases very dear friends with whom I planned outings to Chicago to visit the Art Institute, enjoy the concerts at the Ravinia Festival, and take advantage of the many superb events that took place in the culturally invigorating metropolis.

Wheaton marked both an achievement and an opportunity in my life. It was an achievement because, unlike so many other Cubans who struggled to survive and join America while stuck in a Cuban ghetto in Miami, I succeeded in getting out. Not only that, I was enrolled in a college and therefore on my way to acquiring an education and a degree, which were the first steps toward realizing a dream that most Americans have but only some realize.

Here I was, a Cuban refugee with no money or family, entering a select college in a country where I had been a mere five months. I felt I was in heaven, but the reality was that I faced at least three serious challenges that could threaten my entire future.

The first challenge, encountered by all immigrants, encompassed both internal and external elements. Internally were the cultural and social shocks I would continue to experience. Externally, there was veiled and sometimes open discrimination by segments of the American population. The second challenge involved the religious impact of evangelical fundamentalism at Wheaton. And the third was the ultimate task of deciding what I was going to do with myself and my future.

5

Foreigner in a Foreign Land
(1962–1965)

Perhaps the greatest challenge I encountered when I came to Wheaton was the exposure to the conservative and insular American Midwest. It has frequently been said that for Americans the only thing that matters is America, and if that is true, it is particularly true of the Midwest. But this provincial attitude is not exclusively found in the Midwest. To this day, I see examples of it everywhere.

When I turn on CNN the only news I hear about concerns American politics and American issues. The only coverage about the rest of the world occurs when the United States is in some way involved, as happened with the conflict in Iraq. Isolationism is a permanent temptation for American society and culture, and it is one that is flourishing with renewed vigor even today. This attitude reminds me of a somewhat similar one adopted in Spain at the peak of the Spanish Empire.

This is nowhere better seen than in the insignificant knowledge Americans generally have of world geography. I loved the map of the world published a few years back in which the United States appears as enormously large on the earth, whereas the rest of the world is very small. (The same effect happens with New York City on a map of the United States, for New Yorkers are as provincial about New York as Americans are about America.) Not that such insularity does not happen elsewhere in the world. It does, but some societies and countries have the excuse that their populations are uneducated and the societies and countries lack the resources to turn things around. But given the position of the United States in the world, and the access to education and travel that most Americans have, it is shocking to find such provincialism in a country where one would not expect it.

At Wheaton I encountered this insularity almost every day. And it was not just characteristic of the students, who, for the most part, came from very provincial backgrounds, often the rural Midwest, where their main source of social intercourse and news was their church. But it was not just students; some Wheaton faculty were just as shockingly ignorant of the geography, let alone the history, of the world outside the United States as their students. For some citizens of the small, self-centered world of Wheaton, Buenos Aires was the capital of Brazil, Chile was Portuguese, and Venezuela bordered the Pacific. This ignorance extended particularly to the Iberian Peninsula.

Many Wheatonites had only the most vague, stereotypical, and negative notions of Spain, even though the United States had fought a war with it as a result of which it ended up with the Philippines and Puerto Rico. The view of Mexico was similarly vague and misguided, in spite of Mexico's location, a history closely tied to the United States, and an increasing number of Mexican immigrants to the country. Indeed, to this day most Americans cannot properly spell, let alone pronounce, most Spanish names, including mine, and this goes even for news broadcasters on television and radio.

The situation was so bad when I first came to this country that for many years I gave up on the idea of getting Americans to pronounce properly my first name, Jorge. Instead, George would have to do. It was not until the 1990s, after Hispanics, Latinos/as, and Latinxs had become a demographic force to be reckoned with, and their influence and importance were generally recognized, that I made the effort to get my friends to call me Jorge rather than George. Still, even to this day most of my colleagues at the university cannot, or will not, do it, although presumably they are part of the American intelligentsia! Imagine what the rest of America is like in spite of the fact that the Hispanic, Latino/a, and Latinx population in the United States is close to 20 percent.

If Wheatonites had no clue about Iberian and Latin American history or geography, the situation with respect to other aspects of our culture was even worse. Consider as simple a thing as food. When I came to this country, I found that practically no one knew anything about Latin American or Spanish food. Mexican food had not yet become as popular as it has since then, but even today, most Americans cannot distinguish between Mexican and, say, Cuban food. It is standard that they regard all

Latin food as being very spicy, when anyone who knows anything about it knows that Cubans and Argentinians in particular hate strongly spicy food. Cuban food is fundamentally Spanish while Argentinian food is mainly Spanish and Italian; in both cases the cuisine, although strongly seasoned, cannot be considered spicy.

The situation was still worse with respect to so-called high culture. In classical music, no one had ever heard of Falla or Granados; in art no one had ever seen a reproduction of a painting by Velázquez or Rivera; in literature they had not run into a Spanish author; and of books, only a handful of my teachers at Wheaton had heard of any author other than Cervantes.

In short, my teachers and student colleagues knew very little, if anything, about the things I considered to be important parts of my history and culture, things that I considered made me who I was and that were landmarks in my cultural tradition and identity. No wonder I felt like an alien, a foreigner in a foreign land. I did not belong to it because I did not share a history and culture with those who surrounded me.

Not that I was a pariah. I was well accepted by the faculty and most students, but I could not be one of them, as I had been in Cuba with other Cubans, where I belonged, where I understood those around me, and where I had buddies and friends whose situation was similar to mine. In this foreign land of the Midwest I did not feel part of the mainland but rather like an island all to myself, alone, and even lonely at times. For the first time in my life I felt inferior because I did not have what those around me had and expected of me, what was a matter of course for Americans and a novelty to me.

What made this worse was that some students shared the view that somehow Latin Americans were inferior. Indeed, there were students who openly subscribed to this view and, when asked how they explained my performance at the college, answered that every generalization has an exception—I was an anomaly. Interestingly enough, I only learned of this through hearsay. No one ever came to me and openly defended the charge. Although in Miami I had encountered signs advertising real estate for rent that warned: No dogs or Cubans.

Most important for me was the language. My lack of knowledge and fluency in English separated me from everyone, and made me feel ashamed. How many times did I have to ask that my interlocutors repeat themselves when they addressed me? And how many times, even after multiple repetitions, did I still not get the difference between "shirt" and "church"? Differences in sound were subtle, and often I could not understand what Americans said because I had never before encountered the words they were using. I felt stupid and embarrassed. I longed for a time and place where I would no longer have to struggle. I wanted to be in a place where I did not have to suffer feelings of isolation and shame simply because I was not an American and did not know English well.

Of course, I knew there was no reason why I should feel that way. Ignorance that is not self-inflicted or a result of stubborn, uncompromising ideology should not cause shame. But I couldn't help but feel shame. And so did most of the other Latin Americans at the college. So it was natural for us to stick together, to find support in each other, and in that way to feel once more like human beings, unashamed and unembarrassed, and part of the mainland.

Interestingly, once I began to better understand what other students were saying, it was clear that I was generally more knowledgeable about the humanities, the arts, and the sciences than they were. Indeed, their insularity and lack of acquaintance with world literature and art, even with plain geography as mentioned earlier, were shocking. And it was not because they had a grasp of their own culture, for often they knew as little about it as they knew about European art and literature, let alone non-Western cultures.

These feelings generated a reaction in me. Yes, I had resolved that I would learn English and adapt myself to American culture, and this required in my view a distancing from everything that could prevent it at least for a while. Instead of joining the ghetto of the marginalized and isolated, I needed to stay away from the group of other Latin Americans at the college.

This was a hard decision that took a great deal of courage and an uncompromising, disciplined will, for it implied not just a few days or weeks, but months and years of pain and isolation from what belonged to me. The solution to my situation seemed to be that I had to become someone else. But could I be so cavalier with my identity?

Indeed, how long did it need to last? I had no idea because it depended not so much on me but on others over whom I had no control. Not that they did not want anything to do with me, although I perceived some resentment when I did get together with them. They were willing to talk to me, to include me in their circles, and to welcome me. And in time I developed good friendships with a good number of students.

It was difficult at first because at the beginning of these friendships many of the Anglo-American students realized it was painful for them to have to repeat themselves and make constant allowances for my linguistic and popular cultural ignorance. Their patience was repeatedly tested, and eventually some of them gave up in the effort. But others worked out of curiosity and interest in my point of view. I was a novelty, and some realized that they could learn something as valuable from me as I was learning from them.

I was exploring uncharted territory, and I was eager to learn American history and culture and be part of the society that generously had given me shelter in the hour of need, the society that had made room for me and was providing me the opportunity to reach the goals that I dreamed to achieve. But at the same time, I could not give up on who I was in order to make room for a new me. There was only so much of me and my past that I could sacrifice in order to become American.

Indeed, in the process I realized that I did not know enough about my own history and the history of my people and about the culture that had sustained me. I was willing to eat roast beef with mashed potatoes and gravy, but I was not willing to give up *arroz con frijoles* and *dulce de guayaba con queso*. Besides, I asked myself the key question of identity: What is it that defines me? And if there is something, what is the proper balance between being Cuban and Latin American on the one hand and American on the other?

This, I thought was the key: instead of drowning in America, I should try to learn to swim in it while still maintaining afloat. It turned out that this was a good strategy. A great part of what kept me afloat was the investigation and appreciation of the great achievements that my culture had produced. So this was my line of defense in order to survive as myself. It also meant that, in order to do it, I had to transcend my Cuban identity without abandoning it. Cuba by itself could not counteract the undeserved sense of inferiority I felt. Cuba was too small and insignificant, too parochial, to balance a scale upon which the United States and Europe occupied the counterweight. Yes, Cuba has Ernesto Lecuona's intoxicating rhythms and José Martí's incomparable verses, among many other jewels of civilization.

But the United States and non-Hispanic Europe had scores of figures that not only boasted enormous achievements in the sciences, the humanities, and the arts, but seemed to dwarf the Cuban contributions, figures who had influenced the world, at times changing the course of humanity. After all, is it not true that most Latin American countries, including little Cuba, modeled their forms of government on some aspects of the American Constitution?

Yes, Cuba had some great achievements. After all, hadn't Cuba been a powerful influence on popular music in most of the world? But that was not the case with classical music. Even in cases where Cuba clearly had made important contributions to the world, the United States surpassed them. It was irritating that my student colleagues, and often their professors at the college, were ignorant of Cuban contributions to the world, but it was painful to see that they did not even know of some outstanding American contributions—and yet, ironically, they thought of themselves as both special and superior.

Matters were made worse because I was a refugee. I did not belong in the country. I was a passerby, almost a tourist, tolerated for the sake of charity, although unlike tourists I did not bring anything with me that I would leave. Yes I had brought the diamond with me, but this was something I would keep. In the end, I had only myself. I could be considered, as many did, a taker, and therefore a competitor for the goods the country had to offer. I was just a cut above so-called illegal immigrants.

I faced two great temptations that exiles, immigrants, and refugees have to reckon with. Both are counterproductive and may lead to failure and resentment. One is the temptation to reject the country where they land and to maintain a strong emotional attachment to the native land. I call this the "temptation of nostalgia." I have observed this phenomenon throughout my life in the United States. I have seen it in Cubans, Mexicans, Colombians, Argentinians, and immigrants from other countries all over the world. A pervasive characteristic of this nostalgia is wrapping the country of origin in a veil of approval, reimagining it as a golden land where one had been happy but that, for economic or political reasons, had to be abandoned.

In contrast with this mythically perfect land that immigrants tend to construct, the real land where they live becomes an object of resentment. All its faults, real or imagined, are multiplied and one regards oneself as a prisoner in a culture in which one does not belong, where one feels humiliated and inferior, a stranger, a foreigner who longs for the mythical native land where happiness was pervasive, the proverbial land of milk and honey.

Some of my Latino friends at Wheaton fit this model, always criticizing the United States, the country that was giving them shelter, and uncritically glorifying the country they had abandoned or were forced to leave. It is easy to succumb to this temptation because it is supported by an imaginary creation of a past that never existed and that has nothing in common with the current reality, which feels harsh and unwelcoming due to linguistic, religious, or other cultural differences.

Even at Wheaton, where I met with kind interest and approval, this was true for some Latinos as well as students from other parts of the world. I remember in particular a sad student from South America who was not studying at Wheaton but who visited us frequently. He was like a rebel without a cause, hating everything that had to do with the United States even though everything he had was made possible because of the welcome he had received in this country.

And I remember a white South African who could not stop complaining about the countless faults he found in the United States and its people, contrasting them with the heavenly picture he painted of his own country, where apartheid was still the rule. Nostalgia can be, and often is, blind.

This is not an unusual attitude among immigrants, particularly among younger men who need to feel part of society, to have friends who appreciate them, their desires, and their ambitions. Being in a foreign land, where they can be easily marginalized and discriminated against, and made to feel like foreign interlopers, they can develop resentment against the country that gave them and their families refuge. This resentment can become a kind of irrational hatred and a wish to undermine and harm the society in which they live.

Feeling rejected by the mainstream, they make matters worse for themselves by exclusively associating with each other in social ghettos that isolate them even further. This in turn encourages ordinary citizens to further reject them and think of them as ungrateful, generating a vicious circle that sometimes results in violent acts on the part of the immigrants or the mainstream citizenry. Some Latin Americans, feeling themselves victims of these circumstances, find fuel for their resentment in the demagogic rhetoric of Latin American *caudillos* and the mistaken and imperialistic policies that the United States has so often had with respect to Latin America. Overlooking the egregious behavior of unscrupulous Latin American leaders drunk with power, whether on the political right or the left, they become their misguided apologists.

Equally nefarious is the second temptation that immigrants, refugees, and exiles face, that of rejecting the past, and making no room for it in the present. Contrary to those who fall prey to the temptation of nostalgia, these immigrants fall for what I call the "temptation of forgetfulness," because unlike those afflicted with nostalgia, they forget all the good that characterizes their native lands. One's roots are firmly tied to one's self, so that it is impossible to completely forget one's past, even if one was so young when emigration occurred that one remembers little to nothing about it.

Those roots survive in our parents, relatives, friends, and in the culture, national, racial, and ethnic ties tethering us to our origins. The effort to sever ties with our past leads to a sickly kind of schizophrenia and even paranoia. Those who succumb to it, rebelling against their original culture, and anything that has to do with it, whether good or bad, because it is their original culture, tend to welcome uncritically everything the new land has to offer.

Here again I saw some of my Latin American friends at Wheaton reject everything that historically belonged to them in favor of everything that sounded American to them, as if everything American was good and required no critical inspection. They were victims of a syndrome similar to the temptation of nostalgia, but in reverse. They built an image of the new land as the Promised Land while viewing their past as irredeemable.

But is any land perfect, and is any land irredeemable? I saw some of my Latin American friends live this mirage, and suffer its consequences, for at some point the past caught up with them and they had to go back and find a place for it in their present. But then it was often too late. They had forgotten it, and the society of those who had not so rejected it was not welcoming to them. In a sense, just like the Nostalgics, they become outcasts of a sort.

I faced both temptations and ultimately rejected them in favor of the recognition of the place that my past had in my life and the place that my present and future were to occupy in the coming years. In order to join the present I had to bracket the past for a while, but only just sufficiently to be able to acquire the tools to join and participate in my new land without forgetting the old one.

In short, I never decided, as some immigrants often do, to reject my identity. I did not give in to the temptation of forgetfulness. Cuba would continue to be part of me, even though many of my personal memories of my life there were painful. I needed to expand myself to include other factors that were also influencing me and of which I had not been previously aware. This included the history and culture of

Spain and Iberia in general, as well as the history and culture of Latin America at large.

This was easy for me, for how could I not celebrate the poems of San Juan de la Cruz, the music of Albéniz, or the temples of Machu Pichu? This constituted my defense strategy, the raft that kept me afloat and that in time became an enormous ship able to withstand any cultural behemoth that challenged it. The impact of American culture was so overpowering, and my situation so perilous, that I needed the entire edifice of Hispanic and Latino history and culture to resist drowning in it. The effort entailed a major change in my conception of who I was, a first step on a road that I have followed since then and which has yielded both great successes and some failures, but which overall has enriched my life in ways that I could not have foreseen and has also made it possible for me to help others who were experiencing similar pressures. In short, I first had to be transformed from Cuban into Hispanic and Latino in order to become American, which is precisely the opposite of what those who succumb to the temptations of nostalgia or forgetfulness do.

Some immigrants are so Cuban or Mexican, say, that, in their sense of themselves, they always stay within those categories. In my case, I became conscious of a strong contrast between my being Cuban and being American. But then, almost immediately, I seemed to become more, namely Pan-American or Latin American. I remember writing letters to former friends who lived in Miami and talking to them about the richness of Latin America and Anglo-America. This was something they did not care to talk about and openly dismissed.

They thought I was weird, maybe even a traitor of sorts, for I was abandoning Cuba for Latin America and Iberia for the United States. Perhaps the reason for their reaction was that they lived in a closely-knit community. To this day, many Cubans in Miami still live in Cuba—mostly a mythical Cuba, a product of their imagination, but still Cuba.

Fortunately for me, almost from the very beginning I had lived outside the Cuban milieu in Miami, so that I was forced to confront another world early on. Now, readers might remember that I said earlier that until I learned sufficient English to communicate effectively, I tried to stay away from anything, and anyone, that had to do with Spain, Latin America, or Cuba. And I did. Only after a year had elapsed did I feel I had developed sufficient confidence in my knowledge of English and the workings of American culture that I went back to the Latin

Americans at Wheaton, ending up with a very nice group of friends that did things together.

Some friends were purely Anglo-American and did not mix with any of the other Latin Americans; some were Latin Americans and did not mix with any of the Anglo-Americans; and there was a group of Anglo-Americans and Latin Americans that got together and enjoyed each other's company. The only Cuban other than myself in the college was my roommate from Miami, who did not impose a personal moratorium on Latin America and Cuba, and paid a price for it.

So what is the best strategy for foreigners who reside in foreign lands and cultures and who are suffering from the temptations of either nostalgia or forgetfulness? There are three possible strategies. One is to adopt a plan that involves *full integration* into the foreign culture and a rejection of the past culture. The result of this strategy is most often frustration and unhappiness, because it is quite unlikely that one can be happy while completely abandoning one's roots. Those who adopt this approach also end up in a constant struggle. The second approach involves *full rejection* of the foreign culture and complete adoption of the past culture, which also results in frustration and unhappiness. Fortunately, there is a third alternative, a middle way, and that is to seek *a discerning adaptation* that satisfies most of the cultural and social needs of the groups in question. This is, in fact, the strategy that I followed not only in my college years but every time since then that I have lived in a foreign land. The result has been a healthy balance—an appreciation of my own culture and the one in which I reside, while at the same time rejecting elements of both that are unacceptable.

This is how identity issues became important to me for the first time in my life. This did not mean, however, that I had any philosophical interest in these subjects. My personal situation and my philosophical concerns occupied separate compartments in my life at that time. The first had to do with my emotional life and who I was or was trying to be. It involved juggling the various cultural claims on me in order to preserve a functional identity.

Philosophy as a universal intellectual enterprise occupied a different place altogether. In this sense, I was trying to learn about the world and how to talk about it cogently, how to articulate arguments for and against its interpretations, and about the history of human attempts to understand it. Philosophically, then, I didn't have a great deal of interest in anything that had to do with Latin America or the Hispanic world at this time. Before a proper integration of these forces could occur, I needed to reject some aspects of the American way of life that stood in the way of successful adaptation to my situation, and further, to develop a deeper philosophical understanding of the forces at play. So much then for the first challenge I had to face and deal with at Wheaton. In the following chapter, I turn to the second.

6

Surviving Evangelical Fundamentalism (1962–1965)

The second challenge I had to face at Wheaton was its evangelical fundamentalism, particularly because I was neither evangelical nor fundamentalist. I was a Catholic and, to make matters worse, a wavering Catholic, what I sometimes call "a roaming Catholic." Wheaton forced me to face the question of faith.

Let me go back a bit. I was nineteen when I landed at Wheaton. Six years earlier, at the age of thirteen, I had decided that religion just didn't cut it. I have never been an atheist, but I certainly have had periods in my life when I have been an agnostic and other periods when I have been anti-Catholic, faithfully Catholic, and existentially Catholic. Even at times when I did not consider myself Catholic, I never adhered to other faiths. I have always thought that if one is going to be religious, being Catholic makes the most sense from a theological standpoint.

I had an existential period in college, when I read Dostoevsky and Kierkegaard, authors who left strong marks on my thinking about religion. This is the sort of view that Arthur Holmes, my favorite teacher at Wheaton, seemed to me to have held, and probably he was unknowingly responsible for having enticed me into it. I have always had problems with orthodoxy, of whatever kind.

The religious tenor of Wheaton enticed students to think seriously about religion. It encouraged some of the most conservative ones to defend extreme fundamentalist views, whereas it motivated progressive students like me, who did not believe in the brand of Christianity that was common at Wheaton, to articulate our views with sufficient rigor to shake up some fundamentalists. Since smoking, drinking, dancing, movies, and the theater were forbidden at the college, some of us spent our time arguing fine points of doctrine or social policy.

Serious discussions were everywhere—at the cafeteria, during work, and of course in the classroom. This created a community of students interested in intellectual matters absent at many secular colleges, even the most selective ones, where a considerable amount of time and effort is spent on drinking and sex.

Christianity was at the center of everything that happened at Wheaton. Daily chapel attendance was compulsory. At midmorning the chapel bells rang, everything stopped, and faculty and students walked to the large chapel where there was always a religious program. This may seem strange to those who have not attended religious institutions, but it wasn't to me. I was used to attending Mass every day, reciting prayers at the beginning of each class, saying the rosary once a day, giving thanks before every meal and sometimes after as well, and religious instruction. Indeed, life at Wheaton was not much different in the mechanics of these matters. The difference was that Wheaton was a college—and it was evangelical and orthodox.

The daily chapel program at Wheaton generally included someone who spoke on some point of doctrinal interest. The services were strong in emotion and testimony. I cannot recollect any of the speakers I heard at those services over the years, but I remember vividly the vigor with which the entire congregation sang Protestant hymns.

Bible courses were required of every student, and for those with stronger religious interests there were plenty of additional courses available. I took advantage of some of these, particularly during intersection in January and during the summer.

Because religion was at stake, these courses did not seem quite as rigorous as other courses, and the teachers were encouraging and lenient. I remember taking courses on particular biblical books, such as Ephesians, which were fascinating.

The instructors were thoroughly conversant with the original biblical languages and the level of instruction was high, even if the standards for student performance were not at the level of science courses. Even the sciences, however, were dominated by a fundamentalist ideology, as were the theology and Bible courses.

Wheaton was interdenominational, but within this general rubric it aimed to be orthodox in all important points of doctrine, although in some instances what was regarded as orthodox differed from denomination to denomination. Apart from chapel every day and the heavy course load focused on biblical studies, Wheaton was heavy on devotion. There were prayer meetings going on at all times, and saying grace before and after each meal was de rigueur. Not that it was required, but not doing it was considered inappropriate and identified those who did not do it as rebels.

Being a rebel at Wheaton was not very difficult, since there were so many rules against behavior that young people like to engage in, but it was not pleasant insofar as those considered rebels were made to feel like fish out of water. I made clear from the beginning that I tolerated the evangelical cartel, although I opposed it for rational reasons, not because I was Catholic.

For some true Wheatonites, being a Catholic was as bad as being a disciple of Satan, or at least of the Antichrist, which some of them identified with the pope. Still, the faculty members were tolerant, and some of them were even a bit on what might be considered the evangelical left. I never felt unwelcome at Wheaton because of my religious opinions, and I was the center of much attention and interest precisely because I was so different from everyone else. I was a rarity. Indeed, for some students I was the first Catholic they had ever met. Keep in mind that this was the time when the main objection against John F. Kennedy's candidacy for president of the United States was that he was Catholic.

It helped my intellectual development that Wheaton and its mission were somewhat schizophrenic. Consider four examples: the theory of evolution, the doctrine of the literal interpretation of the Bible, the doctrine of the inerrancy of biblical texts, and the view that races should not mix.

The first posed a problem for the college because Wheaton wanted to be perceived by the community of scientists as a place of rigorous scientific research, up to date in the latest scientific theories. Indeed, Wheaton had a strong department of biology, but at the same time, because of its fundamentalist religious doctrinal commitments, the college could not openly advocate the theory of evolution, which is generally accepted in scientific circles.

Faculty members were asked to sign a doctrinal statement that required them to reject Darwin's major scientific achievement. At the same time, in order to be accepted by the broader scientific community, they would teach in the classroom precisely what they denied to be true in the doctrinal statement. Biological theory required them to believe one thing, while their faith required them to believe the opposite.

The problem with the doctrine of the literal interpretation of the scriptures similarly created a conflict, indeed a contradiction, between a historical and textual theory that makes sense (and was advocated by Christians from the very beginning of the Christian era), and an absurd view, advocated by nineteenth-century fundamentalists, that held that scripture should only be interpreted literally.

This did not make any sense. Considering the scientific proof we have of the slow development of the universe and the earth, Genesis makes sense only if it is interpreted metaphorically. Catholics, who have fallen into doctrinal difficulties in the past—remember the case against Galileo?—have consistently rejected a literal interpretation of the scriptures, going back to the views of the fathers of the Church, such as St. Augustine.

Ironically, fundamentalist interpreters of the Bible regularly violate their own hermeneutic doctrine when they translate biblical texts into different languages, for there is no translator indeed that is not a traitor, as Boethius maintained. No two languages carve the world exactly alike insofar as their different vocabularies reflect different takes on their surroundings. In this, evangelical fundamentalists are more inconsistent than orthodox Muslims who reject the translation of the Koran from Arabic into other languages. The result is consistent, although rather absurd, insofar as many Muslims cannot read the original language of the Koran and end up memorizing passages without knowing what they mean. In a sense, this approach results in a view of the texts in question as "magical," as well as religions that are eminently ethnic and that reject any measure of rationality in belief.

The problem posed by the doctrine of the inerrancy of scriptures has long been contradicted by textual evidence and historical data. There are mistakes in the Bible. The texts in which these inconsistencies, contradictions, and tensions appear have long been known and acknowledged in the Christian community. We need only read Peter Abelard and his indictment of literalist views and defense of a rational understanding of scripture for a convincing illustration. In his book *Sic et Non* (*Yes and No*), he shows how the scriptures contradict themselves and how they can only yield a sensible understanding if it is based on a philosophical analysis, which for him meant the use of reason and science. Only a critical reading of the text can yield an explanation of the errors found in scripture. Contemporary textual critical theory has proved without a doubt that the text of the Bible has mistakes in it. Needless to say, Abelard was not a favorite of Rome.

Finally, there was the absurd view, based on some misguided interpretations of scriptural verses, that races should not mix. At Wheaton the relevant biblical texts were understood to refer to blacks and whites, and the text was taken as an injunction against marriage between them. Accordingly, mixed dating was out of the question. Because there were very few blacks at the college, it was easy to adhere to this policy without controversy. Still, there were a brother and sister from Trinidad who had black and white ancestry. There were also two brothers, children of the Ethiopian ambassador to the United States, who looked black. So at parties these students had to scramble to find dates that would not be objectionable, such as some Latin Americans, and indeed my roommate from Miami was frequently asked to parties by the Trinidadian students. Other students of color who could not find appropriate dates had to forgo partying.

Even more objectionable was the existence of segregation. I remember once that a group of students were going on a tour, and we stayed at a hotel where we all had to share double beds. One of the Ethiopian students asked me whether I would mind sleeping with him because he was afraid to ask anyone else. He knew quite well the implicit view of racial distinction at Wheaton, even though there was no explicit segregation. Looking black, he felt he might be rejected and publicly humiliated by any Anglo-American students he approached and concluded that his only way to avoid a rejection was to ask a Latin American, thinking correctly that most of us were not as racist as the Anglo-American students. I personally felt very sad for him, but more importantly, to me this did not make any sense in a Christian environment.

Is this segregationist conduct something Christ would have condoned? Surely not. And yet, it was practiced at Wheaton, although very little was said aloud about it. I have found that some of the most blatant violators of the spirit of Christ are often the very same people who tout themselves as the most devoted of his followers. It is particularly paradoxical that Jesus himself, given his Middle Eastern background, would have been rejected had he asked an Anglo-American student to share his bed.

The fundamentalist atmosphere of Wheaton generated a strong negative reaction in some students, particularly those who read and thought about what they were fed in their churches and what they were exposed to in the classroom. This was in spite of the careful management of their teachers, who tried to uphold the letter and spirit of the doctrinal document they were required to sign in order to teach at Wheaton.

I have always wondered about the honesty of some of these faculty members, and surmise that the way they justified their position, at least those who taught philosophy, was by adopting a nonrationalist approach tinged with a kind of existentialism, where doctrine is more a kind of feeling than an understanding.

The fundamentalism of the branch of Christianity advocated at Wheaton, with its antirationalist bias, eventually turned me off and made me appreciative of the Catholic tradition, in which, despite some unfortunate deviations, there has generally been a profound respect for reason. That tradition pointed me toward the scholastics, particularly Thomas Aquinas.

I have never been a disciple of Aquinas or an apologist for him or his views, as unfortunately many Catholic philosophers are, but I became interested in him at Wheaton because if one looks at the history of Christian thought, there are very few authors who reach Aquinas's stature, his rationality, and his clear thinking.

But embracing Catholicism was not enough for me, for as early as the fifth grade I had already found some Catholic doctrines inconsistent and unacceptable. I had always gone to private Catholic schools in Cuba and in spite of serious questions about the Eucharist, for example, I had more or less accepted the views that I had been taught. This accepting attitude began to break down in my first year of high school, when I began to question Catholic doctrine.

I had started reading voraciously the previous year, and reading had become my greatest occupation and pleasure. It also introduced me to thoughts and ideas I did not know existed. What I read was different from what my teachers said, and those incredible stories of bleeding bread and martyrdom we had been fed in primary school now found a counterweight.

I began to critically examine my views and slowly dropped many of the beliefs and practices that had been central to my life. I did not question the truth of Christianity, nor did I not question the goodwill of my teachers. But the first cracks in the edifice they had built and in which I had lived, oblivious to anything else, began to appear. In school I was introduced to ancient history, which I found fascinating. It was the source of a different kind of story. There was gore as well as heroic acts, but the heroism was not for beliefs that challenged our reason, but for honor and virtue. This was a significant difference, and even though I was still immature, I began to appreciate it.

In my second year of high school I experienced a crisis. I had regained my place at the head of the class, with a straight A average in the first year. In spite of the drop in my grades the year before due to a move to Havana from the countryside and a change of school, I continued to read everything I found in my father's library, Aunt Rosario's library, or that was recommended to me by anyone. Some of the books were recommended by my teachers, some I saw advertised, and some were offered by classmates. I bought any books I did not already have. Anything illicit was welcome. I do not mean illicit because it was pornography. In fact, there was plenty of pornography to be had in Cuba, but that was not what I read.

I never spent a penny on that trash. Many of the books I read had been placed on the Catholic Church's infamous Index Librorum Prohibitorum. The Index, for those who do not know, was a list of books the Catholic hierarchy thought dangerous and should not be read except with the permission of the clergy. Practically every important book in Western culture was included in the Index, and so it was inevitable that someone who liked to read would read forbidden books. The result was that I found it incomprehensible why some books, like Victor Hugo's *Les Misérables*, were placed on the Index.

Among the books I read that made important impressions on me was *The Twenty-Fifth Hour* by Constantin Virgil Gheorghiu, the tale of a man who suffers an endless list of mishaps during World War II because he was mistakenly thought to be Jewish based on the fact that he was circumcised. Another was *The Skin* by Curzio Malaparte, a story of the American invasion of Italy. I still recall the vivid images that formed in my mind while reading this book, such as black American soldiers patronizing Italian prostitutes and asking that they wear blonde hairpieces on their vaginas. Even more important was Françoise Sagan's *Bonjour Tristesse*, which had become a kind of existentialist manifesto for young people at that time. The ennui described in that book echoed my adolescent moods.

There are too many books to list, but suffice it to say that I read everything I got my hands on, including biographies of kings, queens, popes, heroes, and artists. Among my favorite biographies were those of

Marie Antoinette and Michelangelo. The stories of the popes were particularly shocking. I remembered the criticisms my father voiced against the leaders of the Catholic hierarchy, but I had not quite believed him. Now I found out that he was correct.

Although it also was a glorious atelier, the Renaissance Vatican was a moral cesspool, which is one of the reasons why the Reformation was so successful. Not that it was the only, or even the primary, reason for its success, of course. Politics and power had as much to do with it as anything else. Luther was no innocent Cinderella. But the state of the papacy certainly gave Reformers a reason for rejecting the Catholic Church's legitimacy.

All of this came to a head when I was thirteen, when I decided that the Catholic Church was a sham. The reason I reached this conclusion was not just that so many of the highest leaders of the Catholic hierarchy had been corrupt but, more importantly, that the doctrine they taught made no sense. The idea of a God who inflicts punishment on his so-called children, whom he is supposed to love so much that he gave up his own life for them, was just unbelievable.

What father would behave in such a way toward his children for any infraction, even an egregious one? What kind of a father, or a god, was this? The idea that he presented himself on earth in the flesh-and-blood form of Jesus, to be crucified and to die for our sins, seemed absurd. First of all, how could Jesus die since he was God and God is supposed to be immortal? The idea, too, that the Virgin Mary never died, and was lifted to heaven in her physical body, seemed equally nonsensical. How can a body be taken to heaven when heaven is not a physical place? The more I thought about these notions, the more that Catholic doctrine appeared to me to be nonsense. Of course, had I been a follower of Tertullian, for whom the measure of faith is absurdity (*Credo quia absurdum!*), this would have had the effect of strengthening my faith as it does in fact with many believers. But I have never been a fan of Tertullian; indeed, he is not one of my favorite writers or thinkers. I believe that for faith to be taken seriously, it has to at least be consistent with reason, and better still, to make sense. As Aquinas argued, faith need not be proven by reason, but faith should be compatible with reason.

But would giving up belief in the Catholic doctrines that appeared to me to be nonsense require that I give up all sense of spirituality? The choice was difficult because when I went to church I was often deeply moved. The procession of the Host on Holy Thursday, the singing of

Thomas Aquinas's magnificent hymn, the *Pange lingua*, together with the incense and the ritual, produced in me experiences that were deep and seemed genuine.

Was all of this a farce? And what of the holy people I knew, men and women who had selflessly devoted their lives to Christ and to the welfare of others? Were they a complete farce too, or were they just stupid? How could I reject the legitimacy of St. John of the Cross's *Spiritual Canticle* or St. Augustine's *Confessions*? At this time I had also begun reading the work of Eastern sages, such as Jiddu Krishnamurti, whose wisdom I felt deeply and further complicated my intellectual situation.

The cracks appearing on the edifice that was my faith kept growing, but I still continued to go to church and engage in religious activities. Rationally, I had become an agnostic: I could not believe what the Catholic Church taught. Nor could I accept the views that my mother tried to press upon me, the evangelical version of Christianity she had adopted after the tragic death of my brother at twenty-two. Indeed, the death of my brother was the source of a revolution in all the members of my family. He was just beginning to live, as it were, and yet he was taken from us. For me this was a catastrophe, because my brother idolized me and I idolized him. I was eight years old when he died, so how could I understand this fact? What had I done to deserve this pain? The pain lasted a long time, and when I became too depressed I would take the horse that he had given me on my sixth birthday for a ride. It was a way of remembering my brother and consoling my pain.

I found these evangelical views aberrant, even more unacceptable than Catholic doctrine, in part because of their tendency to irrationality. Still, I did not stop living as if I were a believer, even though I had not found a solution for reconciling my doubts with my practices.

While I remained at the Marist school, I continued to live as if I believed everything the school taught. In fact, I joined a Catholic Action group and was very active in it, although I tended to concentrate on areas of social assistance, such as helping the poor, rather than on pious acts. For a couple of years I was in charge of looking after an old black woman who was almost blind and who lived alone. I bought her groceries and visited her frequently. She was a fine person, gentle and kind, and the little room where she lived was kept in perfect order.

I also went to religious meetings and talks at which I met a fabulous priest by the name of Durán, who was the epitome of devotion and holiness. He was a Spaniard who had settled in Cuba as a member of one of those orders that have both priests and lay members living and working together in the world. To a great extent, he was the reason I kept the trappings of Catholicism, for he was the real thing. But although we had many talks, nothing was ultimately resolved. He tried very hard to get me to commit to his order, but I could never do that. My temperament is neither that of an activist nor of a religious zealot, and the tension between doctrine and practice was at the time unresolved. There were periods in my life in which I felt a strong sense of spirituality, particularly when I did the Jesuit spiritual exercises in Cuba, but they were always followed by periods in which agnosticism fought for supremacy.

At Wheaton I had to take a stand and, as people say, clean up my act. I had to decide what I did and did not believe, and to put this together with my professional and personal goals. A decisive book for me at this time was Dostoevsky's *The Brothers Karamazov*. This is a story of conflict among three different views of life and faith. The hero is Alyosha, whose approach to faith is portrayed as authentic and non-doctrinaire. He is a symbol of the Christ that is revealed in the scriptures. At the same time, I was reading both Protestant and Catholic theologians who had adopted in some ways an existentialist approach. This gave me the key to my predicament.

Rather than trying to justify the inconsistencies of Christian doctrine, whether in Protestantism or Catholicism, I should embrace the actions and rituals of a traditional living faith, for faith was not about holding on to propositions, many of which made no rational sense, but about living a life based on the Christian commandment to love everyone. Years later I used these ideas in the short book I wrote about tradition, *How Can We Know What God Means?*, arguing that tradition is not a matter of propositions but of actions.

This was the lesson taught by Alyosha's life. In stark contrast is the atheism of Alyosha's brother and, even worse, the cynicism of the Grand Inquisitor who is willing to sacrifice Christ again in order to save the institutionalized Church. Neither of these attitudes was appealing to me. The resolution to my quagmire was, of course, still insufficient and not above criticism, but it would do for the moment. After all, I was young and there were other forces fighting for supremacy in my life.

None of what I have said should imply that life at Wheaton was dull, and that we spent all our time thinking about philosophy and theology. It is true that students had to sign a pledge stating that they would abstain from drinking, dancing, smoking, and going to the movies or the theater while at Wheaton. But I did not feel constrained to honor the pledge because I considered that I had signed it under duress. I did not think one needs to honor pledges extracted under such conditions, or that one thinks are wrong or nonsensical, and it was wrong and nonsensical to abstain from all these forbidden things when some of them are actually good, such as dancing, and going to the movies and the theater.

Indeed, the prohibition on going to the theater, in particular, made no sense. Even drinking can be perfectly good if it does not lead to inebriation. Interestingly enough, I do not recall that we pledged not to engage in sex outside of marriage. Was it because the college administration was so uptight that even a reference to sex was felt to be inappropriate?

In spite of the casuistic arguments I used to justify my rejection of the pledge, I never actually violated it on college grounds or even in the town where the college was located. However, I did not refrain from it out of a sense of duty, but out of a sense of courtesy for the college. In short, I convinced myself that I was free to do certain things that were not allowed as long as I did them outside those locations. My violations were limited in any case because I have a Puritan streak: I've never smoked; I've always been a sensible drinker; and, although I love dancing, I didn't have the opportunity to do it while at Wheaton. My violations were mostly restricted to going to the movies and the theater. Yes, at Wheaton we were taught Shakespeare, but we were not allowed to attend performances of his plays, and this was ridiculous and intolerable.

So much for rationality and consistency! As a final note on my life at Wheaton and my criticisms of the fundamentalist mentality of the college, I want to emphasize that with very few exceptions, the faculty, students, and administration treated me with interest and respect. Indeed, because of the conditions under which I left Cuba, the Bay of Pigs crisis, the continued political tensions between Cuba and the United States, and the scarcity of firsthand sources of reliable information, I was frequently invited to give talks around campus and to churches in the town, and in spite of my fractured English, practically everyone was cordial, understanding, and patient.

Of course, after my college years at Wheaton, I had to face the world outside the ivory tower and make serious decisions about what I wanted to do with my life. The time for playing had ended, and I had to know myself and find my way. And this involved choosing a career or profession.

7

Knowing Myself
(1962–1965)

According to Socrates, the most fundamental, and perhaps the most difficult, task of philosophers is to know themselves, that is, to discover who we are and how we fit into the world that surrounds us. Indeed, finding the path, career, profession, or vocation, call it what you will, is one of the most significant, difficult, and agonizing decisions we are expected to make in our lives. To make matters more difficult, we are asked to make this decision when we are too young and often too immature to make it. Indeed, how can seventeen-year-old kids, barely out of their home, be expected to choose what they will be doing for the following sixty years?

In places like Cuba, where one is required to jump into a narrow field without sufficient exposure to a variety of career paths, not only does it seem absurd to expect it, but it is also absurd to think that the choice made will ultimately be successful and satisfying for life.

The world is full of disgruntled people locked into professions that they despise and that make them unhappy. This is a personal tragedy of enormous proportions that affects them and their families for life. It is sad to see that only a small minority is satisfied with that choice while the majority spend the rest of their lives trying to escape it. They find passing relief in vacations, hobbies, and often alcohol or drugs. But none of these really work, so they live miserable lives of desperation, undecided about who they are and what they should do.

In the United States, thanks to the college system, young people have a few more years to decide on their career, and it helps that during their college years they are introduced to a variety of fields before making a final decision. This saves some. For me, of course, that help was not available in Cuba, and the entire process of choosing my path was worrisome and traumatic.

When I chose architecture as my career in Cuba, I thought I had made a decision that would shape the course of my life. I felt a bit like Caesar when he crossed the Rubicon—the die was cast and there was no turning back. Little did I know that forces over which I had no control would soon be unleashed and my future would take an entirely different direction.

So much for the view that we control our destiny! Obviously, I was not destined to be an architect, although to this day I take an interest in architecture and follow contemporary developments in the field. All my doubts about a future career over which I had agonized in Cuba returned, and with greater intensity, but more delight. College was a uniquely wonderful experience for those who are curious and want to learn. There was so much to choose from!

The courses that impacted me the most my first semester at Wheaton were English literature, writing, and music appreciation. I loved classical music, and I also loved popular music for dancing to in the Havana nightclubs, although I found it too boring for listening. The first time I heard Rachmaninov's first piano concerto, I felt as if I had an epiphany.

I can't count the number of times I've listened to it since then. Its romanticism, hypnotic power, and magnificent structure overwhelmed me. I memorized entire phrases of it and would have given anything to be able to play it on the piano. We had a piano at home, but boys were not encouraged to play the piano in Cuba because male pianists were considered effeminate. The piano was for my sister, who banged on it once in a while, but with her children and other duties, she never got past the stage of beginner.

At Wheaton I didn't have time to learn to play the piano or any other musical instrument, but the music appreciation class made up for it by giving me the rudiments of how to distinguish different historical musical periods and how to identify the greatest composers. I very much enjoyed this particular course and looked forward to it. It helped that the teacher was engaging and funny.

The freshman course on writing was very difficult for someone like me, who did not know English, but the teacher was tolerant and, understanding my plight, required me to do exercises that would help develop my skills while also encouraging the flights of imagination that were part of my nature. I thrived on the challenge. But it was the literature class that was my favorite and that had the greatest impact on me.

We read extensively, but three assigned readings had the greatest impact on me. One was Joseph Conrad's *Heart of Darkness*. This is a magnificent work written by an author whose native tongue was not English, so I was predisposed to sympathize with his work from the outset. The plot, with its slow penetration into the heart of Africa, awoke in me feelings and images that had been alien until then, at least superficially. I read it not as a narrative of a trip in Africa but rather as a diary of a journey into my African subconscious. I found every passage to have personal significance. Then there was John Milton's masterpiece, *Paradise Lost*. I had never before appreciated poetry as much as I began to then, in spite of the fact that poetry was something my family loved. The exposure to English sensitized me to the sounds of language, and this long poem satisfied my longing for a greater variety of sounds organized in magnificent verses about a thrilling hero. This was psychology at its best; the psychology of good and evil. The epic character of Satan, who is without a doubt the tragic hero of the poem, is unequaled in world literature. Finally, Sophocles's *Oedipus Rex* was the tale of the tragic life of a hero who paid a dear price for his inquisitiveness. I had always had a thirst for knowledge, and I found in Oedipus a kindred spirit and a warning of what could happen to me if I followed in his footsteps.

Would my own search for knowledge and meaning end in tragedy as well? And what of the role that destiny plays in our lives? After all, I had already seen how a strange combination of will and chance had affected the course of my life in unexpected ways. The course became more than just the accumulation of literary facts; it turned into an odyssey of sorts in which I was the traveler and my destiny was a mystery known only to the gods.

But how could I get over my difficulties with English? How could I master this insufferably beautiful language? Spanish, my native tongue, was very different from English. It was phonetic, that is, it was written as it sounded, as happens with the word *gato*, which sounds as it is written. And similar combinations of letters sound alike. *Gato* always sounds the same, whether we are talking about an animal or a tool to change a flat tire. This made it easy. But English was nothing like that.

Words like "strong" and "Strachan" (a street in Toronto) that are spelled differently sounded the same to me, and words that have different meanings are often spelled in the same way, like "read," the past tense of "to read," and "red," the word for a color. Then there were linguistic phenomena in English that did not occur in Spanish, such as words ending with certain consonants like "ham" or "young," and sounds available in English and not in Spanish, such as the sound of the "y" in "you." This made for very funny situations, for example, when I wanted to say "sheet" but pronounced the word as "shit," and vice versa.

The only viable solution to my predicament seemed to be practice in talking and reading, as much as possible. So I took every opportunity to talk with other students and read every printed page I could lay my hands on. Indeed, the key to the process was reading, because I could learn to associate the written word with the spoken one.

So I read and read, often understanding practically nothing of what I read, but identifying phrases here and there that I had heard spoken, which helped me to figure out the meaning of the text. It was particularly helpful to try to think only in English, putting together sentences that I would later use in conversation, often erroneously, which would end in embarrassing situations. Still, all of this was useful in that I would try not to repeat the same mistakes.

One problem was that I was not used to recognizing and distinguishing certain sounds. So, for example, I mistakenly associated the word "dear" with the word "there," and for a while I was saying things like, "Hi, dear!" when I actually meant to say, "Hi, there," which made me appear excessively familiar. And there were more embarrassing moments.

I remember once when I was giving a talk in a local church about my escape from Cuba and how I had brought as many things as possible, including a sheet, which I called "a shit." Imagine the commotion in a fundamentalist congregation!

The fact is that I did not have an adequate vocabulary to express myself. So the dictionary became my constant and faithful companion. The work was painstaking, sometimes ending in exasperation. And yet every day I learned something I did not know before, and slowly it was not just a few things that I learned, but many, because what I learned one day opened new doors the next.

The papers I submitted in class came back full of red annotations by the teacher. Still, she was able to figure out what I wanted to say and where I was going. Her patience had no limits, probably because she had briefly been a missionary in Cuba and had similar experiences with Spanish. She was committed to my success and I paid her back by always giving her my best. Indeed, the very first summer I was at Wheaton I took two courses in American literature, where we read some of the great classics.

The grade point average I achieved thanks to the summer courses made it possible for me to take honors courses and seminars beginning in the fall semester. The literature course also made me decide to change my major from mathematics to mathematics and English literature. I could not pass over the greatest challenge that I faced by doing so. But the best was yet to come.

The following year I took a course in philosophy with the legendary Arthur Holmes. He was a great actor in the classroom, a teaching virtuoso, and the way he presented himself and the texts that we read were enticing. More significant perhaps was that he squeezed out of texts a content that should have been obvious but that students missed. He also related authors and texts in such a way that we could see the history of human thought developing in front of our eyes. The difference between what the instructors of literature courses did and what Holmes did was enormous, and I wanted more of what he did.

The problem with literature teachers was that they seemed to function like bad philosophers. I had come to literature not because of its philosophical content, but because I was intrigued by what made a text a literary work as opposed to something else. Some of the questions I needed answers to were about form: Why is *Paradise Lost* a great work of literature? Why did *Heart of Darkness* have such an effect on me? And what was the solution to the plight of Oedipus in *Oedipus Rex*?

Other questions were about the audience's understanding: How do we get at the meaning of these works? How do I know I have understood them correctly? What is the author's role in the composition of a work of literature? These were questions that were going to occupy me for decades to come and which I tried to resolve in books like *A Theory of Textuality: The Logic and Epistemology*, and *Texts: Ontological Status, Identity, Author, Audience*.

Of course, in philosophy there are no definitive answers. As philosophers, we are forever engaged in an unending inquiry. Being oblivious to the general answers to these questions has to do in part with the form a work takes. It is the form, the sounds, the vocabulary, and how these are woven into a tapestry that make a work unique and invite an audience to think in unique ways. It is not primarily because of a particular thought conveyed by the work, although the thought is part of what makes a literary work great.

But no class of literature I took at Wheaton ever addressed anything other than the thought, that is, the meaning of the text. The instructors spent their time trying to extract from the texts a kind of philosophy, but they did not know enough philosophy to do so effectively, nor did they take into account the contributions to meaning made by the shape and structure of the literary text.

When I took Holmes's course I realized that, although I would continue to be interested in the form and hermeneutics of literary texts, a major part of what interested me was, paradoxically, the thought they conveyed, and yet in order to get at the thought, one needed a philosopher, not a literary critic. And that did it: this is why I dropped mathematics from my double major and instead became a philosophy and English literature major.

I had taken logic and philosophy in my last year of prep school and had loved both, but there was no place in Cuba where one could seriously study or practice hard-core philosophy. There were not enough institutions to make room for philosophers to teach at the university level. And their programs and degrees turned out to be as heavily literary as their names suggested: *Filosofía y letras*, that is, Philosophy and Literature. Indeed, the one philosopher of note who did some hard-core philosophy in Cuba was Enrique José Varona, a positivist who was not very sympathetic to philosophy as a whole.

Cuba has produced some extraordinary poets and essayists, such as Jose Martí, but very few philosophers of note. Discussion and dialogue have clearly been essential to philosophy from the very beginnings of the discipline. But if one is a philosopher, what can one do in a country where there are so few others with whom one can engage in a discussion of ideas? What can one do by oneself? This is one of the reasons I had not seriously considered philosophy as a career in Cuba. I didn't have enough conviction to follow through, and thus betrayed that initial inclination to become a philosopher.

Now, however, I was coming back to it, and with sufficient force to devote my entire life to the discipline. The United States had what Cuba lacked, an abundance of well-trained philosophers who addressed the main problems that had been explored in the discipline throughout the ages—and it had a well-established community devoted to it. To boot, it was possible to earn a living teaching philosophy, although not the kind of living one would earn in better-paying professions.

My situation in the United States opened the possibility of seriously considering devoting my life to philosophy. At the same time, Castro's Revolution closed my sources of income in Cuba. I had lost my inheritance when the Cuban government despoiled me of the properties I had inherited when my father died. In the United States I felt free, unfettered by social constraints or family responsibilities.

In a way, philosophy fit my entire intellectual history up to this point, because one of the problems I had faced until now had been that I was interested in too many things and was talented enough to undertake any of them with some credibility. Although I was not a dilettante, I appreciated almost any area of human learning. And philosophy is the only discipline that takes into account every other discipline insofar as no subject matter is alien to it. Pick anything at random and you will see that it can be the object of philosophical investigation. Don't we talk about a philosophy of mind, psychology, colors, morality, and so on? One can compose a philosophical treatise about words, lines, figures, paintings, art, texts, history, minds, literature, ad infinitum.

Philosophy puts together our knowledge and fills the gaps in our understanding of areas that are not discussed in other fields of learning such as logic (the study of reasoning), ethics (the study of how we should act), metaphysics (the study of the most fundamental categories), and epistemology (the study of knowledge). Nothing falls outside the purview of philosophy, because philosophy is the pursuit not just of wisdom narrowly understood but of knowledge in general insofar as the human experience of everything is relevant to it.

Nevertheless, I should acknowledge that at the time I did not have complete theoretical clarity in my mind about what all this entailed. I was too busy living to reflect on the contribution of philosophy to my life. It took me years to get a sense of it. Still, I was sure of one thing: I wanted to become a philosopher, and the primary motivating factor was the impact that learning English was having on me. This in turn led me in a new direction, although not in a straightforward way. Nothing about humans and their goals is ever straightforward; everything is complicated and embedded in an unpredictable set of factors that influence it, and contribute to its clarity (or lack thereof) and depth.

At Wheaton I found myself immersed in a strongly fideistic environment that was difficult to accept. Particularly difficult for me to understand was the antirationalist tendencies of both the faculty and the students. My turn toward philosophy may have been indirectly affected by religious factors in that I felt I needed to understand the place of religion in human life, and Wheaton had much to do with making me think about it. Karlin, of course, knew that this was going to happen, but she hoped that I would become a born-again Christian and embrace some version of evangelical Christianity as a result. In spite of her strong convictions about her faith and the fact that she was greatly disappointed because I did not embrace her beliefs, we continued to be dear friends until her death. She lived an exemplary life, and I owe her a great debt. Her enthusiasm about everything in which she got involved was contagious. Although I did not agree with her about becoming a born-again Christian, which I never did, she awakened in my life the need to resolve some religious issues. Unfortunately for her, her hopes were dashed.

Indeed, it was particularly ironic that being at Wheaton not only helped me turn toward philosophy and away from the kind of religious fundamentalism that Karlin favored, but that it made me appreciate the contribution of medieval philosophers such as Thomas Aquinas and William of Ockham, among others, to the understanding of the relationship between faith and reason.

There was at least one serious rebel cell of students at Wheaton—some Protestant and some who eventually became Roman Catholic. Motivated by their religious faith, they took a particular liking to Thomas Aquinas. By contrast, my appreciation of Aquinas was motivated by the same impulse that eventually led me to medieval philosophy: I realized that most of the basic concepts of philosophy that we today consider to be the fundamentals of Western philosophy were framed in the Middle Ages—concepts such as essence, substance, nature, category, quality, relation, and so on. These concepts come ultimately from the Greeks (in Latin/Roman translations), but the bridge between the Greeks and the United States is the Middle Ages.

The Middle Ages was the period of history in the West when modern languages were formed, and when the first treatises and discussions of how these fundamental concepts relate to each came into existence. I became convinced that in order to do philosophy—and I have always wanted to do philosophy rather than to be merely a historian of philosophy—I had to go back to the Middle Ages to discover the origins of the fundamental philosophical concepts that we study today. Indeed, my trajectory, without knowing it, was not very different from the one traveled by Martin Heidegger. Recall his turn to the Middle Ages for his dissertation, which was the same turn that I eventually took, although I was not aware of what was actually happening.

All this fit well with the strong interest in language I had developed after coming to the United States. I had arrived with a very limited knowledge of English, and the immersion in it caused an unexpected intellectual revolution in my personal world. I wanted to know more about how language works and how we communicate effectively through the medium of language. Remember my struggles with literature that I mentioned earlier?

This was one of the reasons why I became attracted to logic and eventually to Wittgenstein and other philosophers who favored a linguistic approach, including an emphasis on ordinary language. Indeed, to this day, in my philosophical writing I avoid philosophical jargon as much as possible and try to philosophize using ordinary language and ordinary examples. At Wheaton, this interest was decisive in moving me in the direction of the history of philosophy in the Middle Ages. But to get there was not easy by any means. First I had to go to graduate school, and that meant going to Chicago.

8

Make Love, Not War
(1965–1966)

The motto "make love, not war" dominated the latter part of the 1960s in the United States. The opposition to the war in Vietnam and the growing frustration in the country exploded in marches, complaints against the government, and social unrest. This was the time of the hippies, smoking marijuana, and chanting antigovernment slogans. Without knowing it, I was to live the reality of both sides of the motto. It turned out that I avoided the war, even though it had not been my calculation to do so. And it was a decade of love for me, because it was during this time that I fell in love with Norma, the woman who would become my wife.

The three and a half years I spent at Wheaton had passed very quickly. In no time I was taking the GRE tests and applying to graduate schools in philosophy. On the advice of my teacher Arthur Holmes in particular, I took a gamble and applied only to the top ten schools in the country. And I was lucky in that not only was I rejected by only two schools, Yale and Northwestern, but the school of my choice, the University of Chicago, accepted me and made it financially possible for me to enter their program.

The reason I wanted to go to Chicago was the presence of Richard McKeon (the teacher of Richard Rorty and Marshall McLuhan, among other notorious intellectuals) on the faculty. He was a legendary pioneer in the study of medieval philosophy, and a very broad thinker with interests that in many ways I was to develop later. He had studied for a while with Etienne Gilson, whom I was going to meet in Toronto, and had edited a two-volume anthology of medieval philosophical texts that became a classic, dominating the medieval philosophy anthology market for decades.

After reading parts of this text with enthusiasm, I developed a reverence for "the great McKeon." It was only years later, when I had learned Latin and had checked McKeon's translations of the original Latin texts, that I realized how high-handed he had been in his translations.

Nowhere is this more evident than in the language of individuality, in which he proceeded to ignore the nuances of different terms in favor of a standardization that in many cases distorted the meaning of the original. Still, one has to take into consideration the times when he was working and the tendency of his contemporary medievalists and their critics to gloss over the fine distinctions that medieval theologians and philosophers had made.

In fact, the presence of McKeon became irrelevant for me once I got to Chicago, because, as it turned out, he was of retirement age and well on his way to that phase of his life. To compound the irrelevancy, he was on leave for at least a year. Initially, I was very disappointed; things were not turning out as I had thought, but actually I was fortunate, for unpleasant rumors about McKeon circulated among students. Perhaps the most ominous of these was that, although he had some famous students, he had destroyed many of those who had worked, or had wanted to work, with him because of his harsh criticisms of his students and his intolerance of other points of view.

In spite of McKeon's absence, I was able to take a course on medieval philosophy with a member of the college faculty, a man by the name of William O'Meara, who was a good teacher but had not produced much scholarship in my areas of interest. Only four students had registered for the class I took with him. Most students were taking courses with other faculty on hotter subjects: Robert Coburn on Ludwig Wittgenstein's *Philosophical Investigations*, Eugene T. Gendlin on Kant's *Critique of Pure Reason*, and the most popular by far, Alan Gewirth on early modern political philosophy.

I loved O'Meara's course and wrote a paper on matter, which turned out to be a favorite individuator among medieval authors. This was my first introduction to individuation, a topic to which I was going to devote a good portion of my philosophical efforts for the remainder of my career.

Chicago also had another medievalist of sorts, for Gewirth worked on Marsilius of Padua and published an English edition of the *Defensor pacis*. He had a brilliant mind and was an engaging lecturer. I was awed by the sharpness of his intellect and, after Wheaton's fideistic existentialism, by the radical rationalism that informed his analytic method.

Gewirth had a theory about how to evaluate ethical judgments, which he called the PGC, or the Principle of Generic Consistency. It was a clever scheme that every visitor to Chicago tried to defeat in vain. Gewirth seemed to have an answer for all possible objections. Indeed, in many ways he reminded me of another great philosopher and undefeated logician, Anselm of Canterbury.

Had I stayed at the University of Chicago, I would have tried to study with Gewirth, although his interests had shifted toward ethics and politics, which have never been my priorities. Given my interest in medieval philosophy, I did not see a future in working with him in spite of my admiration. In fact, his and O'Meara's advice was to go to Toronto, where the Pontifical Institute of Mediaeval Studies was at the time the main center for the study of medieval philosophy in the world. It had been founded by Etienne Gilson and included such well-known medievalists as Anton Pegis and James Weisheipl, and the members of what I like to call PIMS' Holy Trinity: Joseph Owens, Armand Maurer, and Edward Synan.

Then there was also Reginald O'Donnell, an expert on Latin and Latin editions who inspired terror in all of us students. The Pontifical Institute was the centerpiece of Gilson's plan to revive medieval philosophy. He had proposed to Harvard the creation of an institute devoted primarily to the study of medieval philosophy. Although Harvard offered him a job, it rejected his proposal, which was later accepted by St. Michael's College at the University of Toronto.

The institute had a program of complete immersion in medieval studies in preparation for concentration in particular fields. Students had to take yearlong courses on canon law, paleography, art, vernacular literatures, theology, medieval Latin, and philosophy. This sounded fascinating to me and right for the program that I was considering pursuing, which was the study of the development of the philosophical language and fundamental concepts in the Middle Ages.

It was all very exciting and I went ahead and applied to the institute. My plan was that, if accepted, I would stay in Chicago until the end of the summer, when I would move to Toronto. I would pick up an MA in philosophy during the remainder of the school year, earn some money during the summer, and then leave for Toronto early in the fall. This script did not go according to plan, however. Several events were to complicate matters considerably.

One of the unanticipated factors that threatened to wreck my entire plan was the Vietnam War. It was 1965 when I arrived in Chicago, and the war was beginning to heat up. Demonstrations in Chicago and other cities were becoming common. In Chicago, the university became a hotbed of antiwar sentiment. Like most young people at that time, I was strongly opposed to the war and participated in marches and other events. This in itself did not threaten my plans, but something else did: the draft.

When I arrived at the United States in 1961, I was registered as a refugee. This status allowed me to apply for permanent residency at any time. At first I was too busy doing too many things to worry about my status in the United States, but eventually I felt that I should become a permanent resident of the country and in due course, after a period of five years, become a citizen.

This country had given me shelter at a critical time in my life and the democratic ideals on which it was founded, the freedom of thought, and the progressive thinking of its Founding Fathers made me want to join it fully as a citizen. Accordingly, I applied for permanent residency as a first step in that direction and it was granted.

One thing that I had not anticipated was that as a refugee I was free to join the army to fight in Vietnam, but it was not required. However, as a legal resident I could be drafted, and this is precisely what happened shortly after I was granted resident status in the United States. Of course, not everyone was drafted. Most children of well-established families found a way around the draft, or found ways of serving that did not require them to fight in Vietnam, as we know happened with many of our politicians. Moreover, exemptions were regularly granted to college students and to those enrolled in programs leading to degrees in certain professions.

The hard reality, however, was that a good number of those who served were young people who did not have social connections. It must be recalled that draft boards were local and they made decisions based on local considerations. In my case, I was doomed from the start in that, as required by law, I registered with the Wheaton draft board as soon as I received my residency papers.

Unfortunately for me, the town of Wheaton was a prosperous suburb of Chicago with a population of primarily professional people whose children were in school and therefore exempt from the draft. Indeed, even if they were not in school, their parents found ways to sway members of the draft board. By contrast, I was a nobody, a recent refugee who had no connections to anyone in the community, a passerby who was ideal for the draft. Indeed, my absence would hardly be noticed. The board was desperate to fill their quotas of draftees, and I was the perfect case of someone who could easily be asked to serve.

When the letter informing me that I was required to report for the draft arrived, I thought that my plans to go to Toronto were doomed. I was given a date to take the required physical examination. Young men were doing all kinds of things to make sure they did not pass the required physical, including claiming that they were gay. Indeed, one of my Wheaton friends did just that, and was somehow exempted. But I did not use any of these stratagems. I did not feel I could lie to the country that had generously opened its doors to me and that I had been willing to join. True, I was against the war, but to my mind that was not a good reason to not answer the call.

The notification informing me that I had passed the physical examination and should report for duty came in January, and the date of reporting was a few weeks hence. Just a few days later, I also received the letter of acceptance from the Pontifical Institute as well as notification that I had been awarded a scholarship to make it possible for me to enter the school for the fall semester. I was devastated, but what could I do?

My future, which had looked so promising, was crumbling. I immediately asked for an extension to at least finish my degree before I joined the army. I explained that I would like to finish out my year at the university so that I could complete my MA, and this request was granted. This gave me a respite, but it was not a solution to my predicament. I would still have to go to Vietnam and forget about my dreams of going to the institute. Was there a way out?

Lots of young men were avoiding the draft by leaving the United States and not coming back. But that was illegal, not to mention it would be an ungrateful gesture on my part toward this country. I bit the bullet and went to talk to the board at Wheaton, where I presented my dilemma. At first, the answer I received was simply that I would have to serve.

The members of the board were sorry and sympathetic to my plight, but there was nothing they could do. As a permanent legal resident I would have to serve. Fortunately, as has happened so often in my life, there was once again a caring person who was able to suggest a compromise. One of the members of the board explained that it was legal for me to resign my US residency and leave the country, and that this would not prevent me from reapplying for residency at a later date, nor would it be a black mark on my record. The catch was that this plan would work only if Canada granted me residency, which sounded like a tall order.

A guardian angel must have been watching out for me, because I applied to Canada for residency and in a few months received it. This solved what appeared to be an unresolvable predicament, making it possible for me to leave the United States legally in order to pursue my studies in Toronto, while leaving open the possibility of immigrating to the United States after I was done. Perhaps my dream was coming true after all!

My stay at Chicago had been far from happy, another reason why I was eager to leave the school. The gloomy and gray Gothic architecture of the school oppressed me. My finances were in terrible shape—I really did not have any deserving of that name. They were tight because, although I received a scholarship that covered tuition and fees, I still had to pay for food and lodging. I had worked during the previous summer and saved as much as I could, but it was not enough, and during the year I could not afford to work. My priority was doing well in school, but Chicago was way harder than Wheaton had been.

Chicago was not only hard, it was a sad school, gray, cold, and competitive. It certainly was one of the best schools in the country, but its philosophy program had a reputation for being tough. Unlike colleges such as Harvard, which had a very selective admissions process but made every effort to keep students well and happy after acceptance, Chicago was not an Ivy League school and had an inferiority complex. It made up for that by accepting more students than it could support well, and then encouraging them to fight among themselves for limited resources. It was a system based on the survival of the fittest—not the kind of atmosphere that would be helpful for someone who did not even know the language properly. To make matters worse, while we were at the bank, a gang had held us up. Fortunately, I had thrown my wallet under some furniture before they paid any attention to me, and my wallet was saved.

Moreover, even though I had been at Wheaton for more than three years, I still had difficulties when it came to writing in English. Besides, the philosophy faculty at Chicago were primarily analytic in orientation and of very high caliber, whereas at Wheaton there was not a single serious analytic philosopher. Arthur Holmes, who was the best philosopher of the group, was an existentialist, and analytic rigor and attention to detail did not characterize either his teaching or scholarship. In short, I didn't have the proper background, and I felt it keenly. It is surprising that I did as well as I did, getting some decent grades and passing the MA examination.

For the second time in my life, there were many days when I was hungry. I was desperate for money and went so far as subjecting myself at least once to a very unpleasant medical experiment for the meager sum of twenty-five dollars. I was enticed to do it by one of my friends who had done it repeatedly, but for me it was a disaster. I felt so poorly and weak afterward that I had to go to a restaurant and eat a big steak, which took most of the money I had just earned. So much for that experience. Still, I survived, and every night I managed to have a dessert I had never tasted in Cuba: cheesecake. This was a comfort and the major extravagance in which I indulged.

I frequently had to borrow money, which I paid back as soon as I could. And I depended on others for entertainment. I was fortunate that I lived in the International House, a large dormitory for foreign students and for Americans who were interested in meeting foreign students. It was not the most fun place in the world, but I met several students from Latin America who were part of a group studying economics and business administration. They had generous scholarships and often invited me to share their riches.

Occasionally, when I was too hungry, I went back to Wheaton to spend a weekend at the home of Blanche Way, who fed me as much as possible, trying to fatten me up, for I was becoming skeletal. I was working too hard, sleeping poorly, and eating less than I needed. This was not an ideal situation, and it could not be maintained for long.

There was also a student who lived in the tower of the International House and he had plenty of money. He became what I thought was a good friend and we spent time talking about various interesting subjects. He was a student of literature, and the literati have always had a weakness for philosophy, even though they seldom understand it. He invited me to dinner, to the theater, and the occasional concert. Unfortunately, after a couple of months it became clear that he had other ideas of where our friendship was going and I had to distance myself from him. Needless to say, he was disappointed and sore and I felt sorry for him.

My life at Chicago was a struggle, and for the first time in my life I lost control over my time. I was worried about my grades—good grades were essential to continue receiving help—which led to continuous studying. I often stayed up very late and then got up in the afternoon of the next day, which was not going to lead to success. However, as soon as it appeared as if I might finally be able to fulfill my dream of going to the Pontifical Institute, my life improved. This coincided with meeting Norma.

She was part of the group of Argentinians and Chileans who were studying economics and business administration. The first date I had with her was on April 1. (I will let readers speculate on whether I was fooled that day, my future wife was the one fooled, we both were fooled, or perhaps it was April 1 that was fooled.)

About that date, suffice it to say that we went to eat at a steakhouse (not surprising since my object was to impress an Argentinian), and afterward to the movies at the Clark Theatre, which was known for showing films that could not make it into commercial theaters. Along with the good movies there were plenty of homeless who went into the theater to sleep, for the entrance fee was very low. I'm not sure what Norma thought of the date, for I have never asked her, but her impression obviously was not too bad since we had another date soon after.

Love is a wonderful thing, and also a kind of sickness, as the poets are never tired of reminding us, and ours was a serious romance. In Norma I found the emotional home I thought I had forever left in Cuba. We spent many hours together, taking walks along the gardens bordering Lake Michigan and visiting the wonders that Chicago had to offer. At the art museum I introduced her to my favorite painting, of which I had a large print in my room: *The Old Guitarist* by Picasso. This is a piece from his blue period that conveys an overwhelming pathos. The romance progressed steadily and it became necessary to reach some decisions about our future. On a leap of faith, just a few weeks after our first date, we decided to get married so that Norma could join me in Toronto. Besides finishing schoolwork, we had to deal with Norma's visa and scholarship, and my lack of funds. So I got a job at the International Harvester factory in Chicago while working madly to finish my MA. As crazy as all this may sound, we had a fallback plan. Norma's parents wanted very much for us to settle in Mendoza, Argentina, where they had several businesses and Norma could return to her faculty job at the university.

The Harvester plant was my first and only exposure to American unionized blue-collar workers. I was hired as a sweeper, but when the supervisor saw my diligence he promoted me to operator of one of the machines that produced steel parts for tractors and other machinery used in agriculture. The workers were members of a union, and the quantity of parts that each worker produced in a work period was closely controlled and watched. As in the case of the janitor with whom I had worked at Wheaton, one had to work very slowly. Naive as I was, the first day I was on the job I produced nearly twice the number of parts as the regular employee who worked the machine produced. He was black and as nice a man as I have ever met.

We hit it off immediately. When he found out the number of parts I had produced, he called me on the side and explained the situation: I was not to produce more than fourteen pieces per work period, otherwise I would violate an unspoken agreement between labor and management. In order to make things appear right, the surplus of parts I had created were set aside as having some imperfections that needed fixing the next day, and in that way the average of parts per day would appear to be what it usually was. Obviously I had not learned from my experience in Miami with the job that involved checking cars.

As a floor sweeper I was being paid over four dollars an hour, but when I became a machinist I was making much more because I was paid by the pieces I made, which added up to about twelve dollars an hour. The year was 1966. This was a great wage that many people would have been glad to have. Indeed, the supervisor, who was an approachable fellow and became a friend of sorts, tried to convince me to stay and move up in the company. He thought I would have a great future if I did, and he could not understand why I wanted to spend more years in school when I had already been in school more years than he had been working at the plant.

I learned many things about my coworkers. One was very defensive about anything that might be perceived as a criticism of Uncle Sam. Indeed, when I said that I was leaving for Canada, one of the guys almost beat me up for deserting the country at a time of war. He had immediately assumed I was a draft dodger; at the same time, he was not sympathetic to me as an immigrant.

It took me a while to convince him that I was not leaving because of the war but because I was interested in pursuing my studies, something that was incomprehensible to him. I was lucky not to have mentioned my opposition to the war. If I had, I'm sure I would have ended up with a black eye and a broken nose. The guy was massive and could have easily made mincemeat of a skinny Cuban like me.

Finally our wedding day arrived in September. The ceremony took place in the university's magnificent neo-Gothic Bond Chapel, while a Renaissance organ struggled to conquer the challenge of playing Wagner's famous wedding march from his opera *Lohengrin*. At the ceremony I gave Norma the ring with the diamond that I had been guarding carefully for several years, and which would now symbolically guard and enrich our marriage. The diamond had found its proper place, which made my mother and me very happy.

The reception at the International House was organized by our friends and Blanche Way at Wheaton. She paid for the cake and the champagne. Holmes, my mentor at Wheaton, escorted Norma to the altar. One of Norma's friends from Argentina made her wedding dress, another lent her an appropriate veil, and there were practical gifts from everyone, many of which we still have to this day. To top it all off, a couple lent us their apartment while they were away on vacation, so we could have a proper honeymoon.

The only sad note was that I had to leave Norma a few days after the ceremony in order to be present at the opening of the fall semester in Toronto on September 9. So we were a little downcast because Norma's

Wedding day, reception at International House. Photograph courtesy of the author.

Canadian visa had to wait until I was residing in Canada and formally requested her to join me. It took three months for that to happen, but we were elated because we were able to be together for Christmas.

The previous three years, just as the three that had preceded them, saw significant changes in my life informed by momentous decisions. Among the most significant in Cuba was the decision to study architecture and leave for the United States. In the United States there were many, any one of which was bound to have had enormous significant consequences: Miami, Wheaton, philosophy, Chicago, medieval philosophy at the Pontifical Institute, and getting married to Norma.

Every one of them opened some doors and closed others. In each case I felt as if I were immersed in a Borgesian labyrinth of forking paths, each of which opened new forks and forced me to make choices whose ultimate outcomes I could not anticipate. Upon reflection, some of these decisions involved serious risks. Certainly the choice of philosophy for a career would open some doors in my future, but it also closed many others.

Philosophy has always been a socially marginal field in which it has never been easy to earn a living, even in the United States. The only way to do so is by teaching, and teaching positions in this field have never been plentiful. Yet, I never gave a second thought to the difficulties I would face as a philosopher. Matters of salary and job security never crossed my mind.

I wanted to be a philosopher and that was the end of it. It never occurred to me that I could fail. Indeed, I did not even have a sense of what failure would mean. Was it not finding a job? Was it failing to produce good philosophical work? Was it being stuck in a small college town with a meager salary? None of these mattered because I loved philosophy, which is to say, according to Socrates, who held that philosophy is the love of wisdom, that I had de facto become a philosopher, unconcerned about the practical consequences of my choice and focused on the goal, namely, the pursuit of wisdom.

And the place where I thought I needed to start on my path to knowing myself was to be found in the Middle Ages. In spite of my dissatisfaction with Chicago, it had turned out that there I had cemented two foundational loves: the love of Norma and the love of medieval philosophy. And both had become fused in my mind as the diamond that I had brought from Cuba, to which a new facet had been added.

Wearing the Pontifical Institute of Mediaeval Studies academic regalia. Photograph courtesy of the author.

9

Becoming a Medievalist
(1966–1969)

The Pontifical Institute of Mediaeval Studies in Toronto was everything that it promised to be. The library was rich with old manuscripts and incunabula that invited the serious scholar to spend hours searching for hidden treasures. Where else could you find an unparalleled collection of commentaries on Peter Lombard's *Sentences*, the established textbook of medieval scholastics?

The faculty was impressive. Its founder, Etienne Gilson, was the most famous medievalist alive, and although he no longer spent much of his time at the institute, he came at least once a year to lecture and meet the new crop of medievalists. The rest of the faculty were distinguished scholars who took their work seriously and were committed to producing the best possible scholarship and to train students as well as it could be done.

The institute offered two degrees. One was a three-year licentiate in mediaeval studies and the other was a doctorate in medieval studies. Very few students completed the doctorate. The majority of students enrolled in the licentiate program, to which I had applied and been accepted. Students came from all over the world, and gave the place an international flavor.

I drove from Chicago to Toronto in a very large Ford Mercury station wagon that I had filled with as many of our belongings as possible. It was so overloaded that the back fender was not more than three or four inches from the ground, scraping the road every time there was even a small bump in it. It was a miracle the car did not collapse during the long trip from Chicago. Among the things I brought with me were a disassembled maple dining room table, a couple of chairs, and the enormous quantity of books I had accumulated during my college years.

When I got to Toronto, I first found a room in a house located on New Brunswick Avenue that rented to students and I arranged to eat one meal a day next door. The arrangement reminded me of my stay in Miami. My landlady was a warmhearted woman, originally from Eastern Europe.

Like my landladies in Wheaton and Miami, she adopted me. She was a dear soul. Her alter ego, however, was the dragon next door from whom I had arranged to get a meal every day. The food was both poor and insufficient. I was not as hungry as I had been in Miami or Chicago, but I was not satisfied. The soups were thin—to find the beef in the stews you had to look at it with a magnifying glass—and the desserts were minuscule and mostly unpalatable.

The only thing that was abundant in the menu were the starches, but even those were not served in sufficient quantities to satisfy a young man of twenty-four. To top it all, I had to put up with listening to the daily string of insults this woman inflicted on her insignificant husband, whom she abused mercilessly.

I tolerated the unsavory situation because of the convenience, my sweet landlady, and the location. I did not want to have to prepare meals for myself, and I did not want to spend my hard-earned meager cash reserves to eat at the university cafeteria, let alone restaurants elsewhere.

The great advantage of my new address was its location, walking distance to the university in an area called the Annex. I stayed there until the end of November, when I rented a cozy attic apartment in a house located on Poplar Plains Road that would accommodate Norma and me. The house was large and like many others had been divided into apartments. The owners lived in a section of the first floor, renting the rest of the house to tenants. This was a common occurrence in Toronto, a city that was beginning to attract large numbers of immigrants.

I set up housekeeping and eagerly awaited the arrival of my recent bride. I bought a few sticks of furniture in secondhand furniture stores on King Street and prepared the nest. We would stay a full year there, before moving to a larger apartment on Winona Drive for which we bought a secondhand living room set, a chaise lounge, and bedroom furniture. The most memorable piece of furniture was the chaise lounge, where we used to watch *Star Trek* every Tuesday evening.

Norma arrived at the beginning of December and we were able to celebrate our first Christmas together in our comfortable attic. We quickly settled into our new routine. Norma got a job. She had been studying business administration in Chicago, and she had an accounting degree from Argentina. We were very frugal, except when it came to food. We ate as well as possible, although we never went out to eat. Given Norma's nationality, it was not surprising that we had lots of steak.

Norma left for work early in the morning and I would go to the institute until it was time for me to meet Norma at our place. After a couple of mismatches, Norma got an excellent job as head of the accounting department in a large company of architects, where her expertise was a major plus and her salary was appropriate. Still, we saved as much as possible from Norma's salary (I called Norma "my brunette scholarship") and my other scholarships——I had both a PIMS scholarship and a Province of Ontario Grant. Our entertainment consisted of going camping and exploring the countryside in Ontario and Quebec in our old and clunky, but thoroughly reliable, Volkswagen Beetle. The main problem with it was that the driver had to be careful not to fall through the floor and land on the road because the car's floor had long ago given out.

It is almost incredible, but it appears that my fate was to end up in Canada. From a very early age, I had always had a longing for Canada. Indeed, after my father's death in 1957, I had almost gone to Canada to study. At fifteen I began to feel trapped in my school and at home. I needed space, a place to breathe unconstrained by all the rules and regulations imposed on me.

I wanted to fly the coop and move away, getting to know other places and people. I longed for a new beginning that would allow me to chart my own course rather than follow the paths that my family and society had predetermined for me. I was sick and tired of my school and of living at home. I was in full adolescent rebellion.

The Marist school in La Víbora was a private boys' school run by a religious order of brothers, and I thought most of my teachers were narrow minded, ignorant, and stuck in the Middle Ages. (It was ironic that after all I would end up in Canada and became a medievalist!) I had begun to read voraciously at an early age, and the contrast between the world described in books and the limited horizons imposed by my teachers suffocated me. To make matters worse, after my father's death in 1957 (I was fourteen at the time), the influence he had over my mother had been severed and she gave free rein to her religious zeal. For a young man in puberty, her religious piety seemed to be intolerable fanaticism.

My original idea had been to leave Cuba altogether and go to Switzerland or Canada, two countries I admired, and where I had read about extraordinary prep schools for young men. I did not think of a school in the United States—that seemed too blasé and not adventurous enough! Latin Americans have for a long time idealized Switzerland and Canada, countries with impressive landscapes and traditions that are different from the run-of-the-mill, particularly in Latin America.

Not that these impressions are realities, but it is how I thought of them at the time. For someone who had lived under the conviction, thanks to my Francophile relatives, that France was the epitome of culture and sophistication, the idea that I would be able to learn French in Switzerland or French and English in Canada was a great incentive. Little did I know that outside of Quebec, Canada is almost entirely English speaking, and that Swiss French is not quite the same as Parisian French.

It was wonderful that this dream was within my reach. I counted on the education insurance father had left me and with the one-sixth of his estate I had inherited. Of course, I was still a minor, so I needed permission from mother to do anything, but I relied on her to go along with what I wanted if I wanted it badly enough and if my plans had a worthy goal.

By the end of my third year of high school, I had had enough of Catholic Spanish fundamentalism (*a la española*) in school and of Protestant American fundamentalism at home. So I began to implement my plan by writing to various schools in Switzerland and Canada, narrowing down my choices and eventually settling on two schools, one in Fribourg and the other in Windsor, Ontario. After considerable thought I decided on Canada, based on all kinds of gross misconceptions. Had I known then what Windsor was like, I would have had second thoughts. I was also under the impression that I would be able to learn French and English, and neither the Canadian embassy nor the schools I had contacted dissuaded me of my mistaken assumption concerning both languages.

I got the visas, we paid the registration fee, and everything was on course for my departure. We had only to buy the plane ticket and I would be on my way to freedom and adventure. I was looking forward to being liberated from the shackles in which I felt I lived, but my mother was not happy. She was recently widowed and she was lonely. She did not want me to go. She used every argument she could to persuade me against leaving, and finally I relented. So I almost ended up coming to

Canada in 1958, but in the end, I did not take what Borges would have called that "forking path."

My immigration to Canada had to wait for a revolution to sever my ties with Cuba and several years in which I had lived in the United States, quite content and thinking that it would be there that I would spend the rest of my life. But destiny had arranged for me to go to Canada after all, and to a city not very far from Windsor. Indeed, it was extraordinary that Assumption High School, the prep school I was suppose to attend, was run by the Basilian Fathers, the same religious order that ran St. Michael's College in Toronto, where the Pontifical Institute was located. That was another coincidence!

When I finally arrived in Toronto, the city was still fairly small and rather provincial (it was not the sophisticated metropolis it is today). But it was pleasant, and Norma and I made good friends among the students at the Pontifical Institute and their families, and among some of Norma's coworkers. I felt quite at home in Toronto and was grateful for the cosmopolitan atmosphere at the institute and the courtesy typical of Canadians. There was also a liberal, progressive attitude that was amenable to both Norma and me. The university is located on wonderful grounds and the institute enjoyed all the facilities that a research center is supposed to have.

I did not miss either the strife that had characterized my year in Chicago, or the narrow religious horizons of Wheaton. The student population of the institute was composed for the most part of Roman Catholics and Anglicans who appreciated tradition but were liberal when it came to social issues and doctrine.

The faculty was primarily made up of clergy and laypeople whose religious affiliation was never a matter of discussion. Rather, everyone was interested in the scholarly work associated with the Middle Ages, not on religious agendas. The goal was to become a first-rate scholar of that age, and religious commitments were treated as a personal matter. The members of the institute had an irrevocable faith in the value of the Middle Ages and never challenged the need to study its thinkers.

Students at the Pontifical Institute had come to it because they had badly wanted to. They were committed to the education that was imparted there, and they worked very hard not for grades but for learning. Some were philosophers, but many were social historians, art historians, paleographers, specialists in various languages, scholars of canon law, theologians, and so on.

Still, the core of the institute was philosophy. After all, the institution had been founded by a famous philosopher, Etienne Gilson, and it counted many well-known philosophers among its faculty. One of them was the rather engaging figure of Anton Pegis, who was still going strong when I entered the program.

Educational institutions become great due to the excellence of their faculty, for the most part, but a key factor that should not be underestimated is the students. This was quite evident at the institute. The dedication of some of the students, the high caliber of their minds and research, and their uncompromising high ideals were as important as the quality of the faculty. I had the privilege of studying alongside Paul Spade and John Chamberlain in my class, and met others such as Calvin Normore, who was not part of the PIMS program but took courses at the institute.

In the first year of the licentiate program students studied the history of medieval philosophy, paleography, medieval Latin, art, and history. Of course, the emphasis was on a general understanding of the period and on mastering the tools required to do firsthand work on medieval sources.

Latin was a basic tool that had to be mastered at whatever cost, and so was paleography—it was considered essential that one could date and read manuscripts insofar as most primary sources from the Middle Ages are accessible only in manuscript form. We were also taught how to do critical editions of medieval manuscripts. Library tools and skills were necessary for success in the program. Indeed, we had to learn to find our way around old libraries in Europe. I found the studies difficult, but everything connected to the institute was a great deal of fun. How many people outside this tiny circle of specialists had any idea of the things we were learning and doing? Certainly not philosophers, even most of those who considered themselves specialists on the Middle Ages.

At the Institute I learned how shabby most scholarship on medieval philosophy in the United States was, and is, and not just on medieval philosophy but on every period of the history of philosophy. Americans are generally uneducated in languages and history, as I was, and jump into texts without proper linguistic and historical training. Indeed, I find it frightening that people who present themselves as historians of medieval thought lack the basic tools to do any serious primary research in it.

How many can even understand Latin? How many are able to read a manuscript from the Middle Ages? How many have the minimum understanding of the medieval period, the all-important medieval Church, the way manuscripts from the ancients survived and were made available in the West? I would not be surprised if American medievalists have no idea of the libraries they need to check or of the way to find materials in the libraries that they are able to identify.

This situation is no less than a scandal. Most of these people present themselves as scholars when they are no more than dilettantes who put forward interpretations of medieval authors without a clue as to what they are actually saying and what it means. They rely mostly on translations and, since many teach at presumably good schools, they are regarded as knowledgeable when in fact they are nothing of the kind.

The absurd comments I have heard uttered by scholars at major universities about the Middle Ages are disgusting! And then some of those who are recognized medievalists, although they can read Latin and have some substantial knowledge of the Middle Ages, fail miserably because they lack proper training in philosophy and logic. Yet, logic is an indispensable requirement, as Peter Abelard said so well, of doing good philosophy. Medieval philosophy is cast in a very sophisticated foundation of logical theory and depends heavily on the sources from the ancients that have survived.

On this last point I found a pleasant surprise, namely, the key role that the Iberian Peninsula played in the Middle Ages. It was a bonus I had not anticipated aligned perfectly with my intellectual and emotional needs. For it was the ethnic complexity of Goths, Celts, Romans, Jews, and Muslims, to name just a few of the many groups of people who passed through the Iberian Peninsula or came and settled on it, that was responsible for the preservation of ancient cultures and the development of new ones.

Glorious thirteenth-century Paris, Oxford, Cambridge, Cologne, and Bologna could never have existed had the Iberian Peninsula not played the role it did in the preservation and transmission of ancient sources. It was thanks to Muslims like Averroes who gave new life to Aristotelian texts, to translators such as the Jew Domingo González, who first attempted to make available the ancient thought salvaged and interpreted by his Muslim predecessors, and to the flock of scholars from all over the West that converged on the Iberian peninsula to profit from the newly discovered manuscripts that had been rediscovered thanks to the reconquest of Iberian lands from the Moors.

The quest for my cultural roots had miraculously found sustenance in the study of the philosophy of the Middle Ages, when in fact it had been motivated by a desire to understand the role of language in our knowledge of the world. This was fortuitous in that it brought together the two major strains that had motivated my intellectual quest.

Without anticipating it, I had found in the Middle Ages the source of pride and satisfaction I had been looking for, which now was not just a matter of my culture and ethnicity, but of my identity and part of the universal quest for knowledge and understanding. Thinking about the treasures that were waiting for me to read and engage, I could not avoid thinking about the diamond in Norma's ring as an antecedent of the treasures I would enjoy in the Pontifical Institute.

My work at the Pontifical Institute developed along two tracks that functioned as one. From the moment I arrived, I had fallen under the influence of three of the institute's stars. Above all was Joseph Owens, whose metaphysical depth, joined to an incomparable intellectual humility, spoke to me of authentic wisdom. From Owens I learned to love metaphysics, which from then on has informed everything I have done philosophically. Next was a consummate historian, Armand Maurer, who in his commentaries followed texts wherever they led, opening vistas that lesser exegetes could never reach. Maurer's scholarly virtuosity gave me an appreciation for the value of careful textual research. The third was Edward Synan, whose love of history extended well beyond texts of philosophy, bringing to bear on it their circumstantial and ideological contexts. From him and his sense of humor and irony I learned to love history.

Parallel to and adjoining this track was another that was directed toward the investigation of authors who were part of my cultural tradition. I explored the texts of Domingo Gonzáles, Gonzalo the Spaniard, Peter of Spain, and, more important, the Catalans Raimundus Lulius (Ramon Llull) and Guido Terrena. Domingo was particularly interesting because he had been challenged by precisely the same linguistic issues that had fascinated me at Wheaton, when I was first learning English and which had taken me to philosophy.

Indeed, one can easily see in his texts his struggle with the difficulties he encountered in trying to find Latin equivalents to the Arabic translations of the Greek made by Islamic scholars. The way in which he translated them reveals both insights and failures, but in all cases a determined struggle to go beyond the surface. I knew this process quite well from personal experience, and found in him a brother in arms.

Gonzalo made me understand the controversial doctrine of the various intellects (parts of the mind) that work together to yield knowledge. This was a universal problem that needed as much attention at that time as the contemporary version of it, namely the philosophy of mind, needs today.

In Llull I found an attempt at developing a conceptual method, which he dubbed "the art," intended to produce results from original postulates in an almost mechanical fashion. It was the antecedent of Leibniz's famous *ars combinatoria*, and maybe of our contemporary computers. I wrote papers on all these, most of which were published in specialized journals only a handful of people read, a fact that did not bother me in the least insofar as I believed that I had understood something that others had bypassed. I also wrote papers on figures that did not fall into the cultural roots track, such as Thomas Bradwardine, on whose philosophy of mathematics (on ratios, that is, proportions) I wrote a paper. But it was in Guido Terrena and his question on universals that I found the greatest inspiration.

The problem of universals is perhaps one of half a dozen, fundamental problems that all philosophers worth the name encounter at some point of their intellectual path. It was at the core of the struggles in which Plato and Aristotle were engaged, and has continued to be unavoidable to anyone who is interested in the fundamentals of philosophy. The problem is simple. It asks for the status, or reality if you will, of the referent of universal words, such as "cat" and "leg."

We do not have a problem saying that the referent of "Peanut my cat" is "Peanut my cat," that is, the individual cat I loved. But what is the referent of "cat"? It does not seem that it is any existing individual cat such as Peanut or Chichi. And for Plato this applies to such important terms as "justice." Are universals realities in the world? Are they concepts in our minds? Or are they merely words? Philosophers asked these questions in the Middle Ages and philosophers still ask them today.

At stake is the validity of our knowledge and science, for if universals are mere words or concepts, not realities, then science is about words or concepts, and not about anything existing in the world. But if universals are realities, how are we to understand individuals, since they seem to reduce to bundles of universals? If cat, coat, and leg are universals, and Peanut is a cat and has both a coat and legs, is not Peanut a universal as its components appear to be?

For my licentiate thesis I wanted to do something that was philosophically interesting, something that had some relevance in the history of Hispanic thought and included something for which language and modes of expressions were relevant. Guido's questions on universals were perfect for this project. The thesis consisted in a critical edition of the Latin text and a study of the views it proposed. Because only one manuscript of Guido's questions has survived and it is corrupt in some places; producing a good edition of it would be a challenge.

As mentioned earlier, the Pontifical Institute had a distinguished faculty in philosophy, but it included many top scholars in other fields as well. It was primarily an interdisciplinary center. And so I developed a taste for interdisciplinary work in line with the broad interests I have had since I was in prep school. The emphasis was on scholarship with a big "S." Particularly big was learning to work with manuscripts in the critical edition of medieval texts and I became fascinated by the scholarly rigor it entailed.

For my doctoral dissertation at the university, however, I chose something less technical and more fun: first a more controversial topic, evil, and second an author who was a minor thinker whose work had a popular and literary bent. Francesc Eiximenis was a very minor philosophical figure of the fourteenth century who embarked on the composition of a major encyclopedia entitled *Lo Crestià*, which was never finished. It was intended as a compendium of all the philosophical issues relevant at the time. I picked the third book where he discussed evil, and particularly sin. This fit my interests in that it had a metaphysical root—is evil something or nothing? It also fit because Eiximenis tried to produce a book that was accessible to the common person, and he filled it with stories and anecdotes that are not only philosophically interesting but also amusing. Indeed, I published an article on the hilarious comments he makes in regard to proper table manners.

Another reason for the choice was that I wanted to master the techniques of editing medieval texts, and this work has survived in nine manuscripts, which made it possible to implement many of the techniques I had learned at the institute but had not been able to use in the licentiate thesis because the work had survived in only one manuscript. These techniques included dating the manuscripts, deciphering the writing and abbreviations, setting up a stemma that reveals interdependence, collating texts, correcting grammar, identifying references, and so on—all very boring to most people surely, but fascinating to me.

The dissertation was not meant to explore philosophical concepts in depth, but to develop the skills that are essential for making available the very texts that are the source of philosophical speculation. For me in particular, with my interest in language and the transmission of meaning through it, this seemed a most appropriate project. Again, I was trying to prepare myself for the philosophical work that I thought I would be doing later.

Part of my job in the dissertation was to translate an edition of an interesting part of Eiximenis's text into medieval Catalan, which happily required for me to spend some time in Europe studying and comparing manuscripts of the text. The edition included an essay on the sources of the treatise and its historical significance. All the sources had to be identified in the edition, a task that was time consuming and often resembled detective work. Another essay had to do with the doctrinal content of the book. There were several manuscripts of the treatise spread around European libraries so they had to be collated and annotated, after their interdependence was established. I received a Canada Council Fellowship for two years to write the dissertation, which I finished in Toronto after having spent one year in Europe roaming through the medieval collections of some of the great European libraries.

It is difficult for anyone who has not been involved in serious scholarship of the kind I had undertaken to appreciate and understand how both challenging and fun it is to those of us who have. This just does not make sense to those who have been less fortunate than those of us who have been introduced to this task. The situation is similar to that of those who have never been introduced to wine. That aroma of a good bottle of wine is unique and captivating, and so is the aroma of old books written by hand on parchment. To my mind, there was only one way to study and explore old books in the West, and that involved making a pilgrimage to Europe's magnificent libraries.

10

Pilgrimage to Europe (1969–1971)

Humans are social by nature, and part of being social involves being a member of a group that traces its origins to an ancestral land. This land is often used to explain the origins of the group, so that when members of the group want to tell who they are they turn to it, saying something like, "I am Catalan," "I am Latino," or "I am Cuban." The land not only points to their identity, but also calls them to visit. These trips are not simply tourist outings. They are true pilgrimages central to the social identity of particular groups and sources of pride. Indeed, they explain many of their customs and idiosyncrasies.

Philosophers also have lands of origin and lineages, not of genealogy but of the philosophical ideas that constitute their thinking. For a philosopher with my background and scholarly interests, my first trip to Europe was a true pilgrimage to the land of the philosophers to whom I owe my mental discipline and whose works serve as my sources of inspiration.

I cannot think of Suárez without thinking of Salamanca, of Aristotle and Plato without Athens, of Aquinas without Paris, and of Wittgenstein without Vienna. It is not a matter of religious faith but of intellectual belonging and personal history. Indeed, the same applies to most American and Latin American philosophers, regardless of our philosophical sympathies or racial and ethnic origins, because we have been throughout our careers, or at least for some part of them, heavily influenced by Europe.

Spain, Salamanca, university, front view, 1905. Photograph courtesy of the Library of Congress.

No matter what may we say and what efforts we might make to ignore our European roots, we cannot avoid them. Indeed, despite our rants against Eurocentrism, European colonialism, and European imperialism, both economic and cultural, we cannot help but depend on philosophical tools we borrow from Europe in order to develop our philosophy. We might complain about what Europe has done to us, but we do it mostly with the very tools that Europe has bequeathed us.

Our philosophy is nothing if not European, which does not mean that there are no valuable philosophical strands in pre-Columbian thought in Latin America, for example, or in deep-rooted African cultural currents. Yes, we Latin Americans have every reason to complain about Europe, for the Americas had a good number of culturally rich societies that were pitilessly trampled on by the Iberian conquerors, even by those that were trying to save some parts of it. Indeed, in the colonization process, sometimes ignorance was worse than intention.

Of course, for a medievalist like me, not only could Europe not be avoided, it was at the center of everything I did. And so I longed for a time when I could visit the places that had produced the thought I was trying to comprehend. Paris, Bologna, Salamanca, Cologne, Oxford, Cambridge, Rome, and so many other places were almost sacred, and after three years at the institute studying artifacts produced in those lands I was ready to walk the streets where Abelard, Aquinas, and Suárez had walked and visit the places where they had taught.

What would it be like to walk into Notre Dame and St. Peter's? I needed an excuse to visit Europe and to have someone pay for the trip. Fortunately for me, my very studies amply justified the trip, for my proposed dissertation required that I study and collate the surviving manuscripts of Eiximenis's *Terç del Crestià*.

The Canada Council Grant I received for the dissertation carried a generous stipend of $4,500 plus the cost of airfare that, added to the Province of Ontario grant of $1,200, and another smaller stipend of $1,000 from the Pontifical Institute comprised a very generous sum. With these grants and our savings, Norma and I were able to plan for a yearlong stay in Europe. We planned to spend the largest amount of that time in Barcelona, that lucky city where Antoni Gaudí produced his whimsical architectural miracles.

This city, and to a lesser extent Valencia and Madrid, were where most of the manuscripts I had to study were located, but fortunately there were manuscripts in other parts of Europe that I also had to consult. This justified trips to England, Italy, France, and Germany in particular. In order to facilitate all the traveling and save on hotels, we arranged to pick up a new Volkswagen camper in Munich upon our arrival in continental Europe. We traveled first to London, again to check some manuscripts and do some sightseeing.

We were traveling with our seven-week-old daughter, Leticia. She had been born on July 18, the day of my own birthday. What a gift my wife gave us both! We were elated, but not everything was wonderful. Because the baby had been born with a malrotation of the intestine most likely caused by a vaccine administered during pregnancy, she required surgery a couple of days after birth. This caused us tremendous anxiety and put our travel plans on hold. Norma was in one hospital recovering from giving birth to our girl, and I was in another hospital across the street where our girl was undergoing major surgery. And all this while the TV screens were showing the first human being walking on the moon, I was shuttling from one hospital to the other, frantically getting reports from the surgeons and passing them on to Norma as we embraced each other tightly, searching for the strength we needed.

The surgeon who operated on Leticia was a tall man with very large hands, which, to us, seemed inadequate to deal with such small patient. And he was blunt with us, giving Leticia a fifty-fifty chance of survival. That night, when I went back to our apartment in the early hours of the morning, despite being exhausted I could not sleep.

I tossed and turned on the bed, following the train of my thoughts and wondering what the morrow would bring. When I couldn't stand the bed any longer I got up, but that did not help. The only relief came when I went to the hospital and asked about Leticia and took the good news to Norma that she had survived the night and her chances of living were improving. Still, the following three weeks were hell, for Leticia had to stay at the hospital, and for a while we could not even touch her for fear of infection. We were allowed to visit her, but could only look at her through a glass. The fear of infection was too great to take any risks. After three weeks the wait was over and we were permitted to take our baby home. After another week passed, the doctor told us that she was out of the woods and approved our plan to travel to Europe. In his own words, "These little critters are tough as nails, and cling to life with surprising determination." After all the waiting and fear, the three of us were together and happy.

In spite of the frightening setback, everything turned out well in the end, and we did not have to alter our travel plans. The feeding tube in Leticia's stomach, placed there as a precaution in case of an emergency, was removed and she began to thrive. The condition of the parents was another matter altogether because of the worry and sleep deprivation. Still, we were in heaven with our little daughter.

We arrived in London in mid-September 1969, where we stayed a few days. I checked the sources I needed to consult and Norma and

I spent the rest of the time sightseeing. Although Norma had been to Europe after her graduation from the University in Mendoza (Argentina), neither she nor I had ever been in London. We planned to cover as much ground as possible, but traveling with a less than two-month-old baby was not easy, particularly because she decided to sleep during the day and stay awake at night.

We had to carry her asleep all over London and then entertain her at night after we had collapsed. To make matters more uncomfortable, it was already cold and humid. The walls of our hotel room dripped with water in spite of the gas heater we had constantly going. Frankly, we were relieved and happy after we collected the brand-new Volkswagen camper we had ordered. It was perfect for traveling with a baby; although small, it had everything we needed.

Next we headed for Spain, camping on our way as needed or desired through Germany, Switzerland, and France. In Barcelona we rented a furnished apartment owned by Galician farmers who had moved to the city and had bought the apartment as an investment. My mornings were spent at one of the libraries that had sources relevant to my work.

Barcelona is a sophisticated, culturally vibrant city, where Gaudí built his most famous architectural structures, the pinnacle of which may be the church of La Sagrada Familia, and where Pablo Picasso had spent some of his youth. Other famous artists such as Salvador Dalí had also lived in the area. Barcelona was a Catalan city, and everyone who could spoke Catalan. One of my tasks was to learn as much of the language as possible so that I could edit the pertinent medieval manuscripts by Eiximenis, which I did. I recruited someone to give me lessons and also established a connection to the Institut d'Estudis Catalans, where I went to study philology and philosophy and where I met some of the most important Catalan intellectuals of the day. My Canadian mentor was Josep Gulsoy, a Sephardic Jew from Turkey who was a well-known linguist and expert in Catalan, like his own mentor, the famous Joan Coromines, who, coincidentally, taught at the University of Chicago.

Some evenings I would have dinner (at midnight or later) with Josep M. Casacuberta, the editor of *Els Nostres Clàssics*, a book series published by Curial devoted to classical Catalan writers. He was helping me with the edition of Eiximenis's text, which he later published in the series.

Catalonia at the time was not what it is today. Francisco Franco, Spain's dictator, was still alive and had not relaxed his control over the country. Catalan was still a largely forbidden language. With few exceptions, business had to be conducted in Castilian, what we call "Spanish" in English but "Castilian" in Spain. Never mind that Catalan was as old as Castilian, and that it has a prolific and superb literature going back to the Middle Ages, which some regard as superior to that in Castilian. Such were the times. The dictatorship and the secret police required one to be careful. Freedom of speech was not encouraged, to say the least.

Still, Barcelona was Barcelona. Las Ramblas was then what it is today, a busy and exciting promenade next to the old Gothic town with its magnificent cathedral, museums, and opera house (one of the largest in the world). The food was as good then as it is today, with Catalonia now boasting some of the most renowned cooks and restaurants in the world. Unfortunately, our budget would not permit any kind of splurge, but we used the weekends to visit the surrounding towns and countryside, where unique Romanesque churches were common and where the food was excellent but cheap.

Interestingly, because the medieval Catalan text I was editing had to do with gluttony, it contained information on medieval food and drink and was read by some of the great Catalan cooks. Years later, when I was in New York City exploring a job offer from Fordham, I got a call from one of the famous chefs in Catalonia who had tracked me down to tell me how much he loved my text and to invite me to have dinner at this restaurant.

I spent seven months working very hard, every day, at various libraries in Barcelona and Valencia, which was not far from Barcelona and was another important cultural center whose libraries contained some of Eiximenis's manuscripts. The winter was supposed to be mild, and it was—as long as you stayed outdoors. Inside the libraries, there was no heat and it was very cold.

The only concession to comfort in the main library were foot vibrators. These were electrical contraptions one could turn on while sitting. They were supposed to stimulate the circulation in your feet and keep them warm. Of course, the vibrators vibrated, but after half an hour there was no alternative but to freeze. My only recourse was to dress as if I were visiting the North Pole: overcoat, wool gloves, warm socks, a scarf, and a warm hat. In order to warm up, I would get out of the library and take the lunch I had brought with me to eat at the Plaza de Catalunya, the main center of activity in Barcelona. It was considerably warmer outside than inside those enormous medieval halls.

On Saturdays and Sundays I took time off and went with Norma and Leticia to visit places all the way to Andorra in the Pyrenees going east, and all the way down to Valencia going west. These exploratory trips formed an unforgettable experience. Visiting the Romanesque churches was a revelation. It was Romanesque art at its best, with the Christ Pantocrator looking down on you from the vault, with his enormous eyes and that simplicity that is so impressive in frescoes from that time in Catalonia.

No wonder the Catalans always had a sense of superiority over all the other ethnic groups on the Iberian Peninsula. No other group has ever produced anything like that, before or since.

I also worked hard on my Catalan. The months passed quickly, too quickly, and at the end of March I had completed the research I needed to finish my dissertation. In the meantime, I had also finished my licentiate thesis, which, as mentioned earlier, consisted of a Latin edition and study of the *Questions on Universals of Guido Terrena*.

At the beginning of April my in-laws arrived from Argentina, ready for adventure in Europe. Norma's father was a Spaniard, born in Ciudad Rodrigo, a medieval walled town in Castile. His parents had immigrated to Argentina when he was nine years old. After giving them some time to get to know Barcelona, we packed our things and took off for the rest of Spain, where we camped for two months in our VW camper—Norma's parents had a tent, while the baby, Norma, and I slept in the camper.

Norma's father was an expert and resourceful camper and he loved the trip. Both parents were very helpful, taking care of the baby while Norma concentrated on being the navigator and I, the driver. After Spain we went to Italy, Switzerland, and France. We celebrated our daughter's first birthday, and my twenty-eighth, at a campsite at the foot of the Matterhorn. Norma's parents left for Spain and then Argentina, while we stayed until we had to ship our camper to Toronto from Bremen.

The trip was something to narrate, but I will restrain myself. Keep in mind that we camped on the piazza in front of St. Peter's Basilica; that I nearly got separated from my family when a door of the train in which we were traveling from Bremen to Paris got locked and it would not open in time for me to join them; that the border guards between Switzerland and Germany did not allow me to enter either one of the two countries because of my Cuban passport, so I was in peril of spending the rest of my life at the border between the two countries; that some friends (one of whom was the daughter of Blanche Way) lent us their fabulous apartment at the Place du Trocadéro for a week in Paris, having left filet mignon steaks in the freezer for us to eat when we arrived hungry and exhausted; that our daughter Leticia took her first steps at Notre Dame; and that she first tasted ice cream, which she called "postre helado" for years to come, in the piazza in front of the cathedral at Pisa.

The trip throughout Europe was a tour de force. We saw everything worth seeing, from the most famous, such as the Sistine Chapel, to obscure libraries hidden well off the beaten path. We traveled everywhere in Western Europe, staying at primitive campsites, cooking under rudimentary conditions, eating endless cans of sardines, and snacking on thin slices of *jamón serrano*, *pata negra*, that my father-in-law had bought in Andalucía. For the sake of convenience and with great levity, he had hung it from the ceiling of our camper, where it traveled safely and ready to be sliced with expertise. The ham was a sensation among fellow campers who were often invited to savor it with a glass of wine

All of this with an eight- to fourteen-month-old baby, still wearing diapers that had to be washed every day and hung to dry on fences and improvised clotheslines throughout Europe. There were no disposable diapers at the time, and the facilities in Europe were rather rudimentary compared to those in Canada.

The trip enriched our knowledge of Western culture and allowed us to visit some of the places our ancestors had lived, in Spain and southern France mostly. Indeed, to our surprise we found that two branches of Norma's family and one of mine had originated a few miles from each other in Tarbes and Hasparren. Could anyone explain how and why the two of us, with origins so close in France, came together so far away, in Chicago?

While we were savoring the last moments of our epic journey, news reached us that my sister and her family had arrived in the United States. They were still far from us, but now it was possible to communicate with them, for we were in the free world, where communication was easy. It had taken them nine long years to get permission to leave Cuba, and they suffered intensely for every one of those years.

My brother-in-law lost his job the moment they requested permission to leave the island and was sent to the country to cut sugarcane, away from his family. And my sister had to cope with the family in Havana. She had four mouths to feed in addition to her own, and no source of income. Her situation was desperate. Fortunately, my mother was still in Cuba and she had a small income the government gave her to make up for my father's retirement—my father had died while I was in Cuba. This had been barely sufficient to deal with her expenses and those of her sister, but now they had to cover her own expenses and those of my sister's family. The story of how they did so is heroic, but that is another story. Consider that they had to sell everything they owned that was not indispensable.

The important thing for all of us was that now they were in the United States and I could hear my sister's voice after nearly ten years of silence. We wanted to help them, but we could be of little assistance as we were then in Paris, and on our way to Toronto. Still, we did manage to send them a check with some funds, although it turned out that they were not in immediate need.

Apart from some help from the United States government, my brother-in-law had a brother who lived in Tampa and was taking care of them until they were settled. Our task now was to look forward to seeing them and celebrating their departure from Cuba and to prepare for the addition of a new member of our family (my sister was pregnant with her fifth child).

They lost no time in securing a well-paying job for my brother-in-law at the company where his own brother worked, sending the children to school, and planning to save enough to eventually buy a home. It did not take very long for the older children to develop the necessary skills to find lucrative jobs or establish successful businesses in the Tampa area. In short, the children found their way, married, and have had children of their own. They certainly are participating in the American Dream.

My sister, Nena, and I were always very close because she was twelve years old when I was born. Indeed, her death three years ago was very painful for me, and I still miss our weekly phone calls, in which we shared anecdotes and memories. Our talks, particularly after she became very sick, were wonderful, full of laughter, mirth, wit, and the best that Cuban humor can provide until the very last. Very shortly before she died, we had a particularly emotional parting. We were sad in particular because she and I were the only blood relatives still alive. Our father had died of a heart attack in Cuba when I was fourteen, and our only brother, Ignacito, had died in an automobile accident when I was eight. Father was an inspiration for us because of his strong ethical standards and love of learning. I remember vividly that he never sat down without a book in his hands. And our brother, both to tease and indulge me, gave me a beautiful mare on my sixth birthday so that I could become

On my sixth birthday with the beautiful mare Yegüita. Photograph courtesy of the author.

a virtuoso on the saddle, as he was. I was able to keep the horse until we moved to Havana. Our reunion was bittersweet because next to the joy of seeing my sister and her family after so many years, we missed the members of our family that were no longer with us because they had died or were still in Cuba.

My sister's arrival in the United States was a fitting end for our European odyssey, and the forthcoming birth of her fifth child was an auspicious sign of a future different from the bitter recent past. Each day of the previous year had brought new experiences and the desire to continue our trip, but it was time to return and finish the dissertation.

We had been in Europe for an entire school year, from 1969 to 1970, and it was time to get back to Toronto. So we settled into a one-bedroom apartment in a graduate student building on Charles Street, next to the university campus.

Norma was able to walk to work every day, for her former employer had asked her to come back to the same position she had occupied before we left, and this was located very close to our apartment. This was a particularly lucky break for us.

Our daughter, Leticia, and I stayed at the apartment. We arranged for someone to take her to the building playgrounds while I furiously worked on the dissertation. The monster had to be completed as soon as possible and in time to apply for a job for the 1971–72 academic year.

I have always been good about focusing and ignoring my surroundings. In fact, Norma occasionally complains about it. And so I was able to concentrate on the dissertation task in spite of the many distractions a one-year-old was bound to create. I closed the doors to the bedroom and the bathroom so that Leticia would not have access to anything dangerous. Her crib was in the living-dining area, with the few sticks of furniture that we considered indispensable, as were her toys. The kitchen had no door so she also had access to all of the lower kitchen cabinets, where we kept our pots and pans.

And I let her entertain herself, wreaking havoc for the entire day. She was a sweet child who was happy to be left to her own devices as long as I fed her when she was hungry, took her to the bathroom when she needed to go, and paid attention to her when she claimed it. I also spent some time playing with her, and was thankful that I could get some work done when she took a nap.

11

Landing a Job, with Verve (1971)

The greatest challenge I faced upon returning to Toronto from Europe was the task of securing employment at a time when there were few academic jobs available in the United States or Canada. For the first time since I had chosen philosophy, and particularly medieval philosophy, as my main field, I had to face the fact that this was not the kind of career, if one can call philosophy a career, in which it is easy to find a position. Philosophy in general had a resurgence in popularity in the late sixties because of the Vietnam War. Young people opposed to the war found in philosophy a justification of their aversion to what was happening in Vietnam and flocked to universities to engage the field.

However, by the time I was looking for a job, a retrenchment had begun in academia, particularly in philosophy. The enthusiasm for philosophy had subsided at the time that universities and colleges ended most requirements at the college level, inspired by the misguided idea that students should have the right to choose what to study, regardless of what their teachers thought they needed to learn. Not taking into account that students were not mature or informed enough to make the right choices, colleges and universities rushed to eliminate requirements, instead allowing students to choose freely what they wanted. The result was catastrophic, and lasted for decades; indeed, we are still living with some of the consequences. It was particularly nefarious for many students who, without proper guidance, chose the easy road in college, taking courses that were merely fun and had no serious intellectual content. The resulting absurdity had no bounds. Instead of the sciences and the core humanities, students wasted their time watching soap operas and thinking about the symbolism of open doors. Of course, part of the motivation for these courses was that they were easy, and many instructors, paying tribute to the antiestablishment feeling of the times, decided not to give grades in their courses, eliminating with one stroke one measure of learning.

Apart from the harm that this movement did to students, it also harmed the universities, for instructors in standard disciplines, particularly those that were rigorous, were no longer in demand. And demand is the key to academia, for the job of academics is teaching and if there is no demand for teaching, there is no demand for teachers. The result of the change in the enrollment in fields like philosophy, which are abstract and hard, is that they were no longer well supported in colleges, and the job market for teaching philosophers collapsed.

The problem for me was compounded because I had not picked a popular subfield in philosophy, like ethics or political theory, or a central one such as epistemology or logic. I had picked a historical field, which was already filled with faculty in universities. When faculty retired, they were not replaced, which meant that the number of job openings dried up.

Another strike against my field was that it was concerned with a period in the West that was regarded as a dark age: the Middle Ages. (The term "middle" refers to this period's location between the two glorious ages of the ancient world and the Renaissance.) Only Catholics and Catholic schools seemed to be interested in this historical period, mainly for religious reasons. Indeed, to this day very few first-rank graduate programs have even one person devoted to the study and teaching of philosophy in the Middle Ages. This is the reason that Norman Kretzmann referred to the field as a ghetto. Under these circumstances, the task of finding a job was daunting.

The year before, while in Spain, I had decided to take a crack at the job search to see if anything would turn up, even though I was only an ABD (all but dissertation). I applied to a couple of positions in Canada and to my surprise I did get one, in the Department of Philosophy at the University of Alberta. Unfortunately, this was not yet a tenure-track line, although the Philosophy Department expected the line would convert into a tenure-track position after I got my PhD.

After thinking about it and discussing it with Norma, we decided that it was best not to take the position and thus avoid the hassle of going from Barcelona to Toronto and moving our things to Alberta, which was so far in the west, when I had not yet finished my dissertation.

Indeed, the move might prevent me from finishing as quickly as I needed to, and then where would I be? Would Alberta renew the temporary job? They certainly were not yet committed to turn it into a tenure-track position, and even if they did, medievalists were a dime a dozen. Indeed, places like Toronto were assembly lines of medievalists.

Yet, I could not postpone the inevitable. I needed a job for the 1971–72 academic year, and I had only a year to get it. I was quite conscious of the difficulties I was up against, and had made some contingency plans. My last line of defense if I could not get a job in philosophy was to get a job as a philologist in a Romance languages department. I had been preparing for this by taking some appropriate courses both in Toronto and Barcelona. And my dissertation was on a fourteenth-century Catalan text, of which I was doing an edition and study. Although the text was philosophical, its great value was that it fell into a genre that may be called "popular philosophy," something that made it appropriate for the faculty of a Romance languages department.

I was a native Spanish speaker, spoke Catalan, knew Latin, and had attended Chicago, which was an important center of Iberian studies. In short, I was well qualified for a job in a graduate language department, even though my main credentials were in philosophy and this was the field I regarded as mine.

I prepared for this by joining not only the American Philosophical Association (APA), but also the Modern Language Association (MLA). The APA was having its Eastern Division meeting, which included the job market placement, in Philadelphia, and the MLA was having its own in New York City. The meetings overlapped, so my plan was to go first to the APA meeting and then to the MLA. I was confident that I could get a job as a philologist, but I was doubtful about a job in philosophy.

The trip to Philadelphia was a nasty affair. Apart from my worries about landing a job, I have always been prone to motion sickness when traveling by bus, which I was required to do because a plane ticket was too expensive. I chose to travel by night in order to save the cost of a hotel room in Philadelphia, while making sure I would be available for interviews in the morning when the job market opened. When I got to Philadelphia I looked shabby in spite of my fashionable gray suit bought at El Corte Inglés in Barcelona precisely to impress job interviewers. A night without much sleep due to the stress I felt and the motion sickness had put me in the wrong mood and made me look pale and sickly. I did not recognize the person I saw reflected in the mirror of the men's room in Philly, but I had to carry on; I did not have time to spare. I tried to make myself look presentable, but even with the snazzy suit the image I saw in the mirror was that of a homeless man. I despaired.

Then I dragged myself to look at the list of advertised jobs. At that time jobs were posted on a board at APA meetings. Neither "Jobs for Philosophers," a printout of job openings, let alone the internet, existed. I went through the list carefully and discovered to my chagrin that there was only one job to which I could apply.

I was a well-trained medievalist, but it was not clear that I was a well-trained philosopher or philosophy teacher; I was very specialized and had never taught a class in my life, even though I had spent a year at Chicago. When I saw that there was only a single listing in philosophy, I almost turned around and walked out.

But of course reason advised that I would lose nothing by trying to get an interview. So I put together my credentials and I wrote a note to the interviewer. In the note I said that I was available for an interview until 1:00 p.m., when, if I had not heard from him, I would leave. It was 10:00 a.m. when I sent the note.

The 1:00 p.m. hour was important because the bus for New York City, which, under the circumstances, I thought was my only hope of landing a job, was leaving at 2:00 p.m., and I needed time to catch it. But lo and behold! Barely half an hour after I sent the message I got a message back saying that the interviewer could meet with me at noon.

I almost collapsed when I read it. Did I have a chance at all? And if I did, how good was it? How many people would apply to the single job in medieval philosophy in the entire United States and Canada? My hopes were dashed when I thought of the probabilities, but I got my things together and showed up to the interview.

The interviewer was William Parry, a logician of impeccable credentials whose teacher at Harvard, the famous C. I. Lewis, is reputed to have said that Parry was the most brilliant student he had ever had. I did not know this, which was fortunate because had I known I would have been trembling with fear.

Parry turned out to be an old man who appeared to be very nervous, perhaps more nervous than I was, which reassured me. He had read my credentials but was particularly impressed when I handed over an offprint of the article I had published on Gonsalvus Hispanus on a topic in the philosophy of mind having to do with the various intellects medieval philosophers talked about. I also had two other articles coming out, one in the philosophy of science, dealing with Thomas Bradwardine's theory of proportions and proportionality. The mere fact that I had a rather long and scholarly piece already in print, and two forthcoming, must have been impressive at a time when practically no students seeking jobs had publications.

Apart from being a logician, Parry was also a Marxist. Indeed, he had been a card-carrying member of the Communist Party and had suffered greatly in the 1950s because of it; his tenure was taken away at the University of Buffalo (that was the name of the institution that is today known as the University at Buffalo) because of his commitment to Marxism. Can one imagine a Marxist in a position of hiring a Cuban who had left Cuba because it had become a Marxist-Leninist state? But the unexpected sometimes happens. The left-wing nut, a communist, hired a presumably right-wing nut from Cuba. The fact is that, far from being a left-wing fanatic, Parry was a sensible and eminently rational man.

And I also was trying to be sensible and rational. My anti-Castro bile had passed, so I could look at the Cuban situation dispassionately, in a thoughtful way. I had and still have objections against the Cuban Revolution, but they are not framed in a kind of personal, emotional fashion.

I did not think the interview went at all well, however. It seemed to me that Parry talked too much and asked me very little. He spent time telling me about the retirement system at Buffalo, for which I did not care a hoot at the time. I needed a job, even if the retirement package was nonexistent.

At the end of the interview he told me that he would report on me to the department and let me know if they would interview me on campus. Frankly, I thought this was a dead end and that night I phoned Norma and told her that I did not expect to hear from Buffalo. Indeed, shortly after the interview in Philadelphia, I took the bus to New York City, where I lined up several interviews in language departments.

Of course, I was wrong about Buffalo. Within a couple of very anxious weeks I heard from Parry and had an interview on campus. Apparently, Parry had not only been impressed with my credentials, but had liked me. When I came for an on-campus interview I stayed in his home, a large and beautiful place next to the street where we would live for our entire life in Buffalo.

The department had thirty-one faculty members at the time. It was down from thirty-nine a couple of years before and up from four from the time the university was a private institution, before it joined the State University of New York system in 1964. I survived the interview process, although there were some unpleasant moments. For the colloquium I had chosen a paper that was historical but had considerable controversial philosophical content. It was on Bonaventure's argument for the existence of God.

I thought the topic was traditional enough and general enough to appeal to everyone in the faculty, and I had a nice criticism of Bonaventure's argument that would satisfy agnostics who were scientifically minded (it had to do with infinity) and those who disliked Bonaventure's Augustine leanings and preferred Aristotelians like Aquinas. Besides, it appealed to analytic philosophers that I showed a penchant for argumentation.

The strategy seemed to have worked, except that later at the reception at Parry's home, one faculty member approached me and asked, "When are you going to stop doing this sort of thing and start doing philosophy?" I responded saying that this is what the medievals thought philosophy was; indeed, that it was the most important philosophical question for them, and that I saw my job as pointing out how it failed.

I can't recall his retort, but next morning at breakfast I mentioned the incident to Bill (by then Parry had become Bill for me), and he said not to worry about it because the person in question was not really a philosopher himself but a linguist. If the particular faculty member had heard what Parry had said about him he would have been very mortified. The idea that this or that other member of the department was not really a philosopher was common among the philosophy faculty at the time, and in fact in the profession as a whole. It certainly was present in Chicago while I studied there, and it continues nowadays in various places, although it is less prominent.

The department was considering half a dozen finalists for the job, but they voted overwhelmingly for me, in particular because George Hourani, who was a distinguished professor specializing in medieval Islamic thought, had circulated a note arguing that I was by far the best-qualified candidate for the position.

Indeed, my credentials were hard to disregard. I was graduating from the highest rated program in medieval philosophy in North America, and most likely in the world; I had already published articles in well-established, specialized journals; I had recommendations from some of the most famous historians of medieval philosophy in the world; and I had a background in contemporary philosophy acquired in one of the top ten philosophy departments in the United States. It was not easy to match those credentials. And let us not forget to add that I was a young man with an interesting personal history, a lovely wife who was pregnant with our second child, and the cutest two-year-old daughter that could be imagined.

While the appointment process with Buffalo was moving forward, I had on-campus interviews with some language departments and had lined up some on-campus interviews with some philosophy departments that had not advertised or interviewed in Philadelphia but were looking for a medievalist. In some cases a language department and a philosophy department intended to team up to offer me a position. I had several offers, but none of them was as good as the one from Buffalo, which was an up-and-coming university. Indeed, it styled itself as "the Berkeley of the East." For me this was an ideal job. One of the best graduate departments in the United States, a large faculty, and a pluralistic approach to philosophy where it would be easier to navigate the often rough tenure waters. Besides, it was just a few miles from Toronto, so we could move our things without much difficulty. That is how I landed in Buffalo. Obviously miracles do happen, occasionally.

12

Buffalo Department of Philosophy (1971–1973)

Getting a job in philosophy had been the greatest hurdle I had so far faced at this stage of my career. Much depended on it. Traditionally, teaching has been the only viable way in which philosophers have been able to support themselves and their families. Of course there are exceptions. But at the time I was on the market there were practically no nonacademic jobs. My only chance to do at least part of what I had been training to do for ten years of strict education was to have a job in a college or university.

I was thrilled to have landed the job at Buffalo. I could not understand my luck, but I was not completely out of the woods. Although the greatest hurdle had seemed to be getting the job, once it was secured I had to make sure to finish the dissertation and successfully defend it. Finishing meant dotting all the i's and crossing all the t's of my five-hundred-page project. The defense was still another hurdle.

I was fairly satisfied with the dissertation and felt confident that there would be no problems with it, but Toronto took dissertation defenses very seriously. I had to face a board of more than a dozen faculty, some of whom were willing to spill student blood to show off. Still, I was fine until about ten o'clock the night before the defense. My dissertation director, a very kind man who wanted to be helpful, made the great mistake of phoning me at that time to wish me good luck. It was nice of him to do so, but when I hung up the phone I felt sick. I had spent years on this project and all of a sudden it occurred to me that I had done a poor job with the dissertation and that this would be obvious to the examiners. I spent the night awake and vomiting. When I looked in the mirror the next the morning, what I saw scared me. I was pale as a sheet of white paper and I had dark circles around my eyes. I looked like a hospital patient after major surgery. The situation reminded me of my placement trip to Philadelphia, and it was comforting to recall that I had survived that ordeal. I got dressed and showed up for the defense and, although there were the usual nasty questions, I was able to get through it successfully. I felt liberated and ran home to tell Norma the good news.

With an approved dissertation and a contract with Buffalo, I convinced Norma that we should buy a home. Even though we had substantial expenses during the trip to Europe, we had been able to save enough to put a down payment on a modest home. Indeed, it turned out that we had more than twice as much as we needed.

We spent several weekends going to Buffalo and hunting for real estate. It did not take long for us to find a relatively small home in Snyder, a suburb of Buffalo with good schools. Norma had jitters throughout the process and tried to convince me that buying a home at this stage in our lives was crazy. But I stood firm and we did in fact put in an offer and secure the place. I wanted to have solid ground beneath me from my start in Buffalo, which would send a message to the Department of Philosophy that I meant business and planned to stay in Buffalo permanently. Of course, our house was nothing like Parry's home, but it would make us feel part of the university community.

The move to the new home, which Norma hated, was simple enough since the sum total of our furnishings was by all standards meager. Our greatest load was made up of books; the rest were odds and ends we had collected over the years. I rented a small U-Haul and drove it to Buffalo. With Norma's help, even though she was pregnant, we got the load into our new home.

We were settled in Buffalo and ready to meet the challenges of a professional life. For me this meant joining a community of philosophers, adapting myself to the local culture, and meeting the expectations of my colleagues. It was three years until my first serious review and six years before a decision about tenure could be made. Instead of an end, this was another beginning, and I had to prove myself again, and the conditions of success should not be underestimated. Philosophers are often conceited. Indeed, a good number of them are snobs who regard themselves as above the common rabble of humanity. Some think of

Finally settled in Buffalo. Photograph courtesy of the author.

themselves as part of an elite group that should rule the world. Consider, for example, Plato's idea that until philosophers are kings and kings are philosophers, the world would continue to be a mess where justice is rarely found. Moreover, in spite of an often-repeated appeal to "principles," philosophers are frequently just as biased as the rest of humanity.

Of course, there was no reason for me to expect that my colleagues would be any different than philosophers elsewhere. Indeed, I had many handicaps that could create trouble for me with them. I was a trained medievalist, a field that is not generally regarded as important by contemporary philosophers. Also I was Hispanic, and Hispanics, just like our language, have never been considered active participants in the great traditions in philosophy—for the majority of philosophers, there is not a single Hispanic philosopher of the first rank in the history of the world. Finally, I came from a Catholic background, and this for many philosophers is a great strike against anybody, for they equate Catholicism with narrow-mindedness, persecution of non-Catholics, and many other abuses. The deck was stacked against me and, realistically speaking, I expected a rough ride.

Norma also had her own serious challenges to face. For one, she was pregnant and expecting to deliver a baby before the year was over, and in fact did so on December 2. At the same time, my friend from Toronto, Paul Spade, was visiting us in response to an invitation to the department from me. Norma had quit working to take care of our older daughter, Leticia, and the coming baby, and this also was a new situation. She was an educated and professional woman that now would have to transform herself into a full-time housewife and mother, at least for a while.

Even more important, she was expected to join the American community, our neighbors, and the community of my colleagues. Both she and I were quite aware of the important role that spouses can play in the careers of their partners. And, of course, my family fit the bill perfectly: Norma was gregarious and open; Leticia was a gentle, lovely child eager to make friends; and the newborn, Clarisa, was a fat healthy baby and a bit timid, which made her irresistible.

A lovely and pleasant wife would be a great asset to me, but this role was completely new to Norma, having been born in Argentina and having lived there all her life except for the years after our marriage that we spent in Canada and Spain. But Canada is not exactly the same as the United States, and Canadians have plenty of peculiarities. In fact, we were no different than the many immigrants that live in Canada. And in Europe we were tourists rather than residents, although I was always taken for French and Norma was taken for Greek or Italian.

In the fall Norma's parents came in order to be present for the birth of Clarisa and to help us settle down in the new home. The house needed a considerable amount of work, and Norma's father and I worked steadily until they left for Argentina in January. We painted the house inside and out, added a fence, repaired the roof, and carried out many other improvements.

Here I was, a complete neophyte in the art of house repair, doing everything that was required. I had been introduced to manual labor at Wheaton and had found that I liked it. Indeed, later in life I devoted a good amount of time in the summers refinishing nineteenth-century furniture, which eventually found its way to our daughters' homes.

The Buffalo department was very large and there were plans to make it even larger. Indeed, the original plan called for offices for faculty and students. The number of graduate students alone was quite a few, and increased every year by about twenty.

But the program had already begun to shrink in response to the diminishing demand in the field. Only Catholic schools maintained a strong commitment to philosophy because of the philosophical component of the Catholic intellectual tradition, which had been well established and developed by a host of first-rank philosophers from the early Christian era such as Augustine, towering medieval figures such as Anselm and Aquinas, and important contemporary authors such as Elizabeth Anscombe.

I felt the shock of my new situation from the very beginning. I walked through the door and Dale Riepe, a very sardonic and funny faculty member who styled himself a Marxist-Leninist but was a member of the Buffalo Club, the ultimate capitalist enclave in Buffalo, came to greet me with a smile on his face. He had a copy of *Telos*, a radical journal published by Buffalo graduate students. He had it open and after greeting me, said, "I want to give you an idea of the place where you have walked in. Look at the title of this article." It read, "The Phenomenology of Fucking."

I had come to Buffalo from Toronto, a rather stodgy city at the time, and had been for several years at the Pontifical Institute, where everyone was rather prissy and formal. Indeed, my teaching uniform for several years at Buffalo consisted of a jacket and tie.

So imagine what I thought about Riepe's comment! Eventually, I discovered there were faculty who smoked marijuana, engaged in all kinds of sexual liberties and liaisons between faculty and students, and a generally relaxed view of bourgeois morals. Of course, I have always been progressive in politics, but I have also been somewhat moderate when it comes to my personal habits. So this was the place where I had come? Riepe's encounter made me wonder.

In a department as large as ours, the faculty naturally broke into groups according to philosophical preferences, methods, and traditions, not to mention personal sympathies and animosities. There were half a dozen Marxists—an unusual number at the time for an American department of philosophy, along with progressive liberals, and conservatives.

The late 1960s were turbulent times. The Vietnam War had stirred up passions, creating a climate of political strife throughout the academy in general and the University of Buffalo in particular.

In some cases the political divisions translated into divisions between younger and older faculty members. Large public protests and demonstrations and heated demands for an end to the war took place to the extent that some faculty from our department ended up in jail. At least one of them was a conscientious objector who served time in prison because of his refusal to serve in the armed forces.

Others were concerned with the rights of women. Passions ran deep, for and against certain causes, all of which resulted in sectarian exchanges between faculty and students. Indeed, the relations became so strained that the faculty and students prepared a voluminous set of bylaws to help prevent, and settle when they occurred, serious disagreements.

Part of their intent was to recognize the rights of both faculty and students. We needed a good lawyer to deal with the bylaws' intricate details and regulations. Fortunately, Thomas Perry was a lawyer and a specialist on the philosophy of law, so we kept him busy. When I became department chair I kept a copy of those bylaws in one of the drawers in my desk, ready to be pulled out, if need arose.

An important division in the department was between historians and non-historians. The department's ambition was to cover all basic periods of the history of philosophy, including ancient, medieval, Renaissance, early modern, the nineteenth century, contemporary, and American, as well as specialists in Islamic philosophy and Eastern philosophy, particularly Indian, Japanese, and Chinese. This resulted in a rather large number of historians in the department. I was hired as a medievalist to fill an existing gap.

Other divisions had to do with subfields in the discipline, such as logicians, ethicists, political philosophers, metaphysicians, epistemologists, philosophers of science, and so on. Divisions among traditions were perhaps the strongest, giving rise to sharp disagreements. On the one hand were analytic philosophers who worked in traditions prevalent in Anglo-American philosophy, and on the other, philosophers who were part of the traditions dominant in continental Europe, such as phenomenology (i.e., Germany and France mainly).

In this partisan and sectarian context, accusations of not being a philosopher or not doing philosophy were frequently made. This phenomenon typical of the field of philosophy, although it is sometimes found in other disciplines as well, particularly the social sciences. Philosophers are very prone to accuse each other of not being philosophers because, as Richard Rorty pointed out, the title of "philosopher" is considered honorific. Instead of saying that some philosophers are simply bad philosophers, their critics claim that they are not philosophers at all. According to this perspective, no true philosopher can be bad.

Elsewhere I have called this "the technique of dismissal." It is frequently used by some philosophers to undermine and disenfranchise some other philosophers. I should mention that the members of the department that most frequently used the technique of dismissal were analytic philosophers. Indeed, the question I was asked when I interviewed on campus by one philosopher clearly supported this claim. He disqualified my historical work from being philosophical, and Parry disqualified him in order to undermine his accusation.

I was lucky that, as far as I know, no one publicly accused me of not being a philosopher (perhaps they thought it or said it behind my back), in spite of the frequency with which the epithet was used. I was probably saved from this accusation because from the very beginning I was understood to be a specialist in the history of philosophy who had an interest in the pursuit of philosophy, not just its history, and considered myself a philosopher, not just a historian.

Indeed, the history of philosophy I have done, and I have done much of it, has always been guided by the goal of understanding and clarity. It must have helped also that I had training in analytic philosophy at Chicago and that I was familiar with some continental thought from the time I had been at Wheaton.

My success at Buffalo was also helped by the fact that my family and I fit well into the social life of the department, despite being foreign born. Most philosophy departments are deserts in terms of a social life. Some faculty members become jealous of the success of their peers, have strong ideological disagreements with them, or just detest them personally. In order to avoid quarrels, then, they distanced themselves from their colleagues as much as possible, attending the least number of common gatherings as possible.

Fortunately, at that time the atmosphere was quite different in Buffalo. Of course, there were groups of faculty who liked each other and engaged socially with each other and not with others. But there were some, primarily junior members of the department, who liked to socialize with everyone. Also important was the fact that the faculty was quite diverse in term of ethnicity, nationality, race, origin, and almost every social group one could think of.

Norma and I fit well with the younger members of the department and their families, regardless of the traditions within which my colleagues worked—people such as John Kearns, James Brady, Richard Hull, Kenneth Barber, Carolyn Korsmeyer, John Corcoran, and James Lawler, among others, became friends in various degrees. I was fortunate in being able to make true and lasting friendship with some, although in other cases they were interrupted for various reasons.

Having come to Buffalo in the same year, it was easy to develop a close friendship with Carolyn Korsmeyer. She was very active in the department and when she became director of graduate studies in 1980, at the time when I became department chair, we had a lot to deal with together. John Kearns was another faithful friend even though his field, unlike that of Carolyn, was not very close to my own.

Kenneth Barber was also a close friend, although occasionally we got mad at each other because we both had tempers and when he was director of graduate studies in the eighties and nineties I did not always agree with his policies and decisions and I repeatedly complained. But our friendship continued to be very strong. In part this was a result of the fact that he came from Nebraska and was very sympathetic to the philosophical group known as the Vienna Circle. Indeed, he wrote his dissertation with the legendary Gustav Bergman, one of the members of that group whom I particularly admired.

Barber was an extremely sharp philosopher, but his commitment to perfection, and the fact that he seemed to have read everything, did not give him confidence and he lagged as a publisher. Indeed, it took me quite a bit of effort to get him to coedit a volume on a topic of mutual interest, "individuation in early modern philosophy," and it took me even more effort to have him write the introduction to it. Barber served for many years as director of graduate studies and died unexpectedly when he was getting ready to retire. I missed him deeply.

There were also smaller groups of faculty, such as those around Newton Garver, in which we were very socially active. Norma and I were invited to almost every party. Perhaps our Cuban and Argentinian backgrounds helped in that we were not typecast as this or that, politically or otherwise.

The fact that Norma was an educated, professional woman who went back to full-time work when our two daughters went to school helped considerably. In spite of Buffalo's reputation as a low-growth town, Norma was able to find good jobs in the city, and early on became treasurer of a savings and loan institution. Later on she supervised the financial reporting department of a major bank, and eventually moved on to become executive vice president of a venture capital firm.

It was a department tradition to give dinner parties and invite some colleagues and their spouses or significant others. Some faculty, like the Houranis, had dinner parties every two weeks, and most other members of the department had at least one dinner party per semester.

The tenor of these parties differed from group to group, but often they were elaborate affairs in which the food was superb and everyone dressed up for the occasion. It was common for the ladies to wear long formal gowns and good jewelry.

Not that everyone did this or was as friendly—it took more than three years for me to meet every member of the faculty. And we had the usual group of marijuana-smoking hippies who often stuck to themselves. Still, mostly everyone was friendly and warm. Of course, some people were formal, and even distant, but somehow, Norma and I did well with almost everybody.

This made our lives pleasant and helped a great deal when it came to my position in the department. You cannot easily turn down for tenure and promotion someone whose spouse greets you with a kiss. This may have been one of the reasons I was never regarded as an outsider, and least of all as a non-philosopher. I fit.

Not everything was a bed of roses, however; the roses were occasionally mixed with poisonous thorns. In fact, the department had gone through a rough period just prior to my joining it. Part of it had to do with the country's politics. Conservatives fought with progressives, and this was reflected in our small community in the election of department chair.

There were also disputes between the younger members of the department on one side and the older members on the other, and there were cliques that voted together as a block on various issues. As a junior member of the department who would, at some point, have to go up for promotion, I had to tread carefully.

To become an enemy of one of the "bosses" of the department cliques would surely make it difficult to get a promotion. One has to remember that in social groups of the sort academic departments are, no single person or group can ensure the promotion of a particular faculty member, but it is quite likely that just one senior member of a department, or a small group of members, can prevent a promotion. The best strategy for junior faculty is to be friendly with everyone, even when they hate someone's guts. There is plenty of time to get even after promotion to associate with tenure, and better still, after promotion to full rank. Vengeance should wait for the appropriate time. Indeed, the best policy is to forget your gripes and work toward harmony and on behalf of the entire department. Harmony works best for everyone, while strife is usually counterproductive.

The very first year that I joined the department I was put in charge of the undergraduate program. This job was reserved for junior faculty, and I imagine that it was expected that I prove myself not only as a philosopher and a teacher but also as an administrator—another area in which I had no experience or interest. One advantage of the job was that it came with a teaching load of three courses per year rather than four.

Nonetheless, although it was interesting in some ways, the job was demanding and a headache. I was in charge of choosing the courses to be taught every semester and produce the teaching schedule. With the large number of faculty, we offered sixty-two courses, and for undergraduate students another sixty-two, more or less, depending on the number of graduate students enrolled in the program.

This meant a schedule of 124 courses per semester, more or less. Now, even more difficult and unpleasant was that I was in charge of problems and complaints affecting undergraduate teaching. This also included advising undergraduates and dealing with graduate students who taught regular courses and those who assisted faculty. There were constant lines of students streaming into my office.

Considering that I had never taught a course before coming to Buffalo, and that I had no idea of how to put together the course offerings for a department of thirty-one faculty and a good number of graduate students, the job was exhausting. Indeed, at the time I wondered whether Peter Hare, who had taken over as chair from Parry, had given me this job to prove that I had it in me to succeed. Originally, Hare had some doubts about me and was not sure how to handle me, although it did not take very long for him to become one of my greatest supporters in Buffalo.

In any case, I survived the experience of director of undergraduate studies, but I did have to suffer considerably. Some of the problems I had to deal with involved sexual harassment or inappropriate behavior in class. One of our student instructors, for example, taught a course in which he dealt with sex and love and several students came to see me to complain that he not only illustrated various kinds of sexual behavior with his own personal experiences, but asked students to fill out questionnaires asking for highly intimate information about their sexual lives.

Another graduate assistant decided to save money by moving into the office he shared with another graduate student. Apart from this being unfair to his officemate, it was not appropriate to use one of the common men's rooms to wash and dry his underwear, particularly when he hung it so that it was the first thing you saw when you entered the men's room. When this came to my notice I met with the student and explained that this was not appropriate or acceptable, but I was not nasty—I did understand what it meant to be a student without much money. The matter was resolved when he found appropriate quarters to share off campus with another graduate student.

Another job in a graduate program that I did not anticipate early on was directing dissertations. Of course, I knew this had been coming, but I had thought it would be at least a year or two before it started. But there was already one student that was waiting for me. This was Peter Redpath, who is now retired but is still very active.

After we met and I had talked to him, I suggested the topic: "The Ontological Status of Time in the *Sentences*, *Summa*, and *Physics* of Thomas Aquinas." I found the topic fascinating, and I did not know of anyone who had applied my ontological approach to time. Perhaps I could rely on help from some of my teachers to guide Redpath. He had already been working with George Hourani on some preliminaries when I joined the department, but nothing had been settled when I arrived at Buffalo. Hourani was not a specialist in metaphysics or the Latin medieval authors—his work was in ethics and Islamic thought. Naturally, I took over the work and, given my general interests, I steered Redpath toward metaphysics, Gilson, and the Pontifical Institute folks. I had to do this, because I was as green as green can be, and afraid that I would misdirect Redpath.

The major challenge posed by Redpath's dissertation was that we meant it to be a scholarly contribution about Aquinas's philosophy but also a piece of systematic philosophy. Now, how can this be done? I had already published materials that were primarily systematic and other materials that were primarily historical in value. And I had never run into someone who would explain to me how these two very different goals could be brought together. Yet, here I was, trying to find a way to deal with this dilemma. Of course, Redpath had no answer to this problem himself. And for me this was the first time that I had thought about an issue that I was not going to resolve until years later through the view I have called "the Framework Approach to the History of Philosophy."

Now, the important thing to realize is that the dilemma Redpath was facing had already been internalized by me. My solution at the time was to steer Redpath to follow the historiographical method of Gilson, which was quite reputable, even though it did not answer the problem that I confronted when I was presented with the prospect of Redpath's dissertation. We both learned something important from each other, which was an absolutely necessary condition of the learning process between teachers and students.

Redpath was the first of my graduate students who would work close to areas in which I had philosophical interests such as medieval and scholastic philosophy, metaphysics, historiography, hermeneutics, Latin American philosophy, and popular philosophy. He defended his dissertation in 1974 and I had joined Buffalo in 1971.

Now, Hare, the department chair, was happy with the job I was doing as director of undergraduate studies and as member of the department, and had planned for me to continue, but in the middle of the year I signed a contract with the University of Puerto Rico to join that department as visiting professor for the 1972–73 academic year. They had heard about me and offered me the visiting position to see if they could entice me to go to Rio Piedras permanently.

I was exhausted from having finished a dissertation and from doing administrative work in Buffalo as director of undergraduate studies, so the enticement of a year on the beach was too much for a Cuban to turn down. It was a great opportunity for our two girls also and for the entire family to be away from the brutal Buffalo winters. Besides, I had a good academic reason. As I will mention shortly, in my first year, and with Parry's encouragement, I had developed an interest in Latin American philosophy, and Puerto Rico seemed the right place for the book project I had in the works.

Hare was disappointed but released me for the year. Early on, he had come to the conclusion that in order to keep me he would have to compromise and was prepared to face the fact that I would get many job offers throughout my career. In his view, the best way to keep faculty like me was by throwing goodies at them: early promotion, salary increases, leaves of absence, and support for research.

Hare turned out to be a great mentor and a good friend. His only disappointment as far as I was concerned was that he did not succeed in getting me elected president of the Eastern Division of the American Philosophical Association. He was convinced not only that I deserved it but that I would eventually get it. And indeed, at one point it looked like it might happen. In the year 2000 I was put on the ballot with quite a bit of backing from various groups, but did not get elected. (This was not surprisingly, since I did not even attend the meeting of the American Philosophical Association that year and did no politicking!) After that I became even less sanguine about having my name on the ballot.

Indeed, I did have the opportunity of becoming secretary of the Eastern Division of the Association after Ernest Sosa retired, but I turned down the political machine that assured me I could have the job if I wanted it. I did ultimately become president of other more specialized societies. Hare had a perennial optimism that often interfered with his perception of reality.

Fortunately, I never had a desire to become president and least of all secretary of the association—I did not see myself dealing with the issues I would have to face, and abandoning the work that had attracted me to the profession in the first place. Of course, both jobs would have helped my career, but at what cost? Still, Hare never gave up. When he died in his seventies, he was still plotting to get me elected president of the Eastern Division. For me, however, philosophy was not a profession or career, but a vocation, and one that intrinsically included teaching, rather than administrative work of one sort or another.

13

The Vocation and Profession of Philosophy (1975)

Two of the most important challenges that I faced when I came to Buffalo were teaching and students. I was greatly handicapped with respect to the first because, as mentioned earlier, I had never taught a class, whether graduate or undergraduate. Of course, I had taken many courses in the five institutions that I had attended beginning with college, but those courses had not prepared me to do most of the things that one is expected to do when one teaches. Another problem was that the classes I had taken in graduate school were often too specialized to be properly digested and appreciated by undergraduate students.

At Buffalo I had to teach four courses a year, three at the undergraduate level and one at the graduate level. I could get by teaching one graduate seminar on medieval philosophy and one undergraduate course also on medieval philosophy, but what would I do for the other undergraduate courses? One or two could be logic since I had taken logic both at Wheaton and Toronto. Or I could do an experimental course on Latin American philosophy, following Parry's suggestion, but I did not know enough about this field and had very limited materials to use for it.

There was also a problem in regard to the medieval undergraduate course, for I had never taken a low-level undergraduate medieval course. Even the graduate seminars posed problems because the seminars I had taken in Toronto in this field were very specialized. Consider that when Armand Maurer taught Aquinas's *On Being and Essence* he spent a whole school year on it and did not get to finish the book, in spite of the fact that it was very thin.

In sum, I ended up teaching a graduate seminar and an undergraduate course, using notes from the courses at the Pontifical Institute. Although they were too advanced, I could not do any better. At that time I had not developed appropriate teaching tools, so I am sure the students suffered. I used McKeon's anthologies of texts for the medieval courses together with a brief history and a standard manual for the logic courses. The challenge was to choose texts that would generate some interest. But I felt very bad about the fact that I did not feel sufficiently prepared, and that I piled up a disproportionate amount of work on the students. In the years that followed I would try to be more realistic.

Although I considered my teaching beginnings far from brilliant, subsequent semesters were better planned and more interesting, both for the students and for me. I always had good enrollment in my classes at every level, a fact that was a real surprise. The undergraduate medieval course usually drew more than forty students and some of them were smart and worked hard—the Catholic school prep showed.

I tried to be well prepared and was relaxed and made jokes, and this may explain why students felt comfortable and liked to participate in class discussions. At some point I even received an award for my teaching, and students consistently gave me good marks on their course assessments, but the reasons remained mysterious to me. Maybe they liked my accent and easygoing Cuban style. One student in one of the courses thought I had a British accent—probably the first and only time that happened to a Cuban!

The only course in which I had open student dissatisfaction was the logic course taken primarily by student nurses. A few times I was exasperated with students that could not understand the importance of the topics we needed to deal with, such as Venn diagrams. In time, I expanded my teaching topics in experimental directions, such as teaching philosophy through art, race and ethnicity, metaphysics, categories, ancient philosophy, Latin American philosophy, interpretation, and many more.

Occasionally, I used the very successful textbooks published in the Blackwell series on popular culture and philosophy edited by my former student William Irwin. Indeed, elsewhere I also edited one volume on *Mel Gibson's Passion and Philosophy*. The frequent success of these experiments made me happy because I did not have to teach logic to unreceptive students, even though teaching logic was easy and some parts of it were fun. I was also particularly satisfied because I was teaching courses on topics in which I was working and I could see how they contributed to my research.

The second major challenge I faced had to do with the students themselves. At the undergraduate level they were fine, with few exceptions, although their standards had already begun to decline, a process that has not yet reached bottom. But none of this mattered too much to me because I enjoyed teaching a diversity of undergraduate courses and particularly graduate seminars and I worked with graduate students on dissertations.

Now, when I wrote about philosophy and the Buffalo Department of Philosophy in the last chapter, I said nothing much about the role that students generally play in philosophy as I conceive and practice it, which means, of course, about the role they have played, and still play, in my life and my view of philosophy and philosophical methodology. Indeed, remarks in the last chapter may have given the idea that in the case of research institutions like Buffalo, I believe the faculty is the backbone of the institution and the role of students is somewhat unimportant in comparison.

But this is far from being the case. Indeed, I hold that students have key roles to play in a university in general, and particularly in philosophy. True, both graduate and undergraduate students to some extent come to a university or college to be taught and trained by the faculty, often in technical fields, but this is not meant to be their exclusive role, and it is unfortunate that many, both faculty and students, believe it is.

In my view, the fundamental role of students, both at the graduate and undergraduate levels, is to engage with their teachers in projects that will not only teach them the facts, methods, and history that they are supposed to learn from their teachers, but also engage in projects that will help them learn by themselves and expand the field in which they are cooperating with teachers.

The ideal teachers, as Plato so well conceived them, manage things so that they learn as much as students in the educational process. Plato had many ideas about how to do this and why, which we need not necessarily accept and for which we do not have space here, but the core idea is indubitably the best form of teaching.

So I made its implementation one of the main goals in my new job. In practical terms it meant that I would try to integrate students' research, particularly that of graduate students, into my own work, as well as the reverse, that is, have students integrate in their work those of my ideas that I thought were particularly appropriate to achieve their goals. Whenever possible I would try to include the research goals of students into my goals and vice versa.

This resulted in jointly authored publications, such as articles, books, and collective volumes that include both the work of students and my own work. Of course, if one has students who are sharp and willing, the results of this procedure can be extraordinary; but if they are not, the outcome is a missed opportunity.

In short, I have tried to relate my own work as much as possible to that of my students, particularly of my graduate students. I have directed twenty-two doctoral dissertations, and the authors of sixteen of them are still active in philosophy.

Practically all of those who are still active developed fruitful careers and I think benefited from the teaching method mentioned above. The key, I think, is that apart from having worked with me in their dissertations, they partnered on an equal basis with me in some of my other projects. From my point of view, this was a valuable outcome for me and my students in that they and I profited considerably from this symbiotic relationship.

I explicitly began to put this program in place from the very first semester in which I began teaching the undergraduate courses I had been assigned, and I was given teaching duties at the graduate level.

After Redpath's dissertation in 1974, the dissertations I directed followed two patterns of topics and method that combined what I had learned at the Pontifical Institute and in my first experiences at Buffalo. Historically the dissertations continued to follow the patterns of research I had started on Francisco Suárez and other medieval and scholastic authors. They dealt exclusively with metaphysical subjects that had been neglected. At the same time, I began exploring texts from Latin American philosophy that were even more neglected.

In terms of methodology, the work involved translating previously untranslated texts from Latin and Spanish, as well as following the systematic analysis I had used in my work in the seventies and early eighties. The dissertations and the work with students also followed this pattern and often resulted in joint publications, as said above.

At this point, my new methodological ideas on doing philosophy and its history had begun to crystalize. The translations were preceded by an analytic introduction to help with the understanding of not just the history of the problems posed by their topic, such as individuation or good and evil, but also the philosophy of it. This was an excellent launching pad for historical and philosophical research by students and for my expansion of the work on Suárez and other historical figures.

I found receptive responses to this approach in other graduate students who were looking for dissertation materials. The earliest in this group was Woosuk Park, who continued the work on Suárez I had started but became interested on Duns Scotus and the principle of individuation in "Haecceitas and the Bare Particular: Study of Duns Scotus' Theory of Individuation" (1888). He used this research as a springboard to criticize various interpretations of Scotus, including my own interpretation of his theory of individuation, which prompted me to respond. Following the Platonic view on teaching, I think it essential that teachers encourage their students to argue against them. This is at the core of the teaching process.

John Kronen was also part of this early group. He was interested in preserving some continuity in fundamental issues while moving forward, so he chose "substantial unity" rather than "individuation" as his dissertation topic and exchanged Suárez for Scotus in "The Substantial Unity of Material Substances" (1988). At that time we also worked together on a couple of minor projects, and John successfully developed interests in post-Suarezian early modern scholastic philosophy, still a much neglected field of study, but which another student of mine, Daniel Novotny, was going to explore in the context of the topic of "beings of reason," such as chimeras and the like.

The fourth graduate student in this group, Michael Gorman, continued to cultivate an interest in medieval philosophy, but his interests expanded to fundamental philosophical and theological issues. Again, we cooperated on a couple of projects, but he took a step in the direction of systematic rather than more purely historical work, although he did integrate historical materials in his systematic work. His dissertation was titled "Ontological Priority" (1993).

The work on dissertations continued to yield fruit in the research on medieval and scholastic philosophy, but most research had moved in some interesting directions following my own various interests on purely systematic work after the Middle Ages on the one hand, and on the other in directions that follow the increase in my systematic work on various fundamental topics on meta-metaphysics, categories, and others.

I hope that the previous discussion shows the importance of the relationship between student and teacher in my view and the fact that it really never ends once it has started. Indeed, it does not end even after death, for it goes on in a dialogue in which the memories of both parties are affected.

Former students rejoice in showing mentors that they are doing what they were taught to do, making a partner of the mentor in activities and successes in which the mentor would not otherwise have participated. And for the teacher it is a renewal of the dialogue between teacher and student. Indeed, their ideas are a way in which teachers may be said to achieve a kind of immortality.

The support for these thoughts is clear when the results of teacher-student discussions survive not only in the eternal and unchanging world of ideas, as Plato would probably say, but in tangible works. This is one reason why I have found that cooperative work is essential to the philosopher, for philosophy is a vocation and the core of that vocation is not just passing down views from one to another, but exchanging ideas that will serve as a corrective to ideas developed in solitude. Consider how easily Descartes deviated from truth and common sense in his purposeful isolation.

Dialogue is essential in our discipline, and although this kind of exchange can exist and be profitable with others, it is most fruitful between teachers and students because of their mutual devotion to one another. The bond between student and teacher is one of the strongest that humans can experience.

In part because of the strong belief that philosophy is to a great extent a discipline in which the role of students is as significant as that of their teachers, many philosophers have thought of philosophy as a vocation rather than a profession. Indeed, Socrates's famous words, "Philosophy is the love of wisdom," is a calling to follow a master in the pursuit of wisdom, which in some ways is like art. Unfortunately, a lack of resources in our contemporary world in particular has forced us to act as if philosophy were a profession or a career rather than a vocation.

There is an important difference between being a philosopher and practicing philosophy as a profession, that is, entering the community of philosophers who earn a living by teaching philosophy for a fee, which is approximately what the Sophists did in ancient Greece and which Socrates criticized so sharply.

The first of the hurdles in the profession, rather than the vocation, of philosophy is getting a PhD in philosophy or in an appropriately related discipline, as I described earlier. There was a time in the United

States when a PhD was not a requirement to a successful career in philosophy, as the case of Wilfred Sellars so well illustrates. The highest degree Sellars earned was an MA from the University of Buffalo before the private university joined the State University of New York system in the early 1960s. Indeed, at the time many philosophers who did not have great aspirations in the profession were content with an MA. Most of them were happy teaching at the undergraduate level, and could very well dispense with a PhD. By the time I graduated in 1971, however, a PhD had become a requirement even for the least ambitious philosophers and the most humble jobs. My graduation from Toronto with the required degree, then, was the first professional hurdle I successfully overcame in my career.

An even more difficult hurdle to overcome, particularly at the time of my graduation, was securing a job at the college or university level. I had been able to do this by getting a tenure-track position at the University of Buffalo. The fact that the Philosophy Department at the university was perhaps the largest in the country, and regarded as one of the top twenty in reputation, was particularly important for my professional career, for it had the potential of opening some doors that otherwise would have remained closed. Whether those doors would open, depended, of course, on additional factors. One was the next hurdle in a philosopher's career: promotion to associate professor with tenure within six years of teaching and eventually, in due course, to the rank of full professor.

For colleges whose mission is primarily pedagogic, promotion involves success in the classroom, being well liked by one's colleagues and students, service to the department and the institution, and some evidence that one has not stopped thinking and that one keeps up with developments in the field. In research institutions such as the University at Buffalo (there are only around sixty such institutions in the United States), the key factor is research, although teaching and service also count to some extent.

Research involves developing a successful reputation in one's field backed by appropriate publications and a continued dialogue, through talks and participation in conferences, with other members of the community of philosophers. Professional success in a research university depends to a large degree on success in the philosophical profession as a whole, which in turn involves a good reputation outside one's institution; evidence of professional approval from them must be demonstrated. This translates into publication of articles in well-regarded professional journals and of books in respected presses, as judged by those who are considered knowledgeable in one's specialty within the discipline.

It should not be forgotten that philosophy has many subfields, some of which are quite technical, such as logic and the philosophy of science. As happens with a department, success also involves service to the profession, or in professional societies, as well as being well liked by philosophers who themselves have a national and, if possible, international reputation.

In short, success in the profession of philosophy, not the vocation of philosophy, translates into being accepted in several communities: the community constituted by the department and the college or university in which one teaches, and the community of philosophers outside one's institution, which in turn entails acceptance by the smaller community of specialists in one's subfield. The factors relevant to achieve professional success, whether at a local or national level, are three: performance in teaching, administration, and research. Some of these can be measured more easily than others. Bad teachers and administrators can easily stand out, but when it comes to research the matter becomes more complicated. For one thing, the community of philosophers is divided into groups that do not often respect or recognize what members of other groups do, mirroring the situation described earlier in the Department of Philosophy at Buffalo.

Consider, for example, the groups of analytic philosophers, Thomists, Marxists, historians, and continental philosophers. Like historians, who are subdivided into other subgroups such as those that specialize in ancient philosophy, medieval philosophy, or nineteenth-century philosophy, and so on, other philosophy groups can themselves be divided into further subgroups. Analytic philosophers, for example, may be divided in terms of specialty, say logicians, epistemologists, philosophers of science, metaphysicians, ethicists, specialists in social and political philosophy, and so on.

Similarly, historians are divided into classicists, medievalists, historians of early modern philosophy, historians of the nineteenth or the twentieth century, historians of Asian philosophy, Latin American philosophy, and so on. These divisions in turn are often subdivided according to disciplinary terms (e.g., metaphysicians or epistemologists); at others times in terms of methodology and tradition (e.g., analysts versus continentals); and into other criteria, such as loyalty to particular authors (e.g., Marxists and Thomists.) And matters become complicated because these groups often overlap. You may have analytic philosophers who are classicists or medievalists, and logicians who work on the nineteenth century.

In the United States this is a complex maze and young philosophers need to know how to find their way around it for the sake of promotion and professional success. The key is to understand that these various groups function as communities that have their habits, regulations, traditions, evaluative criteria, favoritisms, and that like families, they often go back to one or more philosophers who are considered to be the founders and models of the communities. Indeed, elsewhere I have argued that these groups function like families in that they favor their own members and engage in nepotism.

In the compilation of a dossier to evaluate an assistant professor's promotion to associate professor with tenure, for example, it would be homicidal to ask a continental philosopher to write a letter for an analytic philosopher (or vice versa), even if both philosophers had credentials in, say, race theory. But this plight is not just a question of promotion. Young philosophers themselves cannot ignore the situation of the profession if they want to get ahead, or even just survive. Should one join the group of Thomists or Marxists? Or should one ignore analytic philosophy and concentrate on continental philosophy, or vice versa? Keep in mind that such decisions may have nothing to do with the vocation of philosophy; rather, they are largely matters of career and professional advancement.

These and similar questions are important because their answers are not merely theoretical, but can affect the life and career of young philosophers. It is important to deal with them early because the need to make decisions on these matters begins as early as college, and they reach a critical point in graduate school insofar as graduate programs in philosophy are quite often divided into those whose faculty is composed of analysts, continentals, historians, and so on.

It is not enough to decide, as I did, to specialize, say, in the history of medieval philosophy. It is also necessary to think about the approach and the school in the United States. For me the question was whether I should go to Toronto, which had the traditional historical approach to medieval philosophy established by Gilson and followed by Anton Pegis, Joseph Owens, Armand Maurer, Edward Synan, and others, or to go to Cornell to study under the leadership of someone who used an analytic approach such as Kretzmann's. Then, after graduation, should one continue to follow the traditional Gilsonian historical path, join the Kretzmann approach, or pick some other methodology?

In making these decisions a junior philosopher needs to realize that it is essential to consider several things about philosophical communities and how they function. One is that, like all human communities, as mentioned earlier, philosophical communities function as families of a sort. And essential to the notion of family are ancestry and tradition. Families have founders, descendants, and become established in traditions. And it is in terms of the relation to the founders and the traditions they have established that the members of these communities are judged to be loyal, and therefore good, or disloyal, and therefore bad. The closer one is to the founders and the community's family traditions, the better one and one's work are judged.

There is also a kind of hierarchy among members of philosophical communities that functions in some ways as pedigree in aristocracies. Consider, for example, the community of analytic philosophers. Among its most distinguished founders are Bertrand Russell, G. E. Moore, and Ludwig Wittgenstein. Of these, probably Wittgenstein stands out as the founder of a successful subgroup of analysts.

Among his most highly regarded descendants were Norman Malcolm and Elizabeth Anscombe. This means that philosophers who can trace their intellectual pedigree to Wittgenstein, be it through Malcolm, Anscombe, or similar immediate students of Wittgenstein, are accepted as members of the family of Wittgensteinians and exercise some authority over other members of the group who have lower familial credentials. How important they are judged to be depends on how far they adhere to core traditions established by Wittgenstein's closest disciples or derived from his original insights.

Consider another example, namely, the community of historians of medieval philosophy that belong to the Gilsonian family, although there are other, less respected authors, such as Jacques Maritain. Etienne Gilson is the uncontested founder of this family, and among its most important members are Anton Pegis, Joseph Owens, and Armand Maurer. This means that those who can trace their intellectual ancestry to Gilson, be that through Pegis, Owens, Maurer, or some other historian who follows the Gilsonian approach, will be considered part of that family and supported by its other members, provided his or her work meets the standards that have evolved within the family over the years.

This is not very different from what happens in an aristocracy, where there is an ancestor who initiates the family. The ancestor sets up a kind of dynasty that is supported and maintained by descendants, relatives, and associates of the founder. In the example just cited, Gilson becomes the founding ancestor, call him king, who was followed by the likes of Owens and Maurer, call them dukes or princes, all the way down the line to their students who have a lower status still, call them counts or marquises, and so on.

One important factor that should be considered in this scheme is that not all families have the same power. The philosophical community is also divided in such a way that certain fields and certain families are more powerful than others. In the United States it is the analytic family that dominates what may be called "the philosophical mainstream" or "the philosophical establishment." And within this family, those who work in logic, epistemology, philosophy of science, metaphysics, and ethics are dominant. Other fields, such as aesthetics, the philosophy of race and ethnicity, and the history of medieval philosophy, are considered less central, even marginal.

This is clear in the fact that these other fields tend to be unrepresented in highly ranked philosophy departments. For example, neither Harvard nor Princeton has a medievalist in their philosophy departments, and aesthetics is frequently absent in what are considered strong programs in philosophy. In some philosophical families some traditional fields are completely rejected, as happens with logic by continental philosophers. Indeed, in the case of the history of medieval philosophy, there is an ongoing battle for dominance between members of the Norman Kretzmann family and the members of the Toronto family founded by Gilson, although there are some medievalists who are well regarded by both families and some who are rejected by both.

Within analytic philosophy, the strength of different philosophical families is generally determined today by the notorious "Philosophical Gourmet Report," which purports to rank graduate programs in terms of their relative strength in particular philosophical subfields. For example, in the field of medieval philosophy places like Notre Dame and Toronto are ranked at the top, while others, such as the Catholic University of America, are not even ranked despite a distinguished history of medieval philosophy. Some of these departments have a good number of faculty members devoted to the field, as at St. Louis, while others have only one faculty member, as at Cornell, Indiana, or Buffalo. In some fields, like the philosophy of race, the ranking is not very meaningful because of the meager number of programs listed and a certain ideological approach that vitiates the list.

Some fields, such as Latin American philosophy, are completely absent from the list, in part because very few graduate programs have even one person who can direct PhD dissertations in it. So far the field is ranked only in what has become the pluralist alternative to the "Gourmet Report," namely, a ranking open to approaches that are not exclusively analytic or to fields that are not traditionally associated with analytic philosophy, such as Latin American philosophy.

Although the "Gourmet Report" in particular determines the value of philosophy programs in the United States, it is clear that it is often a beauty pageant, based on principles that are far from scientific or sound. The rankings are simply the result of canvassing opinions from a reduced pool of philosophers who have all kinds of professional axes to grind. In short, the rankings are based on the opinions of one or a few philosophical families.

The problem with the family system is that it often involves nepotism (i.e., favoring the members of the family over those who are not members, even if they are as well qualified) or simony (e.g., editorial positions, invitations to speak, and other professional privileges that reward those who do favors for the family). It also imposes on its members a narrow conception of the methods that should be used in the discipline, rather than opening new vistas and challenging its members to move in new directions. The authority of the traditions in the group and of certain powerful members of it predominate, quashing attempts that try to go beyond the perimeter favored by the family. Finally, it promotes inbreeding, which is certainly one of the worst things that can happen to philosophy. Philosophy thrives in diversity, criticism, and challenge; it dies in homogeneity, dogmatism, and conformity.

With an understanding of the philosophical community in mind, it is easy to see the challenges I had to face in my career as a philosopher, in part from the intellectual and conceptual challenges that I encountered in my growth as a philosopher. In the first place, my main field of specialization, the philosophy of the Middle Ages and scholasticism, is not one of the core fields in philosophy, not even a core field in the history of philosophy.

Indeed, it is standard in colleges and universities to teach course sequences in the history of philosophy that skip anything from ancient Greek philosophy to early modern philosophy, completely leaving out Roman, medieval, and Renaissance philosophy.

Indeed, the interest in medieval philosophy is limited to those who have some association with the Catholic faith. Departments of philosophy in Catholic schools have strong offerings on medieval philosophy, although too often what they mean by medieval philosophy is merely the thought of Thomas Aquinas. This is sad because it reduces the philosophical richness of the tradition to an ideological commitment because of Pope Leo XIII's declaration that Aquinas's philosophy has perennial value.

Unlike popular fields such as logic, epistemology, and philosophy of science, and to a lesser extent the other core fields listed above, medieval philosophy has always been regarded as a second thought and largely confined to Catholic institutions.

In second place, the obsession with Aquinas in medieval circles has also worked against me. For, although I have always recognized the value of Aquinas's thought, I have never been a Thomist. Yes, some of my views are inspired by the thought of Aquinas, just as some are inspired by the thought of Aristotle or Wittgenstein. But that is very different from what happens with Thomists, who see their role exclusively as promoters and defenders of Aquinas's philosophy.

The situation with metaphysics, however, has been different insofar as this is one of the core fields in philosophy. But here again I have not focused on popular topics such as the philosophy of mind, preferring instead more traditional ones such as universals and individuation. Besides, a good portion of my work in metaphysics was done historically rather than systematically, and was likely to be ignored by those who knew nothing about the history of metaphysics and are only interested in metaphysical problems of contemporary relevance. It was not until later in my career, in the eighties, that I began to work systematically on metaphysics. So here again I was at a disadvantage.

Much worse was the interest I developed in Hispanic, Latino/a, Latin American, and Latinx philosophy. This field is not yet a recognized field by the American Philosophical Association (although it is recognized by the *Stanford Encyclopedia of Philosophy*) or the "Philosophical Gourmet Report." And the situation has been made worse for me because the majority of those interested in this field are either dilettantes whose main area of work is something else, or who work in the continental tradition, which is poorly regarded by the analytic mainstream. Moreover, it has not helped that the fields in which I have focused my attention in later years had similar problems. Historiographical theory, interpretation, aesthetics, and the philosophy or race and ethnicity are not highly attractive to most mainstream philosophers.

In spite of these hurdles I have been able to establish a record of achievement and to receive some important recognitions of my work. This is particularly surprising when one considers that I never chose an area of investigation because it was popular or because it could contribute to making me famous or notorious. Indeed, the search for fame or gain of any kind has not figured in my calculations. No doubt my professional career has suffered because of it, but I am quite satisfied and happy that in Buffalo I have been able to do philosophy for reasons that are not mercenary but vocational. Perhaps the best examples of this have been my decisions to devote a considerable amount of my research time in Buffalo to medieval philosophy on the one hand and Hispanic, Latino/a, American, and Latinx philosophy on the other.

14

Two Alternative Research Programs (1971–1974)

As a young assistant professor fresh out of graduate school, the first question I faced when I came to Buffalo was about what I had to do to ensure that I would pass muster in the high-powered department that had hired me. The first obvious answer was that some of the things I had been doing had proved successful. After all, I had been hired in an up-and-coming philosophy department because of my presumed expertise in medieval philosophy and my publications in the field, so the safe thing to do was to continue along that path.

But I did not feel completely at ease about just staying in the medieval camp. For one thing, I had gone into medieval philosophy because I wanted to do philosophy, not because I wanted to devote my life to the history of medieval philosophy or to the profession of philosophy. I had not forgotten the reasons that took me into the field in the first place. I wanted to understand philosophy by delving into the roots of philosophical language and terminology in the Middle Ages.

Second, although the Buffalo department was somewhat favorably inclined toward history at the time I joined it, the question that one of the faculty had asked me during my interview still rang in my ears: "When are you going to do real philosophy?" Which I took to mean: When are you going to begin to search for philosophical answers to philosophical questions rather than for answers to questions concerned with the views of philosophers from the past?

Third, although I had a solid record of publications for someone at my career stage, the record was all over the map both in terms of topics and authors. I had written articles on the philosophy of mind (Gonsalvus

Hispanus on the intellects), metaphysics (Guido Terrena on universals, Francesc Eiximenis on evil), epistemology/logic (Ramon Llull on necessary reasons), and philosophy of science (Thomas Bradwardine on ratios). I could not afford to continue spreading my efforts in so many directions. From the beginning I was aware that success in research requires focus.

I needed a research plan that would be coherent and focused. In other words, I had to become a specialist in something, that is, I needed to know more about something in particular than anyone else did, rather than knowing a little about many things known better by others. Herein lies the secret of success not just in terms of recognition and fame, with which I have never been much concerned, but for success in advancing the understanding that we, and especially I, have of the world, which is what ultimately moved me.

It seemed clear that in all the disparate inroads I had made, there was a theme that tied much of it together: metaphysics. As I mentioned earlier, in Chicago I wrote a paper on matter, which is one of the favorite individuators for Aristotelians. And at the Pontifical Institute I wrote a licentiate thesis on Guido Terrena's doctrine of universals, which included both an edition of Guido's text and a study of his doctrine. (It was a matter of time before I ran into individuation, a topic that I have explored in many publications for the past fifty years.) I had been fascinated by Guido's discussion in part because preparing the edition of the Latin text had required that I dig deeply into it, understanding every word and reconstructing every argument. Going forward with this appeared prima facie promising. Besides, universals had been at the center of philosophy from its very beginning. They had been the core of the philosophies of both Plato and Aristotle, and it was the core of Aquinas's thought. In short, it did not take much time for me to decide to pursue my interest in universals.

It was in my search for sources on this topic among scholastics that led me to discover Francisco Suárez, the greatest metaphysician that the Spanish-speaking world has produced and one of the greatest metaphysicians of all times. But soon enough I realized that universals were a very popular topic, too popular, and I wanted to explore something that had not been beaten to death by previous historians. Thus the question: What was close to universals and had been explored relatively little by comparison?

The answer was pretty clear: individuals and individuation. The fact that a score of major contemporary philosophers, such as W. V. O.

Quine and Gustav Bergmann, and some lesser ones, like Héctor Neri-Catañeda, had been interested in this topic was a great incentive; it indicated that this topic would facilitate my doing philosophy, not just the history of philosophy, although I thought, and still think, that doing good philosophy is facilitated by knowing the history of philosophy, but more on this in a later chapter.

I began to look around for sources in this area and it was then that I ran into Suárez's *Disputation on Universals*, of which J. F. Ross had made a translation. I was disheartened by this find, because I had immediately thought of doing a translation and study of this work myself. Fortunately for me, the disputation on individuation (*Individual Unity and Its Principle*) had not been translated. So I set to work on it quickly. Translating the text took considerable time, and after I was done with it, I added a systematic introduction and a very extensive glossary tracing the meanings of terms that Suárez uses to their sources in Aristotle and the medieval authors who preceded him.

This was a work of love and curiosity with which I was satisfied and happy, although it has not earned me a great reputation. No matter, I have always done what I think needs to be done, without serious regard for the payoff in terms of career advancement. The price I've had to pay for this has not been insignificant, but I have never regretted it. It has given me a kind of freedom that many intellectuals do not enjoy because of their excessive concern with reputation and recognition. Fortunately, my colleagues at Buffalo and the university administration respected the work I was doing, even if it was different from what other members of the Philosophy Department were doing.

In fact, in spite of a disregard for—maybe even an aversion to—philosophical fashion and networking, I have managed to survive in a profession that is often cutthroat, cliquish, and intolerant of anything new or different, and which often requires paying homage to those who dominate the field at any particular time.

To this day, the historiography of medieval philosophy falls into several categories—it is not the simple field that most of those unacquainted with its substance think. Some historians of medieval philosophy focus on doing editorial work, establishing good editions of philosophical texts that had been written in medieval Latin and survive only in manuscripts. These scholars are often referred to as "text people." Some of them also do translations and occasionally write learned historical articles. Those who engage in this are often referred to as "historians." It is only a very few who venture beyond these scholarly parameters and American historical sources to engage philosophical problems of contemporary interest. These are referred to as "philosophers" and often criticized for not paying sufficient attention to the work of historians.

During my stay in Toronto, and even for the first few years in Buffalo, I tried my hand at all these approaches: previously unedited texts from medieval Latin and old Catalan; translating previously untranslated texts; and writing learned historical articles on neglected authors.

In all cases I brought to bear philosophical concerns, independent of the Middle Ages. I have never forgotten that I am primarily a philosopher, not a historian, and I have come to believe that in order to be a good historian of philosophy one has to be first and foremost a good philosopher. Although at the time I had not yet explicitly held that philosophical understanding, including value judgment, is an essential component of historical understanding, the way I approached historical work was already taking a shape that would later give rise to a theory about philosophical historiography.

If Parry had not been the department chair that hired me, I would have probably and exclusively followed a path leading to metaphysics, particularly individuation, and scholastic philosophy. But chance or destiny often plays interesting tricks on us, and Parry is responsible for one of the most important developments in my intellectual life: the pursuit of Latin American philosophy and everything subsequently connected with this development, including my more recent work on race, ethnicity, social identity, and even art.

Buffalo hired me because medieval philosophy was my field, but in one of the conversations we had, Parry said: "You're Cuban. I'm sure that there's Cuban philosophy, and there's Latin American philosophy certainly. Why don't you look into it and see whether you can teach a course on Latin American philosophy?" My answer was dubious to say the least: "But I do not know the first thing about that. Is there a Latin American philosophy?" Without knowing it, I had asked one of the most important and debated topics about Latin American philosophy discussed by Latin American philosophers.

I knew there was Iberian philosophy in the Middle Ages, and I had read Miguel de Unamuno and José Ortega y Gasset, but Latin American philosophy? Parry was not discouraged by my answer. As he told me, "The solution to that is to learn something about it."

I could not easily dismiss Parry's suggestion. For one thing, he had just stepped down as department chair and his views were highly respected in the department.

More importantly, however, I realized his suggestion fit well with my longstanding emotional needs to explore my culture, and so I ended up enthusiastically embracing the suggestion. But there were difficulties because, with one old exception, no collections of texts that could be used to teach the subject matter existed. That was when I realized the dearth of resources in the field and the opportunity for a well-trained historian, as I considered myself to be, to establish the parameters of the field and open it up to others. This was in 1971 and I found little to indicate that Latin American philosophy had any presence in the United States at the time. Bushy-tailed and bright-eyed as I was, fresh from graduate school and ready to change the philosophical world, I did not entertain the idea of failure. But reality soon enough struck a powerful blow, forcing me to think about my course of action. Maybe I should continue with my original idea of devoting most of my time to medieval philosophy, and leave Latin American philosophy on the side.

15

Medieval Philosophy (1975–1985)

The temptation to devote my time exclusively, or largely, to Latin American philosophy was particularly enticing because I would not have to stop philosophizing in order to implement it, and the need to develop the field in the United States was crying out for attention. Here was something that I could do better than almost anyone else in the United States because I was uniquely qualified for it. Not only did I have the proper linguistic equipment, the rigorous historical tools I had acquired in Toronto, and the analytical tools I had acquired in Chicago, but I also had the necessary connections, both in the United States and Latin America, thanks to Risieri Frondizi, who lost no time in introducing me to all the key figures in the field in Latin America. Besides, unlike a few others in the United States who had done relatively little work in the field and taught in colleges, I had a serious foundation of research and taught in a major graduate program.

However, to devote my life as a philosopher to Latin American philosophy would have confined me to a small ghetto of narrow specialists who until recently had been very marginal to mainstream philosophy in the United States.

Fortunately, I resisted the temptations and stayed away from what certainly would have been a catastrophe for my future. What saved me was my devotion to philosophy and the history of medieval philosophy. I had not forgotten that my original plan had been philosophy all along, and after having spent years of my life in training to do medieval philosophy in order to understand the philosophical issues that concerned me, I could not abandon the Middle Ages, not even for Latin America. Besides, although medieval philosophy was still the Cinderella of the history of philosophy, it was nonetheless an established historical field and area of specialization. Indeed, my work in medieval philosophy helped me establish some credibility for my work in Latin American philosophy.

In a sense, my bread and butter, my stature and recognition as a historian, was not in play because I was actively publishing in medieval philosophy and what I published was recognized as valuable. Still, I needed to put a plan in place that was concordant with the work I had already done, my expertise, and the direction that merited my attention in the future. So I began by taking stock of where I was with respect to my work in the Middle Ages and then turn to Latin American philosophy in the United States.

I had already done considerable work in medieval philosophy, and particularly medieval metaphysics, as mentioned before. I had published two articles on the transcendentals, which has been a topic of interest for me ever since. A small piece was on the logical notion of proposition and another on the roles of faith and reason in knowledge. The most relevant were two articles, in 1977 and 1979 respectively, not only for their content, but because they pointed to future work dealing with individuation and Suárez. In one I pointed out that Aquinas could very well defend himself against one of Suárez's criticisms of his view by making *esse* (the act of existence) the principle of individuation. This claim was largely ignored by the community of medievalists in spite of, or perhaps because of, its radical nature. It eventually caught on, however. Seventeen years later, Joseph Owens seems to have embraced a version of it when he defended an interpretation of Aquinas that emphasized the role of existence in individuation.

Finding Suárez was one of the most significant events in my early career. For me the exercise of translating his *Disputation on Individuation* had been invaluable. I can truly say that I learned what philosophy is all about through it and, therefore, that this project was the foundation of all my future work. Why? Because the concentration, analysis, and effort it required truly turned me not just into a scholar that understands what it takes to try to recover the thought of past ages, but because it also put my mind and resolve to a test. I became a partisan of Suárez and his subtle and inquisitive mind, but I did not become a Suarezian by a long stretch. Nonetheless, I did try to have my students learn the lessons I had learned from him.

I directed three dissertations dealing with Suárez. This marked the first result of the work on Suárez after I had finished the translation on individuation and had started working with Douglas Davis on the two disputations on good and evil mentioned before. The translations were preceded by analytic introductions to help with the understanding of not just the history of the problems posed by good and evil, but also the philosophy of it.

I have never sold my soul to another philosopher, although I have learned much from particular philosophers, but I have always maintained intellectual independence. Indeed, I feel sorry for Suarezians, Thomists, Wittgensteinians, Aristotelians, Platonists and the rest that become slaves to the works and thought of particular philosophers. To do so is one of the most anti-philosophical things one can possibly do. Philosophy is not about authority or intellectual loyalty, but about the pursuit of truth. When philosophers lose their commitment to truth, they cease to be philosophers, becoming something less altogether.

The Suárez project was in a very significant way my first sustained effort to respond to the need that had driven me to the Middle Ages in first place. It was not any of the often-cited reasons why most turn to the Middle Ages, such as faith or religious devotion and the need to defend them.

My turn to this period in the history of philosophy had to do, as mentioned before, with the understanding of the development of the language of philosophy, and both the glossaries compiled for the books on Suárez, and the effort required by the process of translation, took me through the very trajectory I had envisioned, although I had no idea at the beginning how it would be realized. Indeed, it was the effort that answered my inquiry. The results of the compilation of the glossary in particular were general in many ways, for I could not afford to give each entry the space and time it really required.

Nonetheless, it provided a road map of what needed to be done to accomplish my original aim. The next work in which I was engaged carried this program to a higher and deeper level, for it focused on one family of terms essential for the understanding not only of medieval philosophy but, more important for me, the conceptual foundations of recent philosophy.

The work on Suárez prepared the way for my work in the later 1970s and early 1980s. In Suárez I found a critical summary and analysis of what the medievals and scholastics had to offer on individuation, but my obsession with historical roots in order to understand philosophical problems and the vocabularies in which they are formulated led me to the beginning of the Middle Ages. After Suárez and the end of the period, I turned to its beginning, with Boethius.

The result of this work was the first of my books that was not a translation or commentary on some other philosopher, but rather a philosophical study of a philosophical problem that extended throughout several centuries. This work, very different from anything available at the time, established my reputation as a medievalist, although there was plenty of disagreement about its methodology. The first edition of *Introduction to the Problem of Individuation in the Early Middle Ages* appeared in 1984.

I had difficulties finding a publisher for it, no doubt because the study is so different from anything that had been published before. The book broke ground in the medieval field because it was on a topic of extraordinary importance in the Middle Ages but which had not been explored in a book-length study before, except in Germany. Both the topic and the period worked in its favor. But it was an unusual study in at least two important ways.

One is that it was a book-length study of a single topic. Historians of medieval and scholastic philosophy seldom write topical books, tending to write books on particular authors. The reason is that they specialize on authors rather than problems. Some work on major figures such as Thomas Aquinas, Duns Scots, William of Ockham, or even less important figures such as Albert the Great, Anselm of Canterbury, or Peter Abelard. Occasionally, they focus on particular topics, such as being or universals in such and such an author, but very seldom do they write books that cut across time and periods to cover discussions of the same topic. This is precisely what I did. My book covered the period that goes from about AD 500 until about AD 1150, covering the views of such different authors as Boethius, Eriugena, Gilbert of Poitiers, and Abelard. This was something quite novel.

Still more revolutionary than the topical focus, and one of the reasons why the book was rejected by some traditional presses such as that of the Pontifical Institute (this I learned from Owens who confided in me that he had argued for its acceptance and lamented that he could not get it through the editorial board) was its methodology. Instead of following the classic model made popular and perfected by Gilson and his disciples—in which the historian determines the pertinent texts and through a historical analysis compares them, producing a kind of translation/gloss of them—I had done something entirely different, and therefore unacceptable to those who could not envision a methodology different from the one they had been taught.

My first chapter was a philosophical analysis of the problem I was going to deal with, and the analysis was achronic and contemporary. I divided the set of problems that can be identified in a philosophical analysis of individuality, then I identified the main positions that one could take with respect to these problems, and finally I provided arguments both for and against the various possible views discussed. This produced a framework that I then used to compare and evaluate the various positions of early medieval authors, pointing out various ways of understanding their texts and comparing them with the views and arguments stressed by others.

The result is that the larger conceptual frame as well as the agreements and disagreements of the authors were clear and it became possible to judge their historical originality and philosophical sophistication. Naturally, some critics accuse me of trying to lay medieval authors on a conceptual Procrustean bed that did not fit them. And of course, there was a danger in doing just that, but if one is careful, this does not necessarily follow.

Many also resented the style and approach I used, which was generally analytic. This was in part the result of the fact that I tried very hard to find a common vocabulary based on ordinary language so that technical jargon would not get on the way of getting at the core of the views I was examining, making it impossible to compare different views from different times, including those of our contemporaries.

In spite of the difficulties I had publishing the book, once it came out my reputation (good or bad, depending on the source) became established, and the number of reviews of the text was extraordinary: there were more than forty reviews of it, all over the world, some in very prominent journals and written by major medieval scholars, and only one was negative. In short, then, the book finally received the substantial recognition it deserved.

But this was not as important for me, given my position in Buffalo, as the fact that the translation of Suárez's disputation with commentary was thought of highly by the Department of Philosophy and by the profession at large. Of course, medieval philosophy is not the philosophy of mind—it has never been fashionable because the bias against it arises in part from the religious character of most of it. But medieval philosophy had already begun to establish itself at the time because a group of logicians and analytic philosophers had taken an interest in it. I was not part of this group, having graduated from the Pontifical Institute, where a more traditional Gilsonian approach was followed. But the fact that a space had been opened in mainstream philosophy made it possible for people like me to use it.

Another reason was that I was not just a text person, although I had done editions and translations of Latin and other languages and had written some very traditional historical studies—some of them even concerned with how certain manuscripts depended on each other and contained chronologies and the like, topics that historians specially love. I had credentials as a true medievalist, not a second-class scholar.

I had worked on original manuscripts and dug into libraries and long-forgotten texts, but I was primarily interested in the conceptual analysis of the views of historical figures. This, I think, opened doors for me that were closed to other medievalists.

The 1980s opened with a bang for me. The research that I had done in the late 1970s gave fruit in the book on Suárez and the book on individuation in the early Middle Ages, which created a foundation for my program and gave it an impetus that was difficult to stop.

Part of the impetus was realized in my work on medieval philosophy. In addition to the aforementioned books, I published another translation with commentary and a glossary on Suárez's two disputations on good and evil. This was done in cooperation with Doug Davis. I also published various articles, but my major nonhistorical achievement was the publication of *Individuality: An Essay on the Foundations of Metaphysics* (1988), which won the Findlay Prize in Metaphysics. This was my first book-length systematic treatment of the philosophical topic that had concerned me the most over the previous fifteen years. It was the fruit of my research in medieval, scholastic, and contemporary philosophy. I combed the history of philosophy for views on individuality and individuation, but the aim of the book was not to present a history of the problems involved in it.

I had already done that for the early Middle Ages in the previous book. This time I wanted to propose as complete a theory as possible of individuality and individuation. No one had attempted anything of the sort, neither among my contemporaries, nor in the history of philosophy, with the exception of Suárez.

The premise of the book is that the diverse theories of individuation that were debated in the Middle Ages, and that are still being considered in contemporary analytic philosophy in particular, depend heavily on the conception of individuality with which one works. So the book begins by breaking down various problems or issues (metaphysical, epistemic, linguistic, and logical) that can be raised about individuation. I then turn to different conceptions of individuality, and from then on I discuss the other core issues I mentioned. The most fundamental claim is that individuality is best understood as a primitive notion that defies analysis and definition. Once this is understood, it becomes easier to develop a comprehensive theory of it and how it relates to other philosophical problems that frequently accompany it, such as the problem of universals.

The work that I did both in medieval philosophy and systematic philosophy in the 1980s and 1990s attracted the attention of other philosophers and institutions, and with it an endowed chair and a medal. The first was an offer of a job from Fordham University that caused me much soul searching because there was much I loved about Fordham: the fact that it was in New York City, that is was a Jesuit school (the Jesuits have always been my favorite religious order in part because of Suárez), it had a lovely campus in the Bronx, it was a private school, it had a unique didactic mission, and many of my friends were there. Fordham reminded me of St. Thomas Military Academy, the prep school from which I graduated, and the semester we spent in the New York, getting a taste of how fabulous it would be to live there—going to the opera, theater, and checking out the art scene. What else could one wish for? I was sold on the idea of joining the school, and Fordham did as much as they could to help me with a good offer, but Buffalo had some ideas of their own. Simply, at the suggestion of Carolyn Korsmeyer, who was a member of the department executive committee, and with the endorsement of John Kearns, chair of the department, the dean offered me the Samuel P. Capen Chair in Philosophy. This was a counteroffer I could not refuse.

This offer meant money to do all kinds of interesting things, which, in fact, I have been doing ever since my appointment was made. Practically every year since then I have organized conferences on all sorts of topics in which I and others in the department were interested. I brought to campus innumerable interesting intellectuals, I collaborated with many partners that enriched my intellectual life and those of other colleagues, opening doors that did not exist previously, and, in fact, this appointment continues to yield results, for example, in a stack of edited volumes on subjects ranging from the esoteric to the popular. I could not have done this anywhere else or under different conditions. The richness and freedom of action the dean was offering me overwhelming, and I had to accept his offer while regretting that I could not say "yes" to Fordham.

Just writing the last book mentioned above and dealing with the whole Fordham affair should have exhausted me, but rather those events were a source of renewed energy, although the energy was channeled in a different direction. This set a pattern for the future, because I realized that the best way to reenergize myself after the completion of a major project was not to take a vacation from work, but rather to turn toward something new. And this is precisely what I did in applying myself to the study of Latin American philosophy in the United States.

16

Latin American Philosophy in the United States (1939–1985)

I was disappointed, to say the least, perhaps even depressed, at not being able to publish the anthology that Frondizi and I had put together in the mid-1970s, but some events in the 1980s led me to believe that my dream of building up the study of Latin American philosophy in the United States might not remain a dream. In the decade of the 1980s, there were indications that things were beginning to change and there was some interest in publishing materials that had to do with Latin American philosophy. Not that there was a revolutionary transformation of the situation, but there was change in the air. Indeed, the best example of this change was that I was finally able to publish an English translation of the version of the anthology of texts that Frondizi and I had put together ten years earlier, *Latin American Philosophy in the Twentieth Century* (1986).

    This happened because of a combination of favorable factors: first, my colleague Paul Kurtz liked to take publication risks with his editorial business, Prometheus Books; and second, Peter Hare happened to be the series editor for Prometheus's Frontiers of Philosophy series, in which the book was published, not to mention the help and enthusiasm of my student Elizabeth Millán. But let me begin at the beginning so we can understand the vicissitudes of the history of Latin American philosophy in the United Sates and the changes in its outlook.

    Following Parry's advice, that is, to devote serious time to Latin American philosophy, posed a challenge for me and for my career as a philosopher. For, unlike Latin American literature, which is recognized as one of the great world literatures, Latin American philosophy is generally ignored practically everywhere. Indeed, it is even disparaged and ignored by some Latin Americans, such as Mario Bunge, both in Latin America and outside it, not to mention by American philosophers in the United States.

Who does not know or has not heard of the work of great literary authors such as Jorge Luis Borges or Gabriel García Márquez, for example? Their works are read and discussed in every continent and every country involved in literary pursuits. The great boom experienced by Latin American literature in the twentieth century has indeed influenced the work of literary figures the world over. There is no reputable American college or university in the United States, for example, that does not have someone who teaches this literature.

Now the situation of Latin American philosophy was completely different. Latin American philosophy has been generally unknown in philosophy departments, and probably less than a dozen places in the American academic world pay any attention to it. As should be expected, a similar situation occurs in other parts of the world, but my concern is primarily with the situation in the United States and how it affected a budding Latino philosopher such as myself. While some improvements have occurred in the past twenty years as a result of the interest of the growing Latino/a population in the United States, the study of Latin American philosophy is not taken seriously enough, even though it is a philosophical tradition that goes back five hundred years. Let me give a brief summary of the development of this field.

Perhaps the first sign of a sustained interest in Latin American philosophy in the United States appeared in 1939, when the *Handbook of Latin American Studies* initiated a separate and ongoing bibliographical section devoted to the field, under the direction of Risieri Frondizi. This was an indication of interest as well as a recognition by American scholars that Latin American philosophy was considered a legitimate field of study within Latin American studies.

However, the editor of the section was a Latin American philosopher in exile, not an American philosopher or scholar, an occurrence that has, unfortunately, has been occurred too often since then. Moreover, the works listed in the *Handbook* were of Latin American origin, indicating that Americans had not yet made inroads in the field.

Finally, the fact that this publication was a handbook of Latin American studies indicates that Latin American philosophy was considered part of a more general interest on Latin America and not necessarily of particular interest to philosophers per se. It also indicates that, most likely, there was at the time no significant presence of Latin American philosophy in the philosophy curriculum in the United States and that American philosophers were generally ignorant of, and disinterested in, this field; in fact, Latin American philosophy did not seem to have a presence in the United States during the 1930s.

Matters seemed to take a favorable turn in the 1940s. Indeed, there was considerable activity if measured by what had been the case before. Three developments were significant. First was the appearance of two anthologies of philosophical texts, a bibliography, and a volume of essays: *Readings in Latin American Philosophy* (1949) edited by Arthur Berndtson, *A Century of Latin American Thought* (1944) edited by William Crawford, Edmundo Lasalle's partial bibliography of *Latin American Philosophic Thought* (1941), and *Latin American Legal Philosophy* (1948) by Luis Recaséns Siches, Carlos Cossio, Juan Llambías de Azevedo, and Eduardo García Máynez. A significant point to note is that the publications by Crawford and the volume of legal essays were brought out by Harvard University Press, which is something that would not happen today.

The second important development in this opaque history involves three events: the First Inter-American Congress of Philosophy (Haiti, 1944), the Second Inter-American Congress of Philosophy (New York City, 1947), and the Inter-American Intellectual Interchange sponsored by the University of Texas Institute of Latin American Studies (1943). These events, two of which took place in the United States, facilitated the dialogue between Latin American and American philosophers and produced papers about Latin American philosophy, some of which were published in English, in such mainstream journals as *The Journal of Philosophy*, *Philosophy and Phenomenological Research*, and *The Personalist*. Again, I do not think this could happen today.

This record of publication and activity was unprecedented. The appearance of anthologies in particular was a sign that courses were being taught in this field. Moreover, the congresses and the authors of the papers that participated in them were philosophers, some with prominent reputations, such as Edgar Sheffield Brightman and Risieri Frondizi, as well as others with lesser profiles. Still, there was no evidence of sustained activity, such as the existence of a philosophical society for the study of Latin American philosophy, and many of the participants were Latin American. The efforts undertaken in the 1940s seem to be sporadic and restricted to a handful of authors, most of whom taught in departments other than philosophy departments.

Contrary to what one would expect after the increased activity in the 1940s, the decade of the 1950s witnessed a decrease. Perhaps the works produced in the 1940s had saturated a field in which there was still little interest. The publications of this period seem to be the last gasps of the impetus in the 1940s, rather than the beginning of a sustained development, and the philosophers involved, for the most part, were the same as in the previous decade.

Anthologies are always good indications of interest in academia, and in fact, we see the publication of only one anthology of texts: Aníbal Sánchez Reulet's *Contemporary Latin American Philosophy: A Selection with Introduction and Notes* (1954), translated by Willard R. Trask.

Two other books were also published in English, but they concerned a restricted topic (the philosophy of law), and one was published outside the United States: H. B. Jacobini's *A Study of the Philosophy of International Law as Seen in the Works of Latin American Writers* (the Hague, 1954), and Joseph L. Kunz's *Latin American Philosophy of Law in the Twentieth Century* (New York, 1950).

An article on Latin American philosophy by Leopoldo Zea that appeared in Raymond Klibansky's *Philosophy in the Mid-Century* (1958) set an important precedent for future encyclopedias and dictionaries. Moreover, the journal *Philosophy and Phenomenological Research*, published at the University of Buffalo under the editorship of Marvin Farber, continued to publish occasional articles in the field. Such other journals as *The Review of Metaphysics*, *The Philosophical Quarterly*, and *The Journal of the History of Ideas* printed articles on Latin American philosophy. Clearly the editors of these journals had a broad conception of philosophy and an interest in what was happening outside the Anglo-American world. An important landmark was the publication of the first issue of the *Inter-American Review of Bibliography*, a journal that published occasional articles on Latin American philosophy and thought.

The 1950s also saw four pertinent congresses, but only one of them took place in the United States: the Third Inter-American Congress of Philosophy (1950, Mexico City), the Fourth Inter-American Congress of Philosophy (1953, Havana), the Fifth Inter-American Congress of Philosophy (1957, District of Columbia), and the Sixth Inter-American

Congress of Philosophy (1959, Buenos Aires). From this time onwards philosophical congresses and professional meetings became more or less regular occurrences in Latin America, although the participation of Americans in them was usually limited.

One factor that may have played an important role in the decline of interest in Latin American philosophy in the 1950s is that analytic philosophy began to make great strides in the United States and to establish itself as the philosophy of choice for the philosophical establishment. This resulted in less interest in philosophy done in countries other than those that formed part of the Anglo-American world, and particularly in places where the influence of analytic philosophy was weak, as was the case in Latin America. One must keep in mind that ordinary language philosophy became fashionable in the United States in the 1950s, and the ordinary language in question was English.

The 1960s did not show much improvement in the situation of Latin American philosophy in the United States. Several events are significant, but their number was limited: Paul Edwards's *Encyclopedia of Philosophy* (1967), the celebration of the Seventh Inter-American Congress of Philosophy (Quebec, 1967), the Fourteenth International Congress of Philosophy (Vienna, 1968), and the Congress of the Spanish Society for Judicial and Social Philosophy (Barcelona, 1966). These events provided venues for the discussion of Latin American philosophy and the publication of articles related to this field. But again, the authors of these articles were primarily Latin Americans, and they were written in Spanish and obviously intended for Latin American audiences.

Apart from this, *The Journal of the History of Ideas* continued publishing occasional articles on Latin American philosophy. And some general books appeared, such as Leopoldo Zea's *The Latin American Mind* (1963) and the historical introduction to social thought by Harold Eugene Davis, entitled *Latin American Social Thought* (1961). Zea's book was a translation of his work on positivism in Mexico: *Dos etapas del pensamiento en Hispanoamérica* (1963). Indeed, this was not the only translation of a book by a Latin American philosopher at the time; other translations would be forthcoming in later decades, but at no time have they been abundant. To date, most of the work of major Latin American philosophers remains untranslated into English, a serious obstacle to the presence of Latin American philosophy in the United States.

Beyond this there was very little else of note in the 1960s. Still, the items mentioned indicate that Latin American philosophy continued to be introduced into the United States and international forums, although at a very slow pace. That Edwards's *Encyclopedia* took into account Latin American philosophy was significant in that from that point on, no serious dictionary or encyclopedia of philosophy would completely ignore the field, although the substance and range of these contributions were limited in scope and depth. Still, SILAT (the Society for Iberian and Latin American Thought) had been founded and its members organized sessions at various congresses.

The decade of the 1970s showed some improvement. Inter-American and international congresses continued to be held somewhat regularly, and often included the work of Latin Americans or presentations about Latin American philosophy. Yet, most of these events took place outside the United States and reflected very little activity concerning Latin American philosophy in the country. Some other initiatives from the previous decade continued, but not vigorously. For example, William Cooper translated Francisco Romero's *Theory of Man* (1964), but the book, although in English, appeared in the Hague.

Indeed, trying to publish anything on Latin American philosophy in the United States at the time was very difficult, if not impossible. This was the time when I came to Buffalo and was urged by William Parry to teach Latin American philosophy. But was this something I should do? The need was obvious. It was not acceptable to maintain almost complete ignorance about a major part of the world and work written in one of the major European languages. However, given the dismal situation of the field in the United States, wouldn't working on this be academic suicide for me? It could very well be, so what should I do?

Parry was aware of Marvin Farber's interest in Latin American philosophy as part of his general interest in philosophy outside the United States. That was fortuitous, for Farber had published occasional articles on, and by, Latin American philosophers in *Philosophy and Phenomenological Research*, the only journal in the United States that had paid some attention to Latin American philosophy in the United States. This was Husserl's journal that Farber had rescued and brought to the United States after Husserl stopped editing it. Farber also was a good friend of the Argentinian philosopher Risieri Frondizi, who was a member of the board of editors of the journal. So Farber introduced me to him.

This was to be a decisive moment in my intellectual life, for Frondizi was a monumental figure in Latin American philosophy. He was not only a distinguished philosopher—one of the most distinguished

Risieri Frondizi. Photograph available via www.argenpress.info.

at the time in Latin America—but also an important intellectual figure in Argentina. He had been president of the University of Buenos Aires and instrumental in the university reform that changed Argentina's higher education and had repercussions in the entire Latin American continent. He came from a distinguished family of intellectuals. One of his brothers, with whom he had publicly disagreed, had been president of Argentina, and another, with whom Frondizi had also disagreed publicly, was a committed Marxist.

Because of his position and commitment to freedom and human rights, Frondizi, like so many other philosophers and intellectuals from Latin America, had to leave Argentina. So he accepted a position as distinguished professor of philosophy at the University of Illinois at Carbondale. More important for me was the fact that he was devoted to philosophy and interested in issues having to do with Latin American philosophy. Indeed, he had engaged in a debate with Leopoldo Zea on the nature and character of Latin American philosophy that shortly after became a classic in the history of Latin American philosophy.

Frondizi had a reputation of being very proud and intolerant with people he considered incompetent, but with me he was not only friendly and open, but became a dear friend. This could have surprised some, particularly because he was not friendly toward the Catholic establishment in Argentina due to its very conservative views and its alliance with right-wing dictatorships. After all, I was a specialist on medieval philosophy and a graduate of the Pontifical Institute of Mediaeval Studies in Toronto. But he was an authentic philosopher and quickly realized that my fields of specialization had nothing to do with politics or religion.

He welcomed my interest and in no time we had agreed to put together an anthology that would replace the text of Sánchez Reulet, which was dated, out of print, and had some literary slant. This meant that we were to pick up where Sánchez Reulet had left off, although we were quite conscious of the fact that our anthology would be groundbreaking in that it was the first one edited by philosophers working as philosophers in philosophy departments in the United States. Sánchez Reulet taught in a Romance languages department and was never part of the philosophical community in this country.

The extraordinary thing is that Frondizi never treated me like an underling or an upstart—both of which I was. I didn't know anything, and my field was miles away from his field. He had been trained under Romero, perhaps the most important Argentinian philosopher of his generation, and here I was, a medievalist. From this perspective we looked like the odd couple. But, a couple we were, and we were not that odd, in that we worked together extraordinarily well and were well matched—it was an intellectual marriage made in heaven.

In 1972 I went for a year to Puerto Rico to look for sources to develop my new interest in Latin American philosophy and to advance our anthology. This new interest fit well with the sense of Hispanic belonging I had begun to develop at Wheaton and did not undermine my main areas of research in medieval philosophy or in philosophy as such. Indeed, the interest in Latin American philosophy was primarily educational.

Apart from the mentioned anthology by Sánchez Reulet, there were a couple of precedents to our task, but there were no translations available from which we could pick appropriate texts. Keep in mind that Latin American philosophy began early after the European arrival. Indeed, the first philosophical texts produced in Latin America go back to the 1550s, and production of philosophical materials continues uninterrupted to this day. Availability in translation was the wrong way to go about producing a good representative collection.

So we ignored the difficulties and proceeded by choosing texts that focus on the topics that had concerned Latin American philosophers in the twentieth century, a period that had seen a true flowering of philosophy in Latin America, although we added some materials from the nineteenth century. The reason was that much of early-twentieth-century Latin American philosophy was written as a reaction against positivism, a philosophical school that had dominated the second half of the nineteenth century in Latin America. Once we had made a selection of texts, then we would worry about getting translators for them.

Although even under these parameters choices were difficult, we did put together a volume that was intended to be representative of the period that goes from the late nineteenth century to the 1960s. My stay in Puerto Rico helped, although the library was very disappointing. Working in it was a chore in that the temperature was quite hot and the air-conditioning did not work most of the time, so I had to cart materials home and work there. The advantage of this was that we had rented a place on the waterfront, on a beach in San Juan called Sta Teresita, which was a delight. For me, a Cuban who missed the ocean, this was an enormous bonus, as it was for my wife and two daughters. One of our daughters adapted so well that she learned to speak Spanish with a Puerto Rican accent.

The anthology was finished and the Spanish version was sent off to Mexico to be published. But the publication of its English translation became bogged down. I sent it off to publishers that seemed to be sympathetic to the project, but every one of them rejected it. The typical reason for rejection was well articulated by the University of Texas Press, which turned it down because "there was nothing in it" of what I like to call "the exotic." Publishers wanted something idiosyncratic in the anthology, and this was not possible to find because Latin American philosophy since its beginnings in the sixteenth century was pretty much a reflection of European philosophy. Much of it copied European thought, but even the parts of it that did not were not exotic in any sense of the term.

Latin American philosophy was for the most part a branch of European philosophy, except for the religious cosmologies of pre-Columbian cultures. And how could one expect anything different? After all, philosophy deals with human problems and is supposed to be applicable to all humanity. Philosophy, like science, wants to be universal, whether it succeeds or not in achieving this goal.

Indeed, even those Latin American philosophers who claim to have decolonized their philosophizing often merely borrow the jargon and ideas that European philosophers have developed. This does not mean that Latin American philosophy must slavishly follow the lead of European or American philosophy. Latin American philosophy can be, and has been in many instances, original, breaking new ground by responding to the concerns that are more evident in Latin America than elsewhere, and by producing novel arguments for and against responses to these concerns, or doing the same with old concerns. Good examples of this are the topics that were explored in Latin America during the sixteenth century as a result of the encounter between Iberian powers and Amerindians, for they raised questions about the humanity of Amerindians and about their ownership of the lands in which they lived.

In the end, we could not publish the collection in English, and after a while I gave up. This was a tremendous disappointment for both Frondizi and me, particularly because the Spanish version was so successful that a second edition was published shortly after the first edition came out. The English translation had to wait until 1986 to be published, in a substantial revision edited by my student Elizabeth Millán and me.

The experience with the anthology was very discouraging. I felt completely frustrated. I had read many Latin American philosophers and I saw that they were talking about issues that had a direct relationship to some of my own concerns and those of American philosophers. We shared common problems and interests, and although they may have solved them in different ways, we were preoccupied with similar topics, such as social identity, segregation, and social justice.

The fact that I could not convince the American community of philosophy publishers to recognize the value of what Latin Americans were doing was a great blow. The work with Frondizi had convinced me that Latin American philosophy was a worthy field of study and reflection. We had something to contribute to universal philosophy, even though our thought was not exotic, indeed, perhaps precisely because our thought was not exotic. Our problems were worthy of notice and I felt strongly that we could contribute something original, if not "peculiar," to philosophy.

The problem for me was what to do about it. How could I open the American philosophical market to Latin American philosophy? How could I begin to establish the field when it was not recognized to be a worthy area of publication or research? After all, who was I? What power did I have? Who was going to pay attention to me?

Although disappointed, I persevered in my efforts to make room in American philosophy for Latin American philosophy. In the 1970s, I published five articles, two of which appeared in *The Personalist* and *The Journal of the History of Ideas*. The others were published in Latin American journals, including the well-known *Cuadernos Americanos*. And I gave two talks on philosophical anthropology and the relation between philosophy and literature in Latin American philosophy.

More important still was that I attended the Inter-American Congress of Philosophy in both 1972 and 1977. This was a way of establishing relations with other Latin American philosophers and become up to date on what was happening in Latin America and the United States in the area of Latin American philosophy.

Still, my efforts did not amount to much. In the desert that was the study of Latin American philosophy at the time in the United States, they were both significant and insignificant drops of water, depending on how the future would turn out. Of course, if the anthology of texts that Frondizi and I had put together had been published, matters might have been more encouraging, although Millán and I had to compromise on many fronts to publish it at this time, dropping some texts altogether and cutting back others. It was clear that the American philosophical community—and I venture to say the United States as a whole—was not ready for Latinos in general, and least of all for Latin American philosophy. American philosophers tended to be rather provincial and to think of anything that did not come from the Anglo-American or European worlds as not worth looking into. It would take some time and a strong demographic tide to prepare the way for an interest in philosophy coming from south of the Rio Grande.

Here are four reasons that have contributed in the past, and still contribute in the present, to the marginalization of Latin American philosophy in the United States:

First, the philosophical credentials of those who work in the field. Many of them have fields other than philosophy as their main areas of specialty, and work primarily in departments of languages, political science, history, and Latin American studies (more recently in American or ethnic studies). Indeed, most of them do not even belong to the American Philosophical Association and, therefore, are professionally isolated from the profession of philosophy. Disciplinary boundaries can be very strict in the academic world, so it is not surprising that the work on Latin American philosophy, as a result of this factor, has become associated with fields other than philosophy and considered only of marginal interest to American philosophers.

Second, most of those who work on Latin American philosophy teach in borderline geographic areas, such as the American Southwest. This tends to keep the field segregated to certain parts of the country—Florida, Texas, New Mexico, and California—whereas the center of activity in the profession of philosophy is concentrated in the Northeast, the area of Chicago and its surroundings, and the Northwest.

Third, neither Latin American philosophers nor philosophers who work on Latin American philosophy in the United States have for the most part been in sync with the interests of Anglo-American philosophy; at the same time, Anglo-American philosophy, even in cases of Latino/a philosophers, has not had an interest in Latin American philosophy. Latin American philosophers from the beginning have often had a predilection for continental European philosophy primarily associated with France and Germany, and tend to ignore developments in North America and Britain.

Moreover, the majority of philosophers working in the United States on Latin American philosophy have generally ignored analytic philosophy in Latin America and focused on the thought of a few philosophers who are popular for their controversial social ideologies, such as the theology/philosophy of liberation, which is often considered by Anglo-American philosophers to be of little philosophical interest because of its strong continental roots.

Finally, important practitioners of philosophy who happen to be Latin American themselves have often criticized Latin American philosophy and philosophers, going sometimes to extremes that deny even the name of philosophy. Because in some cases these authors have spent significant periods of time outside Latin America, their opinions have circulated widely and have prevented Americans and Latin Americans from treating seriously the work of Latin American philosophers. One example of this phenomenon is Mario Bunge, who repeatedly and unambiguously rejected the value of the philosophy practiced in Latin America by Latin Americans.

Unfortunately, philosophy, including Latin American philosophy, is one of those fields that require strong commitment and the existence of leaders who can serve as examples and mentors to younger generations. Latin American philosophy cannot exist if it lacks the support of leaders who will encourage and inspire new generations of Latin American philosophers to continue the practice of the discipline.

In spite of this bleak horizon, the situation of Latin America has been changing and there are reasons that encourage those committed to making a place for Latin American philosophy in the United States. Some events have given me hope for the future. One of the things that worried me for a long time was that Latin American philosophers did not have many places in which to present their work to American philosophers and discuss their views. So it occurred to me that a volume of papers from Latin American analytic, or somewhat analytic, philosophers would be helpful.

Naturally, I needed some input, which I got from my excellent and patient coeditors: Eduardo Rabossi, Enrique Villanueva, and Marcelo Dascal. This time, given the mainstream analytic work involved, it was easy to publish an English edition with Reidel (1985) in addition to the longer Spanish edition with Fondo de Cultura Económica (1984). Then, in order to exploit the success of Latin American literature and its relation to philosophy, I edited a volume with Mireya Camurati (a colleague from Romance languages in Buffalo) on *Philosophy and Literature in Latin America: A Critical Assessment of the Current Situation* (1989).

Although unfortunately Frondizi had died at the beginning of the decade, I continued to feel his presence, and I reflected on how greatly indebted I was to him for friendship, support, and advice. Because of this and my conviction that he was one of the towering figures in Latin American philosophy, whose example needed to be emulated, I compiled a Festschrift in his honor that gathered articles from both American and Latin American philosophers on a variety of topics: *Man and His Conduct, Essays in Honor of Risieri Frondizi (El hombre y su conducta, Ensayos en honor de Risieri Frondizi)* was published in 1980, by the University of Puerto Rico Press. Later, in 1986, I also compiled a volume of his philosophical essays titled *Risieri Frondizi: Ensayos Filosóficos* (1986).

Apart from these works concerning Frondizi, I was active publishing on Latin American philosophy and engaging the field in other ways. I published nineteen articles on Latin American philosophy and gave thirteen lectures on related topics at various venues, several of which were in this country, including at meetings of the American Philosophical Association.

Two of these lectures were delivered at Inter-American Congresses of Philosophy, where I met Latin American philosophers and coordinated activities and publications with them. In addition, as president of the Federación Internacional de Estudios sobre America Latina y el Caribe, I organized the society's congress in Buffalo in 1987.

An opportune moment presented itself to me when Iván Jaksić, who was working in the History Department at Buffalo, decided to write a dissertation on Latin American philosophy: "The Philosophy of Juan Rivano: Intellectual Background of the University Reform Movement of 1968." This was the first time that I had been asked to work with a student on a dissertation on Latin American thought, and Ivan was a well-trained historian that I could treat as a partner rather than a student. Since I was already doing some work in this field, the opportunity was particularly apropos.

The history of ideas had not been an area in which I was planning to do some of my work, and Latin American thought was a completely new field for me. The result was that by 1981, when Iván defended his dissertation, I had learned much about both the method in the history of ideas and about Latin American philosophy. Iván was originally from Chile and therefore was of tremendous help to me. And I believe I was a help to him because of my philosophical and analytic background.

These common first steps were fundamental for we produced works that were published in English and/or Spanish, and because both of us continued to work on new topics that strengthened the links between American and Latin American philosophers. For example, a revised version of Iván's dissertation was the first book published in the series I had started editing for SUNY Press, and our ideas continued to mix particularly in areas of Hispanic and Latin American thought and philosophy. At the time he was teaching at Berkeley and was actively publishing in the field. Together we edited a volume entitled *Filosofía e identidad cultural en América Latina* (1989) and published it in Caracas. Gary Boskin, Amy Oliver, and I put together a volume on *Latin American Studies and the Social Sciences* (1988), and I also compiled a *Directory of Latin American Philosophers* (1988), with the help of Ricardo Maliandi, Horacio Cerutti Guldberg, Graciela Fernández, Iván Jaksić, and Arleen Salles. These were all Latin Americans devoted to the idea of a Latin American philosophy.

The directory was useful for a while in a field that had nothing of the kind. It eventually died a natural death when confronted with the internet, although it still today contains some information about individual philosophers that is nowhere else to be found. This directory was desperately needed both in Latin America and the United States. There was nothing of the kind at that late date and it was difficult to find basic information about Latin American philosophers, but no one had dared to take up the project of compiling an appropriate directory. Additionally, there were other projects that, although not presently needed, carried with them more glory.

The publication of the mentioned volume on analytic philosophy was unprecedented as well and it was historically significant, being the first of its kind. It had an immediate effect. By showing that Latin America had philosophers sympathetic to what had become the mainstream philosophical current in the United States, it opened a venue of interest in its direction. So it became more difficult to ignore Latin American philosophy in the United States and to dismiss it as not quite philosophy or as a philosophy foreign to the Anglo-American tradition. If Latin Americans knew of Quine and Wittgenstein, then perhaps a dialogue with them was possible! One indication that things were progressing was that *The Philosophical Forum* asked me to edit the 1988–89 double issue of the journal on Latin American philosophy. It had been a long time since this kind of attention had been bestowed on the field, and I felt encouraged by it. This publication also had repercussions, although it was criticized by some groups of Latinos and Latin Americans because it had not paid proper attention to their pet philosophers.

Still, there were problems. One of the most serious was the lack of graduate programs that had faculty who work in and could direct dissertations on Latin American philosophy. One example of this problem as late as the 1990s should suffice.

Elizabeth Millán was a student at a fine college in the Northeast, where she had a superb academic record. She was interested in going to graduate school in philosophy to study Latin American philosophy. Her advisers encouraged her to apply to a good number of first-rank graduate schools in philosophy. In her application she made clear what she wanted to do scholastically. She and her teachers were counting on several acceptances, but she was rejected by every program. This was devastating to her, but she did not give up, for now she understood that the reason that graduate schools had rejected her was because they had no one to work with her. So she went back to the drawing board the following year and applied again, but this time she included Buffalo in her list and was accepted.

When she came to Buffalo, we had a candid talk about her future, and I made clear that if she restricted her goal to Latin American philosophy, she ran the risk of never getting a job. So my suggestion was that she specialize in two fields, one could be Latin American philosophy and the other should be a traditional field with which graduate programs were familiar. In her case, for the latter she chose German Romanticism. But the situation of Latin American philosophy had begun to change. In the 1990s *The Routledge Encyclopedia of Philosophy* was published with Amy Oliver as subject editor of Latin American philosophy, a further step in the regularization of the situation of Latin American philosophy in the United States. Nonetheless, in spite of some successes and efforts toward making Latin American philosophy visible in the United States, there was still much to be desired. Many stumbling blocks remained on the path to the proper recognition of this field in the United States. So I put a question to myself: Should I take the risk of spending my time in a field that did not quite exist yet in the United States? For, apart from the goal of making Latin American philosophy viable as a philosophical field in the United States, I also needed to think about my position and future. Fortunately, things were going well in this regard. Indeed, I was advancing steadily in what might be called "my career." This might make my presence and influence more impactful, creating more space for Latin American philosophy.

Indeed, I received a very interesting offer from Texas A&M. They wanted to make their department of philosophy the primary graduate program on Latin American philosophy and issues related to Latinos/Hispanics in the United States. They thought this could be done with my help and were prepared to be very generous and to give me a free hand in the plans ahead.

Of course, this was tempting. Indeed, it was a unique opportunity to create a center that would not be replicated anywhere else in the United States. There would be new appointments and all kinds of resources. And I would be at the center of all of this. This was not just a unique opportunity for me but for the entire field. And the reputation that I had already built would help. The future visibility would be spectacular. We could attract students from the entire country and Latin America and have doctoral fellowships supported in various ways, in addition to a proper staff. But more important than these was the fact that for years I had been working hard to make Latin American philosophy visible in the United States. And what more could be done to make my dream a reality than to implement the Texas A&M plan?

Unfortunately, there were two obstacles. One was the remote location of the school. Even just traveling there was difficult. Still, this by itself was not enough to prevent me from accepting the offer. In fact, the school was so enthusiastic that they went ahead and had their board promote me to the rank of distinguished professor conditionally upon my acceptance of the position they were offering me. Indeed, the contract they eventually sent me left the dates of the position open for five years in case I wanted more time to think about it. Unfortunately, Norma's health, which originally had been a reason to consider for moving south, became a serious impediment to the plan. Buffalo was bad for her asthma, but contrary to what we had thought, Texas was worse. So we remained in Buffalo, where the university made a very generous counteroffer.

17

From Rookie to Chair (1980–1986)

Institutional advancement in philosophy depends on qualifications and hard work, but perhaps even more on whom you know and who your friends are. Landing a first job in one of the largest departments of philosophy in the United States, and one that lacked a clear focus and styled itself as pluralist, posed great challenges for a recently graduated assistant professor.

Indeed, the department was a minefield and in constant motion: faculty members were leaving Buffalo for what they thought were greener pastures at Emory, Arizona, Rochester, and South Florida, among others. The internal politics was most evident in the election of department chairs, the perennial squabbles between political radicals and reactionaries, and much more.

When Peter Hare followed William Parry as chair in 1971, he seemed unsure about what to think of me. As I mentioned before, this may have been in part because he was not sympathetic to scholastic philosophy, considering himself a kind of humanist, and in part because my appointment had been advocated by George Hourani, a scholar with an international reputation who was the leader of the department historians and who had wanted to be department chair before he had a heart attack.

Hare was also a historian with an international reputation in American philosophy, but he had led the group of those opposed to Hourani's bid to lead the department. Hourani had come to Buffalo with a large salary from Michigan. Matters were made worse between them in that the dean had offered Hourani the job of chair while he was in the hospital recovering from a heart attack, which prevented him from accepting it, leaving a clear path for Hare to take the job.

Philosophers often have doubts about, and are even obsessed with, their own philosophical pedigree and that of other philosophers. Hare was no exception. In his case matters were complicated because of his ancestry, which went all the way back to the *Mayflower* and he was related to several prominent early Americans. Not surprisingly, he considered himself a kind of American aristocrat. More complications came from the fact that he had gone to a private prep school, college at Yale, and was a member of the Anglican Church, even though he described himself as a spiritual atheist.

These accoutrements made it hard for him and those around him to forget his pedigree. They created high expectations for him and his family, and occasionally built fences between him and others. It is true that he never, even for a moment, appears to have thought of himself as superior to others. Nonetheless, it was hard to develop a deep friendship with him in that it was hard for him and others to forget his social standing.

All of this made both of us wary at first. After all, my pedigree in the United States could be considered the antithesis of Hare's. I had come to this country as a refugee, had no family in the country, spoke English with an accent, lacked money and social position, graduated from Wheaton College, specialized in medieval philosophy, and studied at the Pontifical Institute in Toronto. Moreover, I made very clear that, whatever my family and ancestors had been in Cuba and elsewhere, I treated my status in the United States as a blank slate.

At the same time, Hare was insecure about his own philosophical credentials and talents. His high expectations about himself and the fact that most of his publications were done jointly with other philosophers of greater stature, such as Edward Madden, made the situation worse. My opinion, which I voiced to him many times, was that he was content to be less than he could be.

Indeed, I kept pressuring him to do a classic study in his field, American philosophy. The last time I brought the matter up was a few weeks before his death when we had lunch together and laughed at the peculiarities of human nature. Putting all this aside, let me make clear that Hare had many great virtues and I became one of his close friends and allies, a fact I valued greatly and which I think he appreciated as well.

One of Hare's undisputed virtues was that he did not resent the success of others, particularly younger colleagues. Indeed, it is no exaggeration to say that he devoted his life to the promotion of many others he thought worthy of success. Fortunately for me, I was one of those in which he believed. Indeed, until his death he tried hard to help me advance in my career. I cannot but be deeply grateful for everything he did for me, for his unwavering friendship, generosity, and belief in the value of my work. When he became department chair for a second term, after I had stepped down (1986), I became his confidant. Indeed, we discussed things that neither of us could discuss with anyone else in the department. Let's face it, there were many faculty who were troublemakers, whatever job the chair gave them to do. So the question was always about where they could do the least damage. Not that we did not appreciate their intellect and moral character. It was just that they did not seem to be able to do anything without creating trouble.

Hare did not complete his first term as department chair in the mid-1970s because of a dispute with the administration concerning the termination of the contract of a faculty member he had hired a couple of years earlier. This created a potential problem for me in that it was possible that one of the troublemakers would get the job that Hare left vacant in the late 1970s.

I saw the problem that this could create immediately: with the history of the department it was possible that old grievances would resurface and affect the promotions of young faculty, of which I was one. So my strategy was to make sure that the person to follow Hare as chair was George Hourani, who was a senior scholar and a gentleman who could be trusted. Moreover, he had been a mentor for me from the very beginning and always tried to be fair and helpful with everyone.

I was particularly worried about my situation both because I did not have tenure and the department was under fire by the university administration. Philosophy had been put last on a list prepared by the vice president for academic affairs that was supposed to determine the future share of resources, and there was plenty of talk at the time of possible retrenchment in order to survive the endemic financial problems that New York state was suffering.

Because of my vulnerable situation as a non-tenured assistant professor and one of the last faculty to be hired, I was afraid of losing my position. In order to prevent such personal calamity, I got some of the small group of untenured faculty together and convinced them that we should circulate a note recommending that Hourani be appointed department chair. In this way we hoped to prevent the appointment and election of someone who was not going to look out for us.

Hare did not like what I did because he had another candidate in mind, but I think he recognized that it was a political master stroke on the part of the junior faculty, for senior faculty felt they could not oppose the opinion of junior people for fear of appearing callous, whereas if Hourani were named department chair, he would be indebted to us. Personally, with Hourani's election in 1977, I would end up having three successive department chairs with whom I had excellent rapport for my first nine years in Buffalo: Parry, who had said publicly that the best thing he had done for the department was to hire me; Hourani, who had been instrumental in my being hired at Buffalo; and Hare, who had already become a good friend.

In any case, Hourani was willing to serve one term as chair, but not any more than that, feeling, first, that his health was not up to the effort required, and second, and perhaps as relevant, that he was aware of the leftover bruises from the previous fight over the chairmanship. After he was elected chair, however, he made things worse for himself by putting himself forward for promotion to distinguished professor.

One of Hourani's major detractors was Edward Madden, who happened to be Hare's mentor. In Madden's eyes, Hourani had done something he could not forgive, and his reaction was to resign his job at Buffalo as soon as he could arrange for a position at Princeton. But this in the end was a mistake, for the position at Princeton was temporary, and so Madden was left without a permanent position. He would have done much better had he stayed at Buffalo. Indeed, I believe he would have been made distinguished professor, for the following chair would probably put him up for promotion, for he was indeed a distinguished philosopher. Of course at that time I had no idea that the chair in question would be me.

In time, everyone forgot about the election and concentrated on living their lives. I kept working hard and publishing so that in a short period of time I had compiled a substantial vita. Still I was surprised when Hare, who was the chair of the department personnel committee, told me that he thought I could be promoted to associate professor with tenure. This surprised me, but he explained that I had an uninterrupted line of feelers or offers from various institutions and the department felt that they would want to do something to prevent my leaving Buffalo. So they put me up for promotion and I was promoted early in my fifth year at Buffalo, and that changed things.

Indeed, a couple of years after Hourani had been elected chair it became clear that he had been serious about not seeking a second term. Once he resigned, informal discussions began to take place about a proper candidate. I did not campaign for the job; indeed, the thought of becoming chair was preposterous given my age and lack of experience. In fact, this would be the second job for which I had no experience, yet I was surprised to find out that several senior faculty members supported me, including Parry, Hourani, Hare, Madden, Garver, and Perry. These were the most politically savvy people in the department not only because they represented important factions in it, but because they had national and international reputations in their fields.

There were some stumbling blocks to my candidacy, however. Most important was that I was relatively young—a mere thirty-six years old—and there was always the thought that I might be easily pushed around by senior faculty. Another was that I was not yet a full professor, which meant that I ran the risk of retaliation from disgruntled faculty who would block my promotion because they were unhappy with my decisions. Finally, there was a feeler I had received from Princeton inviting me to allow them to put my name on a shortlist of candidates for a position in their philosophy department.

The last one weighed heavily on my deliberations, and to this day I am not sure I made the right decision. I was quite flattered by the invitation, and I thought I had at least a remote chance of getting the job, and if I did not get it I would lose nothing by interviewing with them. I knew some of the competition and it did not scare me, but I also realized that my appointment was a very long shot. In any case, I got my vita ready and answered positively, but it was not to be.

The solution to the three obstacles came from Garver: it was to elect me chair and promote me to full rank as soon as possible after. I had already undergone early promotion to associate professor in 1976. Garver's solution would prevent fears of retaliation by faculty and give me an incentive to withdraw my name from the shortlist at Princeton.

For better or for worse, I played it safe and withdrew from the Princeton list, which I regretted because this was a unique opportunity that would probably never again present itself. But there were many other things to consider. My wife had a fine job in Buffalo that she liked, and our daughters were happily settled here. There was only one thing to do. I sat down and wrote a letter withdrawing my name from consideration, explaining to Princeton the situation at Buffalo.

Perhaps this was a very bad thing I did, but with the Cuban experience behind me, I had come to appreciate that it is better to have one bird in hand than two in the bush. I could not forget that I was a refugee who had to leave my country and emigrate to a foreign one where I had to make my own way. And, of course, I should not jeopardize my family's well-being and comfort for a dubious possibility. So I was elected department chair and promoted to full rank. I was thirty-eight years old and scared out of my wits.

Fortunately, from the very beginning of my first term as chair, my reputation in the department progressively increased. In the first place because I was an active publisher. Between 1971 and 1980 I had published thirty-six articles, edited three books, published ten reviews, and given twenty-seven talks at several American venues. In addition, I had received job offers from several places.

The first was from Puerto Rico on 1971, which I accepted on a temporary basis because of my interest in Latin American philosophy. Then I had a feeler from the Bonaventure Institute. The institute was devoted to preparing critical editions and publishing the works of medieval Franciscan authors such as Duns Scotus and William of Ockham. The appointment was significant because I would be working with the top group of editors of medieval philosophical texts in the United States. If I moved there I would become one of those legendary scholars who are responsible for the state of the texts that constitute the object of our study. Could something better than this happen to a medievalist? But that was precisely the problem for, as much as I respected the work of these scholars, I had never intended to devote my life to this kind of labor. It was too far removed from philosophy. So I did not pursue the job, but other feelers kept coming.

The following year I had a serious feeler from the University of New Mexico. They wanted a specialist on Latin American philosophy. Their specialist in the field, Professor Alexander, had recently retired and, given their location, it made sense for them to hire a replacement. They had two final candidates. One was Fred Sturm, an older man who was actually without a job at the time. And then there was me, who was young, upcoming, and had an appointment at a research university. I loved the place when I visited. New Mexico is a beautiful state and the university has a wonderful location. I calculated the pluses and minuses of the job and decided to accept their offer to visit. Unfortunately, I was not impressed with the department, but the possibility of expanding my work on Latin American philosophy was intriguing.

Still, there were negatives. One was the poverty of their library holdings in medieval philosophy. One of my teachers at the Pontifical Institute, Reginald O'Donnell, had told us never to accept an appointment at any university that did not have a complete set of the *Patrologia latina*, and of course, New Mexico did not have a decent collection of medieval texts, let alone a set of that basic source. O'Donnell was the scariest teacher I have ever had. He taught paleography and made mincemeat of everyone who took his class, not because he was mean but because he knew so much and showed how much we needed to learn. His word was law and his advice that of an oracle.

Other negatives with New Mexico were the overall weakness of the faculty, the very limited graduate program, the isolation from the philosophical centers in the country such as the Northeast, California, and Chicago, and the fact that they wanted someone who would devote himself primarily to Latin American philosophy. Of course, I could not do the last in particular. I did not intend to become just a specialist on Latin American philosophy. My plans were to continue doing work in medieval philosophy and to do systematic work as a philosopher, keeping Latin American philosophy as a sideline.

Fortunately, the decision I faced was taken out of my hands because they did not offer me the job. The ostensive reason, I heard years later, was that they were not convinced that I sufficiently appreciated Latin American philosophy. They particularly mentioned an exchange in which they asked me whether I thought that Latin American philosophy existed, and my answer was that I did not think it existed as American or European philosophy existed at the time. Unimpressed by what I said—they wanted a cheerleader for Latin American philosophy, a devotee that did not look at the field critically—they went ahead and offered the job to Fred Sturm, who had a background that fit well with the area and the department.

Another great advantage was that his specialty was Brazilian philosophy, a field that is usually ignored by Hispanic Latin Americans. He did not have a strong record of publications, but he was qualified in ways I was not, and I did not really fit the department. We were very cordial to each other when we met subsequently.

Years later, I was invited to give a talk in the department and some of the members of the faculty, who had been at my interview years before, told me that some of them had regretted their decision not to hire me. At the time, I was also disappointed I had been not been offered the job, because I had liked the idea of teaching in New Mexico, with its magnificent landscapes and appealing climate. Fred Sturm, the man who got the job, was a very decent man and quite competent in his field, even though he was not a prolific scholar. In the end, I realized that Buffalo had been a better match for my family and me.

At the time I became chair in Buffalo, the department still had twenty-eight faculty members, and some of them were prima donnas. The temper tantrums, including mine, were worthy of a two-year-old who had been denied a sweet he felt he was entitled to.

For example, one particular person sat quietly at department meetings, but it was evident when he disagreed with the opinions being voiced by looking at the changing color of his face, which slowly became redder as he had more and more difficulty controlling an outburst. Eventually he could not control himself any longer and there was an explosion and a tirade and then he often walked out of the meeting. At such times, Carolyn Korsmeyer always played an important moderating, sensible, and elegant role in the department. When the level of testosterone rose too high, she always helped keep it down with an appropriate comment. She had come to Buffalo the same year I did, and when I went to Puerto Rico she inherited my job as director of undergraduate studies. I thought she would be a perfect chair and director of graduate studies (DGS), and when I became chair I asked her to take over the DGS and she did. It was a very smart choice because her temperament was comforting and not confrontational. She was marvelous dealing with faculty and students. Indeed, apart from tantrums, I discovered very soon that some members of the faculty who were my seniors thought themselves entitled to object even to my laughter.

What I have said does not mean that I did not think highly of my colleagues. First of all, their credentials for the most part were superb. I mentioned earlier what Parry's famous teacher had said about him. Newton Garver had been the main student of Max Black at Cornell, and Black was one of the most famous philosophers in the country at the time, even though I think no one remembers him now. John Corcoran was a logician who had taught at Berkeley and an Aristotelian to the core. Marvin Farber had introduced phenomenology into the United States and edited one of the most prestigious philosophy journals in the world. Edward Madden was a well-known historian of American philosophy. And Hourani was a distinguished historian of Islamic philosophy and a respected ethicist. These and others were impressive because of their work and their intellect, and some also because of their presence.

The presence of none of them was as striking as that of Garver, although Hourani had a very distinguished countenance that went well with his British demeanor—but he had a terrible time dealing with uncontrolled colleagues. When I first met Garver, he was still quite young and styled a long beard that I remember as going all the way down to his waist, but that Korsmeyer tells me reached no lower than maybe six inches below his chin. He was blond and the beard was not thick, but looking at him one could not avoid thinking of a prophet from the Old Testament or of a Chinese sage. And then he spoke slowly, with key rhetorical pauses, so that the audience understood that what he was saying was important.

Seeing him interact with other members of the department or the philosophy community was a lesson on how to make oneself be taken seriously. Both department members and members of the university community at large were terrified of him, not just because of his presence but because of his sharp intellect, cutting tongue, and Quaker-inspired lack of patience with double standards and cant. Most people melted in front to him, thereby earning his scorn. Newton never respected those who did not stand up to him. I was lucky because I had what the dean called "a volatile temper" and therefore had no problem standing up to anyone, including him. Moreover, Garver also respected humor and I was able to use my Cuban humor to deflate his constant testing.

When I came to teach at Buffalo I was twenty-nine and had been out of Cuba for ten years, but still, I was, as I am today, Cuban in so many ways. To become the chair of a department as variegated, distinguished, and large as the Buffalo department was a great challenge for me, and I had to put up with some comments that were clearly ethnocentric and in some ways demeaning, although those who uttered them, I am sure, were far from thinking they were, and their intentions were benign; I am certain they just lacked the proper sensitivity. One such persons would call me after every department meeting to tell me that such and such a comment I had made was inappropriate, but mostly to object to a joke I had made or my tendency to find humor in circumstances that for this particular member of the faculty were intensely serious.

This, of course, was a clash of cultures, for although I did not generally behave as a Cuban, one of the things that I have never shed is my Cuban sense of humor. Cubans are eminently humorous, laughing at anything, and making fun of even the most serious matters. It is, of course, a question of survival, otherwise who could have endured the long years of dictatorship under Batista or the even longer years of Castro's totalitarian state? My humor and laughter helped me survive the self-important prima donnas, the vanity and scheming of some of them, and the envy of others who craved power, wrongly thinking that chairs of philosophy departments have any power except for the capacity of inflicting pain on themselves.

More serious was the fact that some faculty wanted to interfere with the right of other faculty and presumed that, because I was junior to them, or because they had befriended me, I had to do their bidding, even if such behavior went against departmental regulations or the rights of other faculty.

I remember the case of a senior faculty member with impeccable philosophical credentials who had become a close friend. Our friendship and that of our families grew steadily, and my wife, and sometimes our children, spent wonderful times with him and his family at the idyllic retreat where he lived. Realizing how intransigent he could be on occasion, I anticipated that our friendship might not survive forever without being seriously tested. And indeed, the crisis came shortly after I became department chair.

Our department had a busy colloquia in which we invited philosophers from all over. The arrangements had to be made about a year in advance. This meant that the chairs of the colloquium committee had to arrange some talks for the year that followed their stepping down as chairs of that committee. In this case the person in question was a continental philosopher for whom my friend had little philosophical respect. After I named him chair of the colloquium committee, he proceeded to organize the colloquia for the year when he took over from the continental philosopher. But contrary to tradition, he did not accept the arrangements that had been made by the previous chair, because, as he explained to me, he thought the speakers the previous chair had invited for the fall semester, when he took over, were not in his view true philosophers. Naturally, I explained that they had already been invited, and therefore we would have to honor the invitation; he replied that he had no objection to have them speak as long as it was clear they were not part of the colloquium series while he was chairing the committee.

In spite of my efforts, there was no way to bring him around. Indeed, he even went over my head and asked the department executive committee to approve what I had already rejected. As expected, the executive committee supported my position. This embarrassed him, and he stormed into my office and announced that from then on our relationship was over and that, although in public he would address me if necessary, in private there would not be any further communication between us since I had betrayed him.

I was not able to placate him, and for ten long years he did not speak to me, except in public. It was only when his wife, a dear person whom both Norma and I loved, interceded that he gave up on his resolve and we became friends again. I was very happy about it and I believe he was also.

This was just one of many other unpleasant episodes I experienced while chairing the department. But I did survive, although when I went to bed at night I told Norma, before we both fell asleep, that I would be completely happy had I not had to chair the department. Some people crave administrative jobs in the academy, and I have had my share of them, but I have always considered them trials with which I put up simply because I feel that everyone in a community should help in administration. I guess I was not cut out to be a philosopher king, or perhaps, if we follow Plato, I was after all, since one of the requirements is that one does not want the job. Yes, I'd rather contemplate ideas than deal with the messy day-to-day of administrative life.

Unfortunately, my tenure as chair had begun under a serious cloud that my predecessor should have dealt with vigorously and expeditiously rather than pass it on to me as a fait accompli. One of the jewels of the department was the journal *Philosophy and Phenomenological Research*, edited by Marvin Farber, the founder of the department and a man who had a national and international profile, having taught at the University of Pennsylvania and having been one of the first American philosophers to take note of phenomenology, which he promoted.

As mentioned elsewhere in this narrative, Farber had brought the journal to Buffalo when Husserl could not keep it any longer. The journal was self-supporting except for the cost of maintaining an office and secretary, which the university president had promised Farber to maintain. In

1979, however, a new dean of the faculty of Social Sciences, where the Philosophy Department was located, decided that he could not afford to maintain the journal and notified Farber of it. Farber was dying of cancer and in a vulnerable position, and this made the situation more difficult.

President Ketter not only did not come to the rescue when Farber contacted him, but simply ignored his plea. This was an insult. Annoyed at his betrayal, Farber contacted an old friend, the philosopher Roderick Chisholm, who taught at Brown, and asked him whether Brown would be interested in the journal. Chisholm was not himself interested in taking it over but his colleague and protégé at Brown, Ernesto Sosa, was. It was at this time that I came in as department chair, but it was too late. I could not put pressure on Hourani or other senior members of the department to at least talk to Farber and the administration, because everybody thought it was too late and some resented that Farber had not given them a role in the publication of the journal.

Hourani had not helped in part because he was not kept informed and he had no sympathies for Farber or the journal, and in part because, being from the old world, he had an exaggerated sense of authority and did not feel comfortable arguing with the dean or the president. The die was cast and when the situation was handed to me, the only thing I could do was to make the transition from Buffalo to Brown cordial, something that was easy given that Ernesto Sosa was Cuban and we understood the situation: Farber had already committed to the transfer of the journal to Brown. This is how the Buffalo department lost the PPR and I began my first term as chair.

The loss of the journal was a major blow to the reputation of the department, and a major event in the philosophical world, but it was not the only one that greatly affected the department. Four senior faculty members died during my tenure, reducing substantially the number of faculty and undermining the reputation of certain specialties: Farber in phenomenology, William Parry in logic, Tom Perry in ethics and law, and Hourani in ethics and the history of Islamic philosophy. Except for Farber, whom I never got to know very well, the three others had become good friends and so I felt the need to do something to remember them when possible.

Farber came from a distinguished Buffalo family and thanks to their generosity I was able to lay the foundation of the Farber Fund, which has been used throughout the years to fund a variety of events.

Hourani had a heart condition and died suddenly. Lelo, his wife, called me immediately after she realized he had passed and I joined her at her home before the body had been taken away. It was later, when I accompanied her to get his ashes, that she showed me a very small piece of paper on which George had expressed his desire that half of their estate, after Lelo's death, should go to the Department of Islamic Studies in Michigan, where he had taught before coming to Buffalo; the other half was supposed to go to the Department of Philosophy at Buffalo in order to support research in the area of Islamic philosophy.

Then Thomas Perry died of a sudden heart attack and in this case I thought we could set up a fund for a dissertation prize for our students in philosophy. In time, these funds have grown and have been used to support many wonderful endeavors that properly honor department members and benefactors. It is a tribute both to them and the department that these faculty members felt sufficiently loyal and committed to the department and to the discipline to set up these funds.

I am happy to report that the tradition continues with more recent gifts from Hare and William Baumer, another longtime member of the department. The philanthropic record in the Buffalo department must be one of the best for a graduate program in philosophy in the United States, for this field generally does not draw much attention in this regard, and I am happy to have played a key role at the beginning of this process, for no chair of the department before me had made any efforts in this direction. There is only one discordant note in this history of faculty generosity, and this is that a few years after the Hourani fund had been set up, the department went to court to change the terms of Hourani's will.

The will stipulated that the yield from the fund was to be used for the sake of Islamic philosophy at Buffalo. However, those terms were changed to include ethics. The result has been that the funds have never been used, with a couple of exceptions, to support the field the Houranis had in mind. Knowing how much they regarded Islamic thought, and how proud they were of their cultural heritage, they would never have given the money to the university had they known that their intentions would be so subverted. In my view, this is a rather sad chapter in the history of our department.

The deaths of so many of my colleagues and friends during my tenure as chair were not the only events that caused me distress. There were also constant attempts from an unsympathetic administration to move lines of funding from philosophy to engineering and other professional schools. In the two terms that I served, and in spite of the losses due to deaths, retirements, and moves elsewhere, we were allowed to hire only one person, who unfortunately did not work out and eventually left the United States. A continuing critical problem was the level of support for graduate students, which had become uncompetitive. I remember complaining to the vice president about a situation I characterized as "a scandal," a term that, I was pleased to know, rankled him.

Things got better when a new university president was appointed, Steven Sample, who in his years here did more than any other of our recent presidents to make Buffalo a first-rank university. He, unlike the vice president, understood well the plight of graduate students and tried to solve it. Indeed, his smart administration almost convinced me at one point to entertain an administrative career as dean. Fortunately, I decided against it. That saved me from the fatal mistake of going into administration. Although from early on in my life, I was often asked to serve in administrative capacities, I seldom devoted my entire time to them.

In spite of all the difficulties I faced while being chair of the department, the faculty members were, in general, grateful for my efforts on their behalf. Indeed, at the university level I was promoted to State University of New York distinguished professor. I was fifty-two at the time, and I should point out that the initiative for this promotion came from the dean. He proposed it to the department chair, Peter Hare at the time, and Hare enthusiastically agreed to move forward with the nomination. However, when Hare talked to me about it my vision clouded, and I said I did not want to be promoted. Indeed, I was happy as I was and was well respected by my colleagues, and even, I would say, appreciated by some. Indeed, when I stepped down, they organized a dinner in my honor in which they roasted me without restraint. It was hilarious and heart-warming, for everything said was in good fun. And to make it more memorable, they gave me a large silver bowl engraved with the following Latin script:

> Jorge J. E. Gracia
> MDMCXXX–MDMCXXXV
> Praetori nostri philosophiae,
> qui impigerque et saepe incachinnum eft
> maximas gratias agim.

The only other case like this I remember took place when Hare retired and the faculty gave him an original, signed copy of George Herbert Mead's most famous book.

Trying to promote me for DP could endanger both my position and the goodwill of my colleagues. And that was the last thing I wanted. In part, I was afraid that the appointment would cause some friction with other department members who thought, probably correctly, that they deserved as much or more than me. Indeed, I had already witnessed similar situations with other faculty that resulted in jealousy and bad blood.

Another of my objections was the descriptive nature of the title. It is one thing to have as one's title the name of a university's benefactor and quite another to go around being called, and calling myself, "distinguished professor." It took more than ten years for me to get used to it. I found the title completely pompous. Besides, I thought the entire process of promotion was embarrassing, and there were no assurances that I would get it.

But there were political reasons for the dean's offer that were out of my hands. At the time, the department did not have any distinguished professors. The only ones we had had in the history of the department were Marvin Farber and George Hourani, both of whom I thought were heavyweights, while I was still too young and my work had not been subjected to the test of time. But it did not look good that the department didn't have at least one distinguished professor. Both the dean and Hare were in favor of promotion. However, Hare, after hearing my objections, went back to the dean to explain them. Nevertheless, my objections made the dean even more insistent.

Still, he said he would be willing to wait a year or so to raise the matter again. Obviously, he had read Plato. So he came back the following year and my response after talking with Hare was that I would be willing to go through the process if it satisfied several conditions. First, there were to be at least fifteen letters from distinguished philosophers outside the university that strongly supported the promotion, and at least half would be philosophers I did not know personally—the usual number of letters was less than half that number—and the number of referees who knew the applicant was sometimes fudged. Second, since I had no use for empty titles, I expected a substantial raise in salary if promoted. This, I thought as well, would make me look greedy rather than puffed up. And third, because the title was clearly connected to research, I wanted to have a teaching load of two courses rather than four courses a year, to be taught during a semester of my choice.

I was prepared for objections about the salary increase and, if so, I would have been happy to forgo the promotion. But neither was necessary. To my surprise, the dean agreed to all my requirements. In fact, seventeen favorable letters were collected—only one referee declined writing a letter because of "prior commitments." Now, I was not supposed to see those letters, but mysterious copies arrived in a manila envelope placed in my mailbox. I read them and put them back in the envelope and in my mailbox. But I put the letters back in an order that would clearly show they had been received and read. I never asked Hare whether he had put them there, but I assumed he had. He would want to make sure that I did not think the letters were negative or that he was playing dirty by having my friends write them. The promotion process took over a year, and the appointment was effective as of 1995.

With UB president William R. Greiner at the SUNY Distinguished Professors award ceremony. Photograph courtesy of the author.

An instructive event that happened while I was chair had to do with an offer of a chair position at the University of Florida at Gainesville. Initially, the position attracted Norma and me because the university is located in a very pleasant, small town and some of the faculty shared interests akin to mine. Besides, being Cuban, I thought this was a good opportunity to reestablish relations with Cuban philosophy and culture. In addition, a good friend, Ofelia Schutte, taught there, and the department had recently hired R. M. Hare, whose book on the language of morals was responsible for introducing linguistic analysis into ethics. I spent most of my time with him and I enjoyed every minute of our time together.

R. M. Hare had moved from Oxford University to the University of Florida for half of the year, but had brought with him the notes for all the courses he had ever taught. It was wonderful to look at these notes, and we hit it off well from the beginning. I spent some time looking at his class notes, and he told me that he had been very impressed with my book on individuation. I also enjoyed the oysters he took me to eat nearby and the conversations about the Gainesville department. So my first visit was quite successful, and I returned home thinking I wanted to move to Gainesville.

But the second visit was catastrophic. Not that the department faculty were responsible. The dean was eager to nail down a yes from me, but he was responsible for the debacle. On our second evening in Gainesville, the dean was hosting a reception and dinner in honor of Norma and me, and our presumed move to Gainesville. But earlier that afternoon I had a final tête-à-tête with him that proved unsatisfactory.

The ostensive reason why I was being brought to Gainesville was to build up the department of philosophy and its graduate program. Now, in order to do that I needed at least a start with one or two more faculty lines because the department had been decimated over the years. Unfortunately, the dean said that he could not assure me of any faculty lines, not even one. He said that there was no problem with getting me whatever I needed to come join the university, including a very generous salary and even an administrative job for my wife comparable to the one she held in Buffalo. But promises about hiring were completely out of the question. So, right then and there I told him I could not accept his offer under those conditions; indeed, I could not even think about coming. We shook hands and went to dinner, which, as one would expect, was a very awkward affair.

So I went back to Buffalo with some goodies added to my salary, grateful for not having left. Obviously, I owe much to the University at Buffalo for making possible the enrichment (in more ways than one) of my life. What else could be more welcome by an academic, a philosopher who has devoted his life to the appreciation of ideas and the search for clarity and truth, than to receive the treatment I have had, not only by my colleagues and my departments (now Philosophy and Comparative Literature), but by several deans, provosts, vice presidents, and presidents? With rare exceptions they have treated me as I never thought I would be treated by the university. Indeed, I could never have imagined it when I disembarked from the ferry that had brought me to West Palm Beach from Cuba.

18

Beyond Medieval and Latin American Philosophy (1990–2000)

In the 1980s I had continued to explore the histories of both medieval and Latin American philosophy, not discarding either one to make room for the other. However, I had broken out of the historical cocoon in which I had largely lived and had fully engaged philosophy in a systematic inquiry with *Individuality: An Essay on the Foundation of Metaphysics*. But this book was still grounded in the historical studies I had been pursuing after graduation, although it was the work on Suárez and the early Middle Ages that had given rise to my preoccupation with this topic.

Toward the end of the 1980s, however, I had begun to examine critically what I had been doing all along, for until then I had not questioned the validity of the enterprise in which I was engaged and its effectiveness. Like most historians, I was engaged in the task of understanding history, without a guide as to how to do it and how to justify it. After the conference organized by Hare in Buffalo it became impossible for me to ignore these historiographical questions and I turned to them in earnest.

I began by writing some tentative articles that explored narrow aspects of more general topics, but pretty soon it became clear that I needed to tackle these questions in the same way I had tackled the questions on individuality and individuation, with a breadth and depth only possible in a book: *Philosophy and Its History: Issues in Philosophical Historiography*. However, after the book appeared in the early 1990s, I was still dissatisfied with what I had accomplished because the matter of interpretation was still unclear to me, and along with it the object of historical interpretation. This preoccupation goes back to my years at Wheaton and my concern with trying to understand how language works and the object of interpretation. This object was presumably the views that past philosophers had developed in their philosophical quest, and the difficulty with it was that we do not have direct access to that object.

The object to which we have direct access is always a text, not the ideas and views it expresses. Consequently, the following conundrum becomes preeminent: What is a text, and how can a text, which is not anything like a view or an idea, make it possible to bridge the gap between the views of a historical author and a contemporary interpreter?

Fortunately, I had not wasted my time, for before then, I had developed a formula for future work. The first step of a proper response to a challenge of the sort I was facing now was to understand that a fundamental issue was one of identity, which in the present case were texts. The second step was to find an answer to the question: How do texts function and how do they produce knowledge? In other words, this was a question about the metaphysics, logic, and epistemology of texts and the related notions of author and audience. As I had done with the historiographical issues that ended up being explored in *Philosophy and Its History*, I began by writing a series of articles and giving talks in various venues on texts and their interpretation. But as had happened before, I found that a systematic, book-length exploration was needed in order to answer the many questions that came up. The result was a very large manuscript that scared publishers, who recommended that I break up the discussion into two books, which I did, since I had no other alternative, although I still think that one volume would have been more effective even if not as profitable to the publisher.

In the first book, *A Theory of Textuality: The Logic and Epistemology* (1995), I focused on the notion of text and its distinction from other related notions such as artifact and art object. I also provided a taxonomy of texts and the conditions under which they are interpreted. The views I worked out helped to solve, in my estimation, many of the puzzles that continued to worry philosophers, such as the hermeneutic circle that posed the impossibility of breaking out of language insofar as any attempt to do so relies on language. The book is original in two important ways. The first is that it is systematic and clear, in contrast to much of the available scholarly literature on this subject; the second is that it takes into account the work of both analytic and continental philosophers. Very few philosophers who worry about the philosophy of language and meaning among analysts ever pay any serious attention to what continental philosophers have to say; and even fewer continental philosophers ever pay attention to analytic claims about interpretation. The book defends original theories of textuality and interpretation in which the social function of texts is at center stage.

In the second book, *Texts: Identity, Ontological Status, Author, Audience* (1996), I turned to the questions listed in its title. These topics had metaphysical and epistemic (hermeneutic) dimensions. Again, one of the major contributions of the book is its comprehensive and systematic approach, which distinguishes it from the piecemeal and ad hoc approach favored by analytic philosophers. Another is its clarity and argumentative character, which examines the pros and cons of current views on the topics with which it deals in an open, clear, and honest way, without playing clever rhetorical tricks on readers. Since the prevalent philosophical climate today is schizophrenic, with two sides—the analysts and the continentals—that ignore and hate each other, the books I had produced were doomed to be ignored, in my view.

This did not bother me much, because from the very beginning I had decided that my primary audience was myself, that is, I intended to solve problems that I found puzzling and that would not allow me to rest until I had some understanding of their causes and solutions. I did not care about selling books since I had a secure income as a professor of philosophy in Buffalo. And yet, although the books did not become best sellers, some philosophers paid attention to them, and with the years more and more of them have found them useful, which has been quite encouraging to me.

The work on these two books was a tour de force, but I did have a graduate student, William Irwin, who shared my interest in these topics and was writing a dissertation on interpretation and authorship. Both of us profited from our work, and we both produced books as a result of our efforts. Irwin's input was useful in another way. After I had finished the project and had published it, he noticed that I had missed an important related topic, namely "tradition." So I took it up as the topic of a lecture I delivered at the well-known Aquinas Lecture Series at Marquette University. And our connection did not finish with that, as I shall point out later.

After finishing two books on texts and their interpretation, I was energized by the fact that in them, as well as in *Individuality*, I had been engaged to a large extent in a metaphysical quest. I had been doing metaphysics. Inevitably, the same type of question about history that had been prompted by my work on historiography now arose in the context of metaphysics. What had I been doing when I was engaged in a metaphysics of texts and their interpretation? Obviously, I needed to sort this out in my mind and the only way to do it—as I had done before with historiography—was to engage in a systematic reflection on the nature of metaphysics.

The resulting book was *Metaphysics and Its Task: The Search for the Categorial Foundation of Knowledge* (1999). This is a meta-metaphysical exploration, as should be clear from its title, showing that I had been moving closer and closer to the fundamental underpinnings or foundations, if you will, of metaphysics and in fact of philosophy as a whole, insofar as metaphysics is the foundation of philosophy.

My first studies at the university in Cuba had been on architecture, and for architects foundations are essential. A building with a weak foundation fails its purpose; it is dangerous and could result in tragedy. A good architect must first be a good engineer. Then comes the building itself, a structure that should be well supported by its foundation and that should reflect both the strength of the foundation as well as the function that it is supposed to have. In a way, I came to realize in my middle years that I had never ceased to be an architect, although I was not constructing buildings where people lived or worked, but rather ideas explored in the mind. All along I thought I had left architecture behind, but in truth by becoming a philosopher—particularly the kind of philosopher that I became—I had in fact turned into an architect of ideas.

Metaphysics and Its Task made me understand, perhaps more than any other book that I have written, the entire edifice of ideas in which I lived, and so it was in many ways an inquiry into my identity. For now I was able to grasp much of who I was and what I had been doing.

I had been engaged in a categorization that tried to put everything in its proper place, relating it to everything else. For the task of the metaphysician is to develop a scheme of most general categories that encompass everything we can think about and in which less general categories can be located. The result is a wonderful model of the universe and how I fit in it, through a deeper understanding of it.

The key is to avoid the temptation to reduce some things to others, a temptation that most philosophers fall prey to. I had avoided that temptation in *Individuality* by understanding the neutrality of universals, as neither exclusively concepts, nor realities, nor words. Now I realized that this was the principle that should inform the message of the new book.

The importance in my thinking about metaphysics and categories was specially underlined in several dissertations I directed and the students' post-dissertation work in various publications, including a volume in my honor edited by Robert Delfino. As I expected, the essays did not pull any punches. The students—Paul Symington, Jonathan Sanford, Peter Redpath, John Kronen, Daniel Novotny, and Robert Delfino—all shined. This was the kind of discussion that gives philosophy its good name, and that honored me more than anything else that could be done. Their evaluations and criticisms showed that they had joined me in the search for wisdom. Indeed, it made me feel very proud and privileged to have had the opportunity to have been their mentor and done justice to the call of philosophy.

The main thrust of the editorial work I did during the 1990s supported the systematic work. With respect to individuation, my colleague Ken Barber and I put together a collection of texts on individuation in early modern philosophy. I also edited two collections of articles on medieval philosophy: one was a substantial collection of articles by key authors on individuation in scholasticism that filled in the gap between 1150 and 1650; the other was an issue of the journal *Topoi* on the scholastic doctrine of the transcendentals. With respect to metaphysics as such, I edited a volume in Spanish on conceptions of metaphysics. I also published articles and gave talks related to these and other areas of research. Thirty-seven were on medieval philosophy, twenty-five on nonhistorical topics, nine on Latin American philosophy, and five on Spanish philosophy.

From the books and articles I authored or edited in the 1990s, and the talks I gave, it is clear that the thrust of my work was philosophical rather than historical. It should also be clear that after a great push in the 1980s, the production of work referring to Latin American philosophy began to decrease. Indeed, after the very active publication record of the 1980s, one would have expected something quite different. So what happened?

Partly it had to do with my consuming interest in core philosophical issues in metaphysics and hermeneutics. Then perhaps one could mention the lack of success, even with the successes mentioned in the 1980s, in comparison with that experienced when I was doing philosophical work. But neither of these reasons is completely convincing. There was something else. At the beginning of my interest in Latin American philosophy I felt enthusiastic and optimistic. This was partly the result of working with Frondizi, who was sensible, direct, clearheaded, and enthusiastic about Latin American philosophy. However, my experience preparing the publication of *Philosophical Analysis in Latin America* was entirely different. It was an unpleasant, negative, and difficult experience, and nothing like my experience with Frondizi.

My experience with a few of the philosophers with whom we had to work on this project was intolerable—their objections, complaints, and most of all their disregard for the deadlines they had agreed to with me and the section editors. Months would go by without their answering queries that my coeditors and I had to resolve. Indeed, the complete insensitivity to the organizers' needs was just too much.

But there was a deeper problem that disenchanted me about Latin American philosophers and made me think that perhaps there was no possibility of real philosophical progress in the field, and even worse, in the appreciation of Latin American philosophy in the United States. This was the unhealthy rift between mainstream philosophers on the one hand and philosophers/theologians of liberation on the other, and in particular the followers of Enrique Dussel. Not that I think Dussel set out to be a divisive figure in Latin America, but he has been all the same.

One reason is that, unlike most other philosophers, he has concentrated his efforts in building up a kind of following, almost a cult, around himself. Wrapping his thinking in obscure and enigmatic language has helped to produce this effect. His tireless efforts to push forward his ideas, in combination with his relentless self-promotion, have turned off most other Latin American philosophers, even some who were originally part of the liberationist ideology. I understand all of this quite clearly, but I also understand, as a well-trained historian, that he has had substantial influence in Latin America and this cannot be ignored; nor can it be ignored that some of his ideas are novel.

For this reason I have not ignored or failed to consider him. Indeed, in the last version of the anthology of Latin American philosophy I edited with Elizabeth Millán, we included a text from him. And I have engaged in conversations with many in both Latin America and the United States who consider him an important philosopher.

This openness, however, has cost me much. For in the eyes of non-liberationists—whether they are analytic, continental, or historians—this is unforgivable. At the same time, since it has always been clear that I do not subscribe to liberationist slogans, least of all to Dussel's versions of them, I have also been considered a professional "enemy" by many of Dussel's followers.

The conflict between philosophical factions in Latin America, in particular between mainstreamers and liberationists, has been devastating for Latin American philosophy, and has also negatively impacted the status of Latin American philosophy in the United States. Indeed, it has for the most part made it impossible to develop the field because, on the one hand, liberationists only think about promoting Dussel's thought, and on the other, non-liberationists will not give him any space. The result has been that the materials published about Latin American philosophy, except for those published by a few nonideological historians, are generally of poor quality. Indeed, it would be difficult to find well-meaning, nonideological, and well-balanced philosophers who would and could write general articles on Latin American philosophy in the United States.

It is very sad to see that there are so few philosophers in the United States interested in Latin American philosophy as such, rather than in this or that ideological approach to it. This was a major reason why I decided to critically examine the value of devoting my time to promoting Latin American philosophy, whether in Latin America or in the United States.

Frankly, after my experience I decided that no matter the value of Latin American philosophy, the injustice of not taking it seriously, and the future that perhaps it could have, I had had enough, and I simply resolved to avoid engagements of a similar nature. However, this did not mean that I rejected Latin American philosophy or its value, as so many others have done. On the contrary, I have continued to try as much as I can to work for the well-being and reputation of Latin American philosophers, although it is still very hard to keep things going, particularly in the United States.

Fortunately, there is another side to my analysis, for at the same time that all this was happening, there were indications that Latin American demographics were beginning to have an impact in the United States. Abandoning my long-standing project of making the study of Latin American philosophy a standard field of study in the United States was impossible for me. I could not abandon it. The situation I have described thus far began to change in the late 1980s, and the changes that took place led to important developments in the status of Latin American philosophy in the 1990s in the United States. Perhaps the most important factor was the appearance in the philosophical world of philosophers of Hispanic or Latino ancestry who were trained in established philosophy programs and who, although often known for work in other fields of philosophy, maintained some interest in Latin American philosophy. Some, like Ernesto Sosa (Pittsburgh) do not have a particular interest in the history of Latin American philosophy as such, but are nonetheless interested in promoting Latin American philosophers because they are convinced that they can do fine philosophical work that therefore justifies paying serious attention to them.

The connections that Sosa established with analytic philosophers in Latin America have been significant for their development and have created interest in the United States for their work. Others, such as Ofelia Schutte (Yale) and myself (Chicago, Toronto), share Sosa's attitude but add an interest in the history of Latin American philosophy.

That these philosophers have been educated in first-rank institutions in North America, have taught or teach in graduate programs, and have a profile in the profession, has helped matters considerably, encouraging younger philosophers to look at Latin American philosophy as at least one of the fields that they could teach and even investigate. Perhaps as important is the fact that some of these philosophers have credentials in mainstream philosophical fields and even, in some cases, Anglo-American philosophy.

Another welcome development has been the addition of translations by Amy Oliver and others of recent Latin American authors such as Leopoldo Zea, and the resulting increase of texts, including some dealing with feminist issues. There has been a steady increase in the number of translations of texts into English and the publication of anthologies. Consider the dearth of anthologies available before this time mentioned in the historical narrative given in a previous chapter of this book. Indeed, for quite some time the anthology by Millán and me was the only game in town, a very sad situation indeed.

But now the situation is largely different. Two of the new additions were the result of a newcomer to the field and her enthusiasm for it: Susana Nuccetelli's *Latin American Thought* (2002) and *Latin American Philosophy* (2004). And also at that time Eduardo Mendieta edited a collection of current essays entitled *Latin American Philosophy, Currents, Issues, and Debates* (2003). The success of these publications planted the idea of a *Blackwell Companion to Latin American Philosophy* in the mind of some philosophers interested in Latin American philosophy.

I was one of those who had thought seriously about such a project after Mendieta had approached me about it. In principle I was excited about the idea of a *Blackwell Companion,* and in fact had begun to think about a plan of action after I met Mendieta at the American Philosophical Association convention. Unfortunately, it became clear after comparing notes that our ideas of what this *Companion* should be were very different. His list of authors to discuss was heavily literary, among other things, so I withdrew from the project.

It was not very long after this that Susana Nuccetelli contacted me about partnering on the same project. And I should say that I almost decided to work with her on a *Companion.* After all, we had worked together organizing an NEH Institute on Latin American philosophy that had been very successful and represented a breakthrough for the field (2005). However, I had just finished publishing, with Timothy B. Noone, a massive *Companion to Philosophy in the Middle Ages* (2006) and could not bring myself to do another *Companion.* Besides, what I wanted to do was philosophy, not philosophy textbooks so that presses could make money.

Perhaps a more obvious phenomenon in favor of the study of Latin American philosophy in the United States was the increasing numbers of Hispanics and Latinos/as or Latinx in the United States, which in turn began to influence their number in the profession of philosophy. The pressure was on, both from without, out of a sense of the obligation to respond to the needs of an ever increasing ethnic group who wanted to know something about its intellectual roots, and from within, in the desire of those who went into philosophy to know something about Latin American philosophy. This in turn encouraged publishers to consider works dealing with Latin American philosophy. America is, after all, the center of capitalism, so if there is demand for something, it is bound to be produced. As a result, there has been an increase in publications in the field, and the quality of publications has gone up.

Early in the 1990s, this pressure prompted the American Philosophical Association to create the Committee for Hispanics in Philosophy, of which I was the founding chair (I continued to chair the committee for five years). This very important initiative was the result of Robert Turnbull, who as board chair of the APA worked hard for to change the climate of the association. This was particularly significant because it gave Latin American philosophy a venue in which to be discussed at the center of the American philosophical profession. The impetus helped the Society for Iberian and Latin American Thought (SILAT), which, in spite of the efforts of leaders such as Oscar Martí and others, had always been considered marginal by the mainstream. In time, panels began to be organized on a regular basis at the three yearly meetings of the American Philosophical Association.

At first these panels drew few people, but with time they began to grow and diversify. Their existence encouraged increasing numbers of younger philosophers to get involved. Of course, the degree of activity has had much to do with the energy and leadership of the chair of the committee. The creation of this committee opened the possibility, which became a reality, of an APA newsletter devoted to Hispanics/Latinos in philosophy, which has become a venue for the publication of articles on Latin American, Hispanic, Latino/a, and Latinx philosophy. Some committee chairs have been very active, whereas others have not.

At the end of the 1980s and early 1990s, it was also clear that we needed a book series devoted to Latin American thought. However, that notion was still too narrow for presses to take a chance on it. Still, I was able to convince SUNY Press to have a series that, while not devoted entirely to Latin American philosophy, would integrate this kind of work. So we compromised and called the new series the SUNY series in Latin American and Iberian Thought and Culture. The first book in the series was Iván Jaksić's work on Chilean philosophy; shortly after that Ofelia Schutte's work *Identity and Social Liberation in Latin American Thought* was published. Along similar lines was the 1999 publication of Saenz's book on liberation by a different press. The SUNY Press series is still going strong, invigorated by a literary influence under the leadership of my coeditor Rosemary Feal, one of my former students. The series recently celebrated its twenty-fifth anniversary, and we have also introduced art into its offerings.

So how could I encourage the new developments without having to suffer what I did organizing the publication of *Philosophical Analysis*? A change of direction was in order, and I began to prepare the foundations for the new perspective. First I wrote a thin volume, *Filosofía hispánica: Concepto, Origen y foco historiográfico* (1998), which fit well within my interest in Latin American and Spanish philosophy. This was the first attempt at making sense in a monograph of the notion of Hispanic philosophy. It was an anticipatory work based on my thinking about issues entitled *Hispanic/Latino Identity*, which would first appear in print in 2000.

This volume represented not so much a shift as a development and expansion in a systematic and philosophical way of the historiographical work I had been doing concerning Latin American and Spanish philosophy for the previous thirty years. So its appearance should not be surprising, since a similar process had happened with others topics I had taken up, such as individuality/individuation, historiography, and metaphysics. In all cases I had begun by doing historiographical work and then at some point I had shifted to systematic work, whereas at other times I did just the reverse, or, in other words, I began as a historian and ended up as a theoretician. At the end of the 1990s then I was poised for another expansion in my areas of reflection beyond medieval and Latin American philosophy. The first encounter was with ethnic identity, followed by racial and national identities.

19

The Call of Ethnic, Racial, and National Identities (2000–present)

At the time I entered the United States in 1961 as a refugee, I considered myself exclusively Cuban, and with few exceptions Cubans also thought of me as Cuban. "Cuban" in Cuba was used exclusively as a national denomination, but in the United States the term was also used as an ethnic and even a racial denomination.

So, while in Cuba I was a Cuban national, but in the United States I could additionally be considered ethnically or racially Cuban. Some Americans, for example, would deny that I was Cuban because I was white, or looked white, and they thought of Cubans as black or colored. And thus for them I did not qualify as Cuban. However, most people, myself included, did not clearly differentiate between these denominations.

In time I thought I would apply for American citizenship, one of the requirements for which was to have been a permanent resident of the United States for five years. So, while I was at Wheaton I applied for residency and got it. But nothing had changed as far as my national or ethnic identity. I still thought of myself as Cuban in both of these senses, although some Americans thought of me as only ethnically Cuban. Then I left the United States for Canada, where I entered as a permanent resident.

Becoming a permanent resident in Canada entailed losing my permanent residence status in the United States. However, I was still Cuban, in spite of the fact that I had become a Canadian permanent resident and was in line for Canadian citizenship, which, in fact I subsequently received, after having spent the allotted amount of time required. But I still thought of myself as Cuban. In short, I thought of myself as Cuban ethnically and nationally, but also as Canadian. Still, I continue to be a Cuban citizen, and the Cuban government to this day considers me as such, with all that entails. A few years after moving to Buffalo I also became a resident and citizen of the United States. So, what am I? Hispanic, Latino, white, American, Canadian, Cuban, or something else?

The first time I heard the term "Hispanic" to describe me was when I applied to the University at Buffalo for a job. The Department of Philosophy wanted the university to recognize me as Hispanic in order to make sure that the hiring took place and so that they could also hire someone else in the area of aesthetics. The year was 1971.

The department chair had kept me informed of the strategy and had asked me whether I had any reservations about it. I said no in the first place because I was used to hearing the term "Hispanic" to refer to Latin Americans from areas of the continent that had been part of the Spanish empire. Indeed, both Latin Americans and Spanish intellectuals had debated the value of this denomination throughout the twentieth century.

Because Cuba was part of Latin America, and after I came to the United States I had developed strong emotional bonds with Latin America, I thought the term was quite appropriate and said so to Parry. Besides, most of my ancestors were Spanish, and Cuban culture presents itself predominantly as Spanish, although with a very strong dose of Africa.

Still, the committee in charge of hiring minorities rejected their petition and said that I could not be considered Hispanic for purposes of hiring. The rationale of the rejection was never clearly explained to me or anyone else who talked to me, and I was not at all clear about what "Hispanic" meant and for what groups of people affirmative action should be rightly applied. Indeed, I had never heard of "affirmative action," let alone understood its rules and regulations.

Thanks to Buffalo, then, I became aware that at least some people in the United States would consider me Hispanic, although others would not accept the term for purposes of affirmative action. Later I found out that the problem may not have been with the label "Hispanic" but with the label "Cuban," because many schools did not consider Cubans deprived and underrepresented, and therefore thought they should not count as minorities for certain careers such as medicine. But none of this was clear to me at the time.

The fact that that I was considered "Hispanic," at least by some, did not mean that I was "American." I had come to Buffalo on a visitor visa for two years, a status that facilitated matters considerably and had tax advantages to boot. I did not have to pay taxes in the United States and I did not have to pay taxes in Canada because, while I had become a Canadian citizen, I was not residing in the country. This status could not be indefinite, and I had to apply for United States residency for a second time.

In time I became a Cuban/Canadian/Hispanic permanent resident in the United States. Presumably, I also was Cuban and Canadian in nationality, and Cuban and Hispanic ethnically. But was I Cuban, American, or Hispanic American? Not likely insofar as I was not ethnically American or Canadian, as far as "Canadian" can be an ethnicity, which is questionable since some Canadians are culturally considered Franco-Canadians and others are considered Anglo-Canadians. None of them are just ethnically Canadians.

All this happened in the early 1970s. In the mid-1970s the United States government decided to use "Hispanic" as a label that would encompass everyone with roots either in the Iberian Peninsula or Latin America, and so the term became entrenched in the United States, although not without opposition to this day. Many Americans of Latin American descent oppose the term because of its association with Spain, the ruthless imperial power that colonized and subjugated Latin America for hundreds of years.

There was also the problem of what to do with Brazil and Portugal. Like Spain, Portugal was part of the Iberian Peninsula and had been an oppressive imperial power, although less oppressive than Spain. Moreover, Brazil was part of Latin America, but not of Hispanic America when the term was used to refer to former Spanish colonies. Still, the term "Hispanic" stuck and still sticks, mainly because some Americans like to be called Hispanics in spite of the fact that many others do not, preferring the term "Latino/a," and more recently "Latinx."

It was not until the United States Congress, in order to accommodate Jewish Americans, decided to allow American citizens also to be citizens of other countries that I decided to apply for citizenship in the United States. I had not wanted to do it before because it would mean automatically losing my Canadian citizenship and I didn't know if or when I would have to go back to Canada. After the experience of being forced to leave my native land, I did not want to expose myself to a situation, such as I had experienced in Cuba, in which I would have no place to go. I thought this would not happen in the United States, but the stories about Japanese Americans during World War II kept me alert to possibilities that appeared remote. Indeed, no country is immune to xenophobia, even this one, as is becoming clear today in the case of Mexicans.

Still, I had been in this country for more than twenty years and I felt a growing appreciation not only for the democratic and free system of government in the United States but for the way of life expressed in mainstream American culture. In many ways I felt more at home here than anywhere else. So why not make my status permanent and join the American nation? This is how I became an American.

So now I was Cuban/Canadian/Hispanic/Latino *and* American. Cuban in nationality and ethnicity, Canadian in nationality, Hispanic and Latino in ethnicity, and American in nationality. So what was I really? A platypus surely! And how do all these labels identify me? How do they mix and influence my identity? How do others think of me because of them, and how do I think of myself?

Bear in mind that labels are important. By identifying people, they boost and deflate their egos, create social personas, and are the source of discrimination and stereotyping, as well as pride and joy. As a Cuban, I could not help thinking of El Morro, a symbol of Cuba and its strength, and that is now unfortunately associated with the dungeon where prisoners accused of antirevolutionary activities were kept. And I can hardly prevent myself from dancing when I hear the intoxicating rhythms of a conga. As a Hispanic, I could not but think of Machu Pichu, the Catalan Romanesque frescoes, and I could hardly contain my feet in listening to an Aragonese *jota* or an Argentinian tango.

As a Canadian, I thought of the urbanity typical of most Canadians and of the imposing renditions of the Canadian landscapes painted by artists known as the Group of Seven. As a Latino, I was moved by the struggles for independence in South America and the plight of Latinos/as in the United States. And as an American I was an inheritor of the Founding Fathers' ideas, for they put together the American Constitution and raised a cry for liberty. Could I do and be all these things? How could I negotiate these various parts of myself and their pull in directions that might not be completely consistent? Could I contain all these identities? Was I a case of multiple personalities and schizophrenia?

As a philosopher, I felt I had to deal with this issue philosophically. That is, I had to integrate myself into a coherent and sensible conceptual framework that would include all these strands and claims on me. How could I conceptually integrate my Cuban side with my Hispanic/Latino side, my Canadian side, and my American side? And how should I think of my nationality and ethnicity? How should I think about all these identities and myself?

My first attempt to bring some order to my thought about identity was in the short book I published in Spanish in 1998 about Hispanic philosophy. This was in line with the long history of similar discussions among Latin Americans, almost from the very beginning of the encounter between Americans and Spaniards. The first relevant discussion began in the sixteenth century, when Bartolomé de Las Casas and Juan Ginés de Sepúlveda engaged in a controversy concerning the humanity and nationality of Amerindians. Were they human and entitled to be treated as a nation, or should they be integrated into the Spanish nation? Sepúlveda argued against integration, and Las Casas argued in favor of it. The identity in question was that of Amerindians, but in raising this issue indirectly, Las Casas and Sepúlveda were also asking about the identity of the conquerors.

Things became more complicated when Spaniards settled in the conquered lands, creating a new class of people, the *criollos*, that is, the descendants of Spaniards born in the colonies. Now there were at least three identities to deal with: *peninsulares* (Spaniards born in the Iberian Peninsula), *criollos* (children of *peninsulares* born in the colonies), and Amerindians (the indigenous populations of the Americas). And of course, matters became even more complicated when just at the start of the conquest Africans were brought to the colonies as slaves. Now there were not only issues of nationality and ethnicity but also of race.

The questions that Latin Americans and Iberians raised as a consequence are still being debated in Latin America, Spain, Brazil, and even the United States. The debate continues in Spain and Brazil because, just like Latin America, the Iberian Peninsula is a conglomerate and mixture of different peoples. Where is the unity then? And is it an ethnic unity, a national unity, or a racial unity? These questions are also raised in the context of philosophy. Is philosophy a matter of nationality, race, or ethnicity? Indeed, to put it in the form of question that has received the greatest attention among Latin American philosophers in the twentieth century: Is there, and can there be, a Latin American philosophy? This question gets complicated when one thinks of the various nationalities, ethne, classes, and races present in Latin America, and the universalist claims that philosophy as a discipline has made throughout its history.

So it was with the question of the identity of Hispanic philosophy that I began the little book. When that book was published, however, I had already completed a good portion of an earlier book in which I tackled the issue of Hispanic/Latino/a identity, and which was going to come out in 2000. The historical importance of this book is that it is the first systematic and comprehensive philosophical treatment of the issues raised by Hispanic/Latino/a/Latinx identity.

Indeed, it is arguably the case that this is the first such treatment not only in the United States but in the world, including Latin America. As such, it has a unique place both in the history of Latin American thought and in the historiography of Latin American philosophy. My book *Hispanic/Latino Identity* also offers the first original philosophical theory of how to think about Hispanic/Latino identity.

The difference between the way these topics had been addressed before is clear when one considers an important book in the historiography of related topics published about ten years earlier. I am referring to Ofelia Schutte's *Cultural Identity and Social Liberation in Latin American Thought*. This volume, which I published in my SUNY Press book series on Latin American and Iberian thought and culture, is the first book-length study on the views of Latin American thinkers on the related topic of cultural identity, but it is not a systematic treatment of it.

There was another antecedent to the publication of *Hispanic/Latino Identity*. In 1998, I had organized with my then colleague, Pablo De Greiff, the first conference sponsored by the Capen Chair, on race, ethnicity, and group rights. And two years later we published the papers that had been read at the conference. The contributors make up a who's who of philosophers working in the areas mentioned in the title: *Hispanics/Latinos in the United States: Ethnicity, Race, and Rights*. This conference consolidated my interests on the issue of Hispanic/Latino identity and helped considerably in the development of my views.

The main thesis of *Hispanic/Latino Identity* is that in the cultural area, and particularly in philosophy, it makes sense to put together the philosophy of the Iberian Peninsula, Latin America, and Hispanics/Latinos in the United States, because of the historical ties among the members of these communities, and the fact that the label "Hispanics" fits this cultural philosophical reality better than the label "Latinos/as," which excludes Iberians from it.

The unity of Hispanics, then, is to be understood in terms of historical ties that give rise to properties in certain contexts that distinguish us from other groups, such as the French or the Chinese. Hispanics can best be understood in historical familial terms, from a philosophical perspective.

This is a good reason why the book uses philosophy as a good example of how this view of Hispanics helps us understand much about ourselves and also about what sets us apart from Anglo-Americans. It also explains why we are perceived as foreigners in the United States while other groups, including blacks, are seen as very much part of the country. It is the history—and the knowledge of that history and its ties—that sets us apart and creates barriers in our professional advancement in philosophy as well as the discrimination we sometimes suffer in our profession. This extends to other professions as well, but it is particularly acute in philosophy because of the nature of our discipline and its claims to a universality that is seldom realized and seldom challenged.

In short, I had solved some of the conceptual puzzles that had concerned me. And now I had a theory whereby I understood how I was Hispanic. However, this did not mean that I had a clear idea of the relation of what I was ethnically as Hispanic and what I was nationally as Canadian and American. Nor did it make clear the role of race in all of this. Race, of course, loomed large in this context because after the changes that had been implemented in the 1960s in race policy in the United States, much thinking had taken place concerning race.

For some, particularly after some important biological discoveries, race was a myth, a pernicious social invention, created for nefarious purposes. Whereas others argued that there was still some basis for race in biology. Scientists were confused, and so the general public was even more so. And I was in the middle of it.

After I had finished writing my book on Hispanic/Latino identity, I understood that I had to settle in my mind how to conceptualize race and relate it to ethnicity and nationality. This gave rise to another book, *Surviving Race, Ethnicity, and Nationality: A Challenge for the Twenty-First Century* (2005).

I had a great deal of trouble publishing this book. It was too sensible to appeal to the crowds that wanted to keep thinking about race as a political plot of whites or those who wanted to go back to the purely biological understanding of it. The manuscript was rejected repeatedly because it argued for neither one of these two dogmatic positions. I was frustrated because I knew what was happening and why.

Indeed, at some point I considered abandoning it and never again writing anything about race, ethnicity, or nationality. But I did ultimately find a publisher, and the book came out a couple of years later than it should have. In the end it did attract attention, since it had a panel at the APA convention devoted to it, with very distinguished participants such as Linda Alcoff and Lucius Outlaw.

The book's main contribution is that it explains the sources of the general conflict among race, ethnicity, and nationality and provides a metaphysical analysis of the three concepts and their relations. The problem with most discussions of these topics is that they are guided by political aims that confuse facts and views, and thrive in conceptual equivocations of an elementary nature.

The ultimate source of the problem is a lack of metaphysical sophistication. Here then, with my background in metaphysics, I set out to clean up the mess and present a lucid theory that would challenge the common fare to which we were regularly exposed. Now, keep in mind that I was motivated by social and political concerns. Who would not be, given the history of discussions of race in the United States? But I worked very hard trying to insulate these concerns from my analyses and maintain a critical point of view. The book is unique in its metaphysical approach, its dispassionate conceptual analysis, and its novel theories concerning ethnicity, race, and nationality.

To motivate the reader, I began by presenting the arguments against and for the discussion of race, ethnicity, and nationality among philosophers, explaining why such a discussion is necessary. Then I characterized the kind of investigation and the flaws in reasoning that are sources of confusion. Next I turned to the presentation of theories of ethnicity, race, and nationality that constitute the core of the book.

I begin each of these topics with a discussion of a prominent but misguided understanding of them. For ethnicity the point of departure and criticism is Corlett's genetic view of race and ethnicity. Instead, I propose a view of ethnicity as familial and historical. Ethnicity is a second-order property based on first-order properties that are historically determined. This opens up the notion to all kinds of different conceptions.

There is nothing constant in all ethne. Nor is there something fixed for each ethnos throughout its existence. This is a source of its confusion with race, for racial conditions can also function in some ethne as their conditions. Being colored may be a condition of certain ethnic groups. But this does not mean that ethnicity is the same as race.

I begin the treatment of race with a discussion and criticism of Anthony Appiah's rejection of both race as ethnicity and of race as a biological reality. Instead of race, he argues, we need to think of racial identity, which is determined linguistically and is not pegged to any set of ethnic or biological features. Finding this view wanting, I instead propose what I call the Common Genetic View of Race. In this way race is conceived as requiring a genetic tie as well as a set of phenotypes that are selected historically. Race then also has, like ethnicity, a familial dimension, but unlike ethnicity it does require a genetic tie.

In contrast with ethnicity and race, I argue that nationality should be understood as a political reality based on a commitment that has nothing to do with phenotypes or cultural properties. This goes contrary to the view of David Miller, according to whom nationality is conceived in ethnic and even racial terms. This is the source of the confusion between nationality and ethnicity or race.

Surviving Race, Ethnicity, and Nationality completed and closed my investigation of the issues concerning race and nationality that I had left pending after the completion of *Hispanic/Latino Identity*. It was an important watershed in my intellectual development. It left pending, however, several issues related to Hispanic/Latino identity that I was going to pick up later. But my preoccupation with these topics did not stop me from engaging other topics that were dear to me.

Between 2000 and 2005 I wrote three other books that were also rounding out my understanding of other issues that I had taken up before. One had to do with metaphysics. It was a short monograph entitled *¿Qué son las categorías?* Published in Spain, it discusses some objections that had been raised by various American philosophers against my theory of categories. More important than this were two books that tied in my previous work on texts to their interpretation.

Old Wine in New Skins: The Role of Tradition in Communication, Knowledge, and Group Identity filled in two important gaps in my hermeneutics and identity theories. This was the text of the Marquette Aquinas Lecture I delivered in 2003. In *A Theory of Textuality* I had given a passing answer to the problem posed by the hermeneutic circle—we can never get out of language, for any attempt to do so is actually mediated by language and therefore we cannot know whether we have transcended it or not. After my former student William Irwin called my attention to the gap in my theory, I took the opportunity to fill it at the Aquinas Lecture. I proposed expectation as a solution to the hermeneutic circle among other philosophy of language issues.

The key to this solution was an understanding of tradition as a kind of action. I argued, contrary to a general belief, that tradition is not a view (or views) but a certain kind of action (or actions). This explains how a set of determinate beliefs is not an essential component of a tradition. Moreover, it explains how we can understand what someone says based on the expectation of particular actions.

A more substantial book was *How Can We Know What God Means? The Interpretation of Revelation* (2001). This book aims to fill in a gap in my hermeneutic theory: the conditions of the interpretation of texts that are regarded as revealed by religious communities. Unlike other authors who use as a measure of interpretation such factors as the author's intention, an interpretation by an authority, or certain uses to which the text can be put, I argue that it is in theology that we find the appropriate way of interpreting texts regarded as revealed.

These three books were systematic studies, but I also edited various others that supported the work I had done in these books and continued to occupy my mind with the topics to which I had paid attention in previous publications.

Without question, interpretation took the lead, expanding its scope and application. With my colleagues Carolyn Korsmeyer and Rodolphe Gasché, I edited a volume entitled *Literary Philosophers: Borges, Calvino, Eco* (2002), which raised the question of the philosophical interpretation of literature and the literary interpretation of philosophy. Other publications on these topics were the two volumes Jiyuan Yu and I published, *Rationality and Happiness: From the Ancients to the Early Medievals* (2003) and *Uses and Abuses of the Classics: Western Interpretations of Greek Philosophy* (2004). To these can be added the proceedings of the international conference we organized at Shannon University in China.

These books introduced a new perspective on the work that Korsmeyer, Gasché, Yu, and I had been writing separately or jointly. In particular, my association with Jiyuan Yu was not only philosophically productive, but personally rewarding. I was honored to be his mentor when he came to Buffalo with recommendations from such high-caliber philosophers as P. F. Strawson. We were both interested in metaphysics and issues of interpretation. Our offices were located next to each other, and it was easy to develop a strong and rich friendship. Unfortunately, however, he died prematurely at fifty-two years of age, leaving incomplete the idea of a project on the relation of culture and philosophy we had been thinking about. His death left a large hole in my life, but nonetheless I had learned much from him, about philosophy, and even more about life and death.

20

A Place for Literature and the Arts
(2005–present)

A rather important event occurred in the fifth grade that was going to change my life radically: I became a voracious reader. It actually began in the fourth grade, when I became addicted to comic books. For a while, all I thought about, apart from religion and school, were comic books, and all I did with my allowance was buy comic books.

The piles of comic books grew and grew to the point that my mother became alarmed. She was also worried because instead of playing or doing other things kids my age do, I just wanted to read comic books. Even when I went to my exercise classes for a presumed case of scoliosis (a popular children's malady at the time—whether one had it or not), I managed to read comic books because I fortuitously found horror comic books at the gym and so I spent time reading them while I waited for the personal trainer, and was very happy if he was late.

Then something even more important happened that completed the cycle started with comic books. I got the mumps and had to stay confined to my bedroom for two weeks. I felt not only sick but also quite bored. I could not even read because of headaches and my eyes were sensitive to light. So my sister, Nena, started reading to me classic stories for children my age. I had always loved the stories I was told, particularly by Mother and Grandmother Dubié, but I had never liked to be read to because I wanted to hear new stories, invented for me on request. I still remember that Mother had developed a never-ending saga about animals to keep me satisfied. Every day while I was small, I curled up on her lap and she would continue the narrative, adding this time the story of a lion that was lame, another time that of a monkey that was too clever for its own good, and so on. There were cows, birds, and even fish and worms in struggles that simulated those of humans and always contained a moral applicable to human conduct. Grandmother Dubié's stories were modifications of the well-known adventures of Sinbad the Sailor, the Knights of the Round Table, and other personages from famous classic books, including tales from the *One Thousand and One Nights*. This signaled an early interest in history, not just a taste for yarns, an interest that would flourish in my college years and beyond.

A new development during my illness was a taste not so much for being read to but for the type of stories my sister had chosen to read. Toward the end of my illness, when I was feeling better, I started reading the stories myself, and this impulse continued after I was well. Eventually I abandoned comic books for classic adventure stories, such as *Beauty and the Beast*, *Ivanhoe*, *Scaramouche*, *Robinson Crusoe*, and *Gulliver's Travels*, and in time moved to literary fiction. Indeed, by the time I reached the age of thirteen I had become a seasoned reader.

I discovered novels like *Gone with the Wind*, and the books of authors like Pearl Buck and Alexandre Dumas, that satisfied my fancy. This transformation was probably one of the most important events in my life, and perhaps the most important intellectual event ever. Reading is the most difficult task that children learn and the one that prepares them best to encounter the intellectual challenges they will face in life.

From the moment I discovered great literature and history, I never stopped reading. In later years, even during times when I was extremely busy or preoccupied with problems, or sad because of tragic events, I kept the habit of reading at least a few pages every night from a good book. This custom has been an extraordinary source of emotional stability and pleasure in my life. For years I had a true passion for literature, although I generally hated literature courses at school, the reason being that we did not read literature in them. Before my father died, he played an important role in encouraging my reading habit, particularly of more cerebral books. Indeed, his example was decisive. There was no time that my father sat down without a book on his lap. And the love of books was demonstrated by the great collection of books in our library. I remember him being the first person that spoke of Marx, in ways that were too advanced for me, and contrary to his political views that were akin to Roosevelt, whose portrait he had hanging on the wall over of his desk.

The object of school courses was to memorize plots about various literary works and information about their authors so that we could pass the official tests to be able to move up toward a higher grade. Except for poetry, we read selections from famous works, but they were snippets, short paragraphs, too short to give a flavor of the works from which they had been taken.

In the meantime, at home, I continued to be a voracious reader, always hungry for more. I read everything available to me, but mostly fiction. Paradoxically, I favored French and English fiction and seldom read any of the great Spanish writers. Indeed, I generally disliked some of their greatest books, such as *Don Quixote*, which I found too boring to ever finish. Perhaps this was because my family had accumulated a good number of the French and English classics and the Gracia-Dubiés were particularly biased toward anything French.

I fed what had become almost an addiction with books belonging to Father or Aunt Rosario. I read everything and never skipped a word, let alone a passage or a line, no matter how boring and uninteresting. The fear of missing something significant was too strong. I felt this as a kind of moral imperative. I considered it bad, almost a moral transgression, to skip anything an author had written. I also considered it a sign of disloyalty, almost treason, so I worked diligently through impossible passages from Victor Hugo and Marcel Proust. If there is a purgatory and I am supposed to atone for my sins there, I am sure that all the pain I endured reading endlessly difficult, sometimes boring, prose will count toward reducing my debt and cleaning up my soul of the traces of sin. Unfortunately, if we are to believe the mechanics of purgatory, I did not consider the pain, failing to offer it as atonement. Maybe I missed an opportunity, like so many others in my life.

The passion for literature did not diminish over the years, and I was never able to reconcile it with the thought of a career, with one exception: for a while I toyed with the notion of becoming a journalist. Many books I read were written by journalists, and novelists were, in a sense, journalists of fictional characters—reporting on their lives and the events that affected them. This is how the idea of becoming a writer grew in me. The power to write well, to communicate my innermost thoughts and in the process grasp something almost ineffable was mesmerizing.

Reading fed this flame constantly, but I was timid about writing. I did try, but felt that I was failing. Instead, I read and read. The reading, particularly of long and difficult books, books that required commitment, skill, and patience, helped me both to strengthen the discipline I had already developed since fifth grade and to develop a focus. Focus served an important function in my studies. It was what turned me from an indifferent student to a top student when in fourth grade I realized that paying close attention to what my teachers were saying made all the difference when it came to understanding the subject matter and of fixing it in my mind. A well understood lecture and diligently done homework were all that was needed to perform well in quizzes and exams. The reading outside the curriculum emphasized that focus and expanded the depth of my understanding. But writing was something on the side; it was not really a career. I investigated all the ins and outs of going to journalism school, but eventually gave that up.

Perhaps more likely to lead to a career was my interest in art. My family was not particularly focused on art. Mother was quite talented and could draw well, but like everything else with her, it was only a passing interest. And Father's interest was in classical music, which mother disparagingly called "funereal." I grew up with very little awareness of art and artists, but when I moved to St. Thomas Military Academy, one of my classmates was a dilettante who dabbled into many things, one of which was painting. Naturally, I was curious about it and started painting myself. But was there an outlet for this? How would my budding interest in art be put together with my other interests, such as psychology and physics?

The interest in literature had been accentuated at Wheaton, where I declared English literature one half of a double major (the other half being philosophy), but in graduate school my interest in literature was drowned by philosophy, and medieval philosophy in particular. It was only in the 1980s when I began work on interpretation and textuality that a consideration of literature appeared relevant, but I did not take it up. I was too busy with the interpretation of the history of philosophy and with the understanding of hermeneutic and linguistic issues that dominated my attention. Still, the topics of author, audience, the identity of works and texts, and other related issues were pointing clearly to a need to explore the nature and interpretation of literary texts. The explorations of the classics, literary philosophers, and popular culture, including film, clearly pointed to the need to take up the questions of literature seriously and in a systematic way, as I had done with philosophy and texts regarded as revealed by religious communities.

There was also an opening to art that I had overlooked before. My personal interest in art had become stronger with the passage of years. When on vacation in Europe and other places where art was easily available, I spend most of my time checking out art galleries. This situation came to a head on a trip to New Orleans, a city that has a large colony of artists. It was there that I decided I was going to start buying art in an orderly and conscious way, rather than just picking pieces here and there as the spirit moved me. When Norma and I came back to Buffalo I began to consider the strategy I should follow. The first strategy I considered, given my love of Canadian art and the tradition established by the Group of Seven, was to collect Canadian art. However, except for the brief periods of my life when we had lived in Canada, and my general sympathy for Canada and its traditions, I did not see a sufficiently strong connection to me or my work that would justify a prolonged effort.

That is when I happened to run into an ad for an exhibition of Cuban art in Buffalo organized by Lynette Bosch, and it occurred to me that this was another avenue for channeling my interest. After all I was Cuban, and although I had stayed away from Cuban things in my many years out of Cuba, I still thought of myself as Cuban in important ways. So I picked up the phone and talked to Lynette and explained my situation. She understood completely because she was Cuban and had emigrated from the island, and she was also a distinguished art historian who had graduated from Princeton and specialized in Cuban art outside Cuba. She was willing to help me, and the first step was to attend the opening of the exhibition she had organized at Buffalo State College.

The show was a tremendous success, and for the first time I saw what exiled Cuban artists had achieved. Of course I fell in love with their generally strong art, and conceived the idea to develop a website, Cuban Art Outside Cuba (CAOC). Immediately, I started building a collection, which as a philosopher I believed had to have a unifying theme or motif. People collect art for diverse reasons. Some do it for decorative reasons: they want to have pieces that beautify their home. Others are interested in profiting from art. In recent years art has become one of the greatest sources of financial speculation. The price of art has skyrocketed, so there is money to be made speculating on art. Still others collect art for nationalistic reasons, to preserve the past of a particular nation or group of people. But none of these appealed to me. I had to find something in philosophy that would justify my collection, some theme or topic that would tie closely to some aspect of my philosophical research in that it would not only be related to it but would help with my philosophical thinking about the topic. So what could this be?

After much thought I realized that identity fit the bill. A few years before I had written a book on Hispanic/Latino identity and I had just finished a manuscript dealing with those topics. What could be better? I had been exploring the very notion of social identity, particularly ethnic, racial, and national, asking myself questions as to what it is, its relation to culture and history, the way we develop and understand it, and their interrelations. And I realized that artists had been dealing with these issues from time immemorial, particularly when they had to emigrate and became minorities in the country of their destination. Cubans, of course, were precisely in that situation, and I was Cuban and had experienced the crisis of identity that all immigrants go through. Why not, then, collect Cuban art?

Now the website I had started took on a different character and so did my philosophical interest in art. Art became an object of research, and so did the idea of building a collection of art that would respond to this interest. The theme of the collection would have to be social identity, and the means whereby I would explore it would be Cuban art. But of course, Cuban art produced by Cuban artists outside of Cuba, since it is in this context that identity most often becomes the source of dramatic artistic expression. The website would include a list of Cuban American artists together with samples of their work, biographical notes, and the transcription of interviews conducted by me and videotaped by Norma. This involved considerable work, but it was both rewarding and enjoyable. It was a great opportunity to build up my private art collection and to get to know artists, some of whom became close friends. Indeed, the interviews often revealed details that had not become public before.

One extraordinary example was the interview of Rafael Soriano, one of the most important Cuban American contemporary artists and certainly the most important artist of his generation. His abstract constructions of luminous veils are not only provocative but also splendidly beautiful. In the interview, which took place when he was quite old (d. 2015), he explained how he had a premonition about Cuba, which put an end to his longing to return to the island. This revelation defined his relation to his motherland and was the source of the style he was to create and which made him famous.

Another example was the interview with Pepe Bedia, one of the great artists that left Cuba in the early 1990s. His masterful blending of African religious traditions in a simple, linear style had made him a common name among Cuban artists. His interview, which took place at his home, reveals the character of the man as he opens the doors both to his home and to everything that it contains. First is the collection of artifacts from Cuba, Africa, and the native peoples of the Americas. And second is the menagerie of animals, which surrounded us throughout the interview, interrupting us with sounds and noises at various points that made me think of the jungle. His tolerance and natural attitude toward them revealed his great sensitivity to everything living and the language that each animal speaks.

All this was happening when Susana Nuccetelli and I were engaged in the planning and organizing of the NEH Summer Institute on Latin American Philosophy for 2005. This promised to be a highly successful event, so I decided to apply for a follow-up NEH Summer Seminar in 2006 that would focus on Cuban philosophy, literature, and art and would be accompanied by an exhibition of some of the works of Cuban Americans collected by (1) art historian Lynette Bosch, (2) the Lehigh collection created by its director, Ricardo Viera, and (3) my private collection. The exhibition was entitled "Layers: Collecting Cuban-American Art," and the NEH Seminar was called "Negotiating Identities in Art, Literature, and Philosophy: Cuban Americans and American Culture." For this I needed not only an expert on art, who could be Lynette Bosch, but also an expert on Cuban literature, which I found in Isabel Alvarez-Borland, a distinguished Cuban literature specialist.

In order to bring in the motive of collecting that had given rise to my original interest in Cuban American art, we would organize the exhibition along three rationales and strategies for collecting art: that of the art historian, that of the philosopher, and that of an institution. The sample case for the first was going to be the collection of Lynette Bosch, for the second my own collection, and for the third, the collection of Lehigh University.

All three focused on Cuban American art, but they had important differences resulting from the criteria used in each case. The catchy title of the exhibition proposed by Lynette was "Layers: Collecting Cuban-American Art." Apart from a handsome catalogue published by the Art Galleries of the University, the three organizers edited a volume entitled *Identity, Memory, and Diaspora; Voices of Cuban-American Artists, Writers, and Philosophers* (2008), with extensive interviews and samples of the work of these authors.

At the same time that these events were taking place, I had been reading and consulting sources on Cuban art. One of these was the fine work edited by the late Holly Block, *Art Cuba: The New Generation*. The artists featured in it were primarily working in Cuba, rather than outside Cuba and quite avant-garde. Among them I found one artist whose work particularly intrigued me. His name was Carlos Estévez and I made a note of him, but unfortunately he was not out of Cuba, so I did not consider him for my collection. What I did not know was that he was in Europe at the time and had decided not to return to the island. Fortuitously, while visiting the art fair Art Miami, I found his work displayed in one of the booths.

The work was whimsical, thought provoking, and aesthetically pleasing, unlike so much contemporary conceptual work, which is inscrutable and ugly. The dealer gave me Estévez's address and I visited him. There I bought my first of his works, *Pensamientos numerales*, which is still one of my favorite pieces of art. Our acquaintance became a friendship, and the philosophical nature of his work gave me the idea for a book in which I would explore both the philosophical interpretation of art and the artistic interpretation of philosophy.

The plan was to use eighteen works by Carlos and see how they relate to traditional philosophical problems. These problems were encapsulated in famous sayings by philosophers and theologians, such as "Know Thyself," "I Am Myself and My Circumstances," "You Cannot Step in the Same River Twice," "There Is No New Thing Under the Sun," "The Will Does Not Desire of Necessity," and "God Has Predestined His Elect." The resulting book is entitled *Images of Thought: Philosophical Interpretations of Carlos Estévez's Art* (2009).

With this book I brought together my work in hermeneutics and my interest in art. In line with the character of my previous work, this was a book of philosophy, not a work of art criticism or art history. A few years later I edited a more traditional volume, also dealing with Estévez's work: *Carlos Estévez: Bottles to the Sea* (2015). This book presents and explores an installation of the artist consisting of one hundred drawings that are put in bottles and thrown into the sea on different occasions. The overall topic is chance.

Much more could be said about how art acquired an important place in my intellectual development. Indeed, the artworks that I had collected went beyond the object of my research, they also became objects that would be part of art collections of such institutions as the University Museum of Binghamton University and the Museum of Geneseo State College. Now, their museums, then, would expose the art to new audiences and help them understand the issues of identity that are essential in the understanding of our Latino cultures.

So much for art. I had finally succeeded in integrating my personal interest in art and art collecting with my philosophical work and reflections on identity. But what of literature? Another project was going to accomplish that and is related to the interpretive volume on Carlos. But how was I to integrate philosophy, art, and literature and the interpretation of these different cultural expression?

How could I fill a conceptual gap that was still incomplete and toward which I had made some headway with the NEH seminar? In order to do it I needed to examine the notions of philosophy, literature, and art, and I needed to get clear on their interpretations, namely, the artistic interpretation of literature and philosophy, the philosophical interpretation of art and literature, and the literary interpretation of art and philosophy.

It occurred to me that in order to make some headway in this challenging project, I had to begin with texts that are literary but also have a philosophical dimension, so that they can be proper subjects of philosophical interpretation, and what best for this purpose than Jorge Luis Borges's stories? Then I needed to consider philosophical interpretations of these stories, particularly some of those proposed by some prominent philosophers and also some that I had undertaken. Finally, I needed to bring art into the project, and this could be done by including works of art that interpret some of Borges's stories. This material then could be subjected to the kind of philosophical analysis that I had developed. And this is what I did, with the resulting volume entitled *Painting Borges: Philosophy Interpreting Art Interpreting Literature* (2012).

So much for the general outline of the project's requirements, but I still needed to turn to concrete choices: I needed to pick a set of stories and a set of artists that had or would create works of art that interpreted those stories. The most difficult part of the project was to find the proper artists. There is no scarcity of artists who have been inspired by Borges, but not many have actually set out to interpret particular stories.

Also the work of many artists who were interested was too abstract to serve my purposes. Splashes of paint on a canvas tell very little about particular literary works. I could have a start with some Cuban American artists, whom I knew through the art exhibition in Buffalo and the interviews for the website on CAOC (Cuban Art Outside Cuba). The originals of the interviews are part of the Smithsonian National Collection of American Art.

But where would I find the others? The obvious place, concordant with my desire to keep these projects within a Hispanic, Latino/a, Latinx identity framework, was Argentina. But it was not easy to find them. It took me three years and several trips to Buenos Aires to find the proper artists who either had interpreted stories by Borges or were willing to create works to that effect. The list of artists was impressive, including the most famous living Argentinian artist, Leon Ferrari, who had created a work on Borges's *El Inmortal*.

My negotiations with the artists generated a list of twelve stories. Each story was to have two interpretations of it done by two different artists. The total number of artists was sixteen. Once I had all these together, I set out to write the book, which includes the artistic interpretations of the stories, short summaries of them, interpretations of the artworks, and philosophical discussions of the issues involved in the philosophical and artistic interpretations of works of literature.

With this book I succeeded in bringing together my early interests in literature and art with my interest in interpretation and textuality in a personal identity context. I had completed an Euganean full circle in which there is return to a beginning that has become enlightening and enriched.

Of course, since the life of the mind need not come to an end, I followed with a book-long conversation with Ilan Stavans on the interpretation of Latino art in *Thirteen Ways of Looking at Latino Art* (2014). This book explores a group of problems that surround the topic of identity and its various expressions in Latino art. The text juxtaposes my non-essentialist views to the essentialism of Ilan Stavans and shows how the issues of identity that are frequently discussed in philosophy and literature also surface in art.

In my case the issues had come about because of my interdisciplinary work in various fields, and this interdisciplinarity was also a reason for the offer of a job in which I was particularly interested, even though as usual, I was not looking for it. This more recent offer was from Brooklyn College, which had received the funds for endowing a chair in the philosophy of culture, and they wanted to fill that position with someone who would qualify for membership in the CUNY graduate program.

The department chair called my office to ask whether I might be interested in the position and left a telephone message. Unfortunately, I have the incorrigible habit of not checking my telephone messages at my office. After a couple of months of not receiving an answer from me, the chair phoned again, and this time, miraculously, I answered the phone.

I was embarrassed and frustrated because I have always been interested in New York City and my behavior made me look like an irresponsible idiot. But she did not mind. She explained the situation and asked me to let her know if I was interested. Norma was not enthusiastic about moving to New York but said that she would not stand on my way if I had a strong interest in moving. Actually the position was perfect for me in many ways.

The donated chair was well endowed and the areas it covered fit my recent research beautifully: interpretation, art, curating, race, ethnicity, culture, and so on. Further, the CUNY graduate school I would be joining was one of the best in the nation. Still, I thought I needed to spend at least a semester in situ to make sure Norma and I felt comfortable in New York.

The department chair was delighted and we started planning our stay for a semester in the city. But things were not to be. My position in Buffalo was extremely comfortable, and Norma and I were at an age in which we should be thinking about preparing for retirement rather than starting a new adventure. So, sadly and apologetically, after considerable soul searching, I told the chair that there was no sense in spending a semester with them and delaying their process of finding a qualified person because my wife and I had decided that we would not accept their offer. Naturally, she tried her best arguments to convince me otherwise, but I did not budge.

The job offer in New York City awakened my attention to the fact that our philosophy department had slowly become somewhat narrower in some areas in which I worked, although it was still strong in such core subjects as metaphysics. Many of the heavyweights who favored a pluralistic approach and the blending of work in literature, art, ethnicity, race, and history, among others, had retired. So would it not be particularly interesting for me to have some faculty who work on art and literature with whom I would share interests, without having to give up my colleagues and friends in philosophy? Couldn't this enrich my experience and work? Indeed, I could profit from establishing connections with them while not abandoning my basic approach to philosophy. And I could use the generous sources of the Samuel P. Capen Chair to the benefit of both programs. This is how I moved half of my line in the Philosophy Department to the Department of Comparative Literature. I must say that things have worked beautifully.

21

From Hispanic to Latino and Latinx Philosophy (2000–present)

As important as the first five years of the twenty-first century had been in terms of my intellectual development and the working out of key notions in my understanding of both myself and my ethnicity, race, and nationality, the following years would be even more important in many ways. One of these was a deeper understanding of myself as Hispanic, Latino, and Latinx and the role that I had been playing in the study of Latin America philosophy in the United States.

I came to realize that the notions of Hispanic, Latino/a, and Latinx carried with them significant meanings and connotations that are important not just for me and my identity, but also for other members of my group and their identity. I also came to realize that my role in the development of the study of Hispanic, Latino/a, and Latinx philosophy in the United States was and is still unique, but that in recent years my efforts are finally bearing fruit thanks to a group of younger philosophers committed to the development and understanding of Latin American, Hispanic, Latino/a, and Latinx philosophy in the United States.

Let me begin with some remarks about what was happening concerning these studies, which are closely related to the work I have been doing in the areas of race and ethnicity. Perhaps the most important new development in the area of Latin American, Latino/a American, and Latinx philosophy, which began developing in the last few years of the 1990s and has since begun to bear fruit, was that Hispanic, Latino/a, and Latinx philosophers began to work in some fields accepted by the philosophy mainstream in the United States, and their input was not only considered important, but it also allowed them to introduce Latin American, Latino/a American, and Latinx American philosophy in their discussions. I am referring to issues that have to do with social identity, race, gender, and ethnicity in particular, although there are others. Because Latin American philosophy has been concerned with these issues since its beginning in the sixteenth century, Hispanic, Latinos/as, and Latinx philosophers have been able to go back to authors such as Bartolomé de Las Casas, for example, and find in them concerns that are pertinent to contemporary issues.

Before I go on to explain what was happening, let me say a bit about the labels I have just introduced. As I proposed in *Hispanic/Latino Identity*, the label "Hispanic" has an advantage in that it signifies the identity of a very large group of people who are inheritors of all that is culturally pertinent to Iberians and their descendants on the Iberian Peninsula, Latin Americans, and Anglo Americans. And whether we like it or not, the term "Hispanics" explains much that other labels cannot, such as the character of Latin American music, the food, the philosophy, and all others that were mixed after the Encounters, that is, the moment in which Iberians and the indigenous populations met in America.

Now, the unsavory part of this label is that it preserves and perhaps emphasizes the contribution of colonial powers and undermines and diminishes the contribution of Amerindians and black Americans. Indeed, it is difficult to accept that the conquerors contributed anything culturally significant or even good for those who suffered at their hands. This is how a label such as "Latino" came into use, because rather than emphasizing the cultural unity of the conquered and conquerors, it emphasizes the social and political conditions suffered by the conquered. But even this label has a negative consequence, namely, that it divides the unity of its reference. The last effort in the direction of picking a label that avoids the disadvantages the others have, is to use the recently made-up label "Latinx," which does not divide us in term of gender. So, now we have three labels, each of which has advantages: "Hispanic" is appropriate for understanding much cultural history; "Latino" is helpful for understanding political and social history; and "Latinx" is appropriate for understanding the relevance of gender.

Although it is popular in certain academic quarters to use one of these three labels and exclude one or two of the others, the exclusion of some labels causes misunderstanding of social phenomena such as race, nationality, ethnicity, gender, and others. Some philosophers who want to open the doors to Latin American philosophy continue using some of the popularly rejected labels. Among those that belong to the generation that seeks to integrate our philosophy into mainstream American philosophy are philosophers such as José María Medina. His most recent book favors such integration and illustrates the advantage of such labels as "Hispanic," particularly in an epistemic context that had not been exploited effectively in the manner Medina does.

My own view is that, given that our aim as philosophers is to understand ourselves and others, I find it prima facie counterproductive to object to the use of any of these labels, for doing so leaves out something relevant in each case. Consider, for example, the case against the term "Hispanic" developed by Linda Martin Alcoff. Her case is interesting because here is a philosopher with credentials in epistemology and race theory, but who, as a Latina, has felt the need to go back to Latin American philosophy and bring into the discussion some of the ideas of Latin American philosophers. In her book *Visible Identities: Race Gender, and the Self* (2006), she integrates the views of some Latin American philosophers into her argument. This has also been part of my own modus operandi, but it became particularly clear in some of my works beginning in the year 2000: *Hispanic/Latino Identity: A Philosophical Perspective* (2000), the edited volume *Hispanics/Latinos in the United States*, and *Latinos in America: Philosophy and Social Identity*.

The main difference between Alcoff's work on the one hand and the work of Medina and mine on the other is that hers is not centered on Hispanics/Latinos, whereas ours is. In the third book mentioned in particular I take up a series of problems that stood in the way of the development and understanding of how the different identities about which I have been writing can be integrated in a coherent set of concepts that serve various purposes.

In the first chapter I take up the question of whether it makes sense to talk about various social identities in addition to a personal identity. I defend the view that there is no reason why this is not possible. The only obstacles to it are two dilemmas that vitiate most discussions of these issues and which are seldom, if at all, explicit. The first pits general identities against particular ones—I cannot be both Latino and Cuban. The other poses a choice between an essentialist conception of identity based on common properties and the absence of identity when such conditions do not pertain.

Both are misguided. The first because more general identities may be compatible with less general ones, just as I can be a member of my nuclear family and also of my extended family. The second, because identities do not imply common properties among all the members who share the identity. Identities are not based on common properties but on familial and historical relations that tie people in different ways but still serve to separate them in other ways. These dilemmas ignore how identities function, how they arise, how they endure, and what an identity is.

Based on a correct understanding of social identities, then, one can effectively address questions about circularity and demarcation and the politics of identity labels, the difficulties that Latinos face in the philosophy marketplace, affirmative action and the question of linguistic rights for Latinos. Finally I come back to Hispanic/Latino philosophy, the philosophy canon, and the way to study the history of Latino philosophy.

As the title of the book indicates, in it I recognize the value of the terms "Hispanic" and "Latino" because of the political and social implications of each. The term "Hispanic" is more closely tied to culture and therefore to the Iberians who colonized Latin America. The term "Latino" for various reasons is more closely tied to society and politics and therefore to Latin Americans both in the United States and Latin America. And *Latinos in America*, unlike *Hispanic/Latino Identity*, focuses on the social and political situation in which Latinos find themselves. Indeed, even when discussing Latin American philosophy, the emphasis is on the social and political situation of the discipline rather than on the historical ties to Iberian philosophy.

This is in part why I argue that it makes sense to employ an understanding of both Latin American and American philosophy as ethnic philosophies, that is, a thought tied to an ethnic group. This explains the disregard of Latin American philosophy among American philosophers and the neglect of it in the European canon. For me in particular, this means a new appreciation and identification of myself as Latino rather than Hispanic, although by no means do I argue that the term "Hispanic" as I proposed in *Hispanic/Latino Identity* should be discarded.

Appropriately, then, this book rounds out and completes the discussion of identity that I began many years ago and makes sense of my identities as Cuban, Hispanic, Latino, American, and Canadian all at once but for different reasons. It also clarifies the sources of the conflicts and problems concerning identity through which Latin Americans have struggled in our history both in Latin America and in the United States, and the conflicts between our philosophies and our ways of looking at ourselves and at each other.

The road that led me here began with a cultural, ethnic analysis of Hispanic and Latino identities; it moved on to explain the relations of these to race and nationality in *Surviving Race, Ethnicity, and Nationality*, and ends up with a social and political analysis in *Latinos in America*. Moreover, as it should be expected after reading about my experience when I first went to college, it is fueled by the misconceptions and misunderstandings I faced at Wheaton. The three books present, then, a comprehensive theory of social identity for Hispanics, Latinos, Latinx, and the various nationalities and races that these groups integrate, including American identity. Personally, this journey solved the emotional and intellectual needs I began to struggle with when I first entered the United States and suffered the shock of being immersed in a society I was not part of but which, at the same time, drew me into it in various ways.

Although this journey began with me as Cuban, at the end it seemed that the Cuban part of my identity had been lost. But had it? I still felt the need to reconsider its place in my life. Also missing were the ties between a theoretical analysis and a more evident hermeneutic and cultural exploration of identity. This is what led me back to the history of Latin American philosophy and into the direction of a new chapter on interpretation, literature, and the arts in this memoir.

Apart from my own philosophical work, other events were taking place that helped open doors to the study of Latin America and Latinx philosophy. Perhaps the most significant event was the organization of the NEH Summer Institute on Latin American Philosophy, which took place in Buffalo with Susana Nuccetelli as codirector.

Keep in mind that this was the first of its kind. Never before had an NEH Summer Institute for teachers on the topic of Latin American philosophy been offered in the United States. But obviously academia was ready for it. The fact that this institute was the first ever, and the only one to this day, that has been organized, speaks for itself.

Part of the importance of this institute was that, apart from the regular sessions, we had time to spend speculating about what was needed to be done for the future well-being of the field. There were strong feelings that the field required a journal, something the field had been sorely lacking so far. How can one argue that there is such a thing as Latin American philosophy in the United States when the only venue to publish in was the APA newsletter, which was quite limited in size and scope? Other articles had to be parceled out to journals that were devoted to other fields. Of course, there was considerable pressure on me to do something about this situation, since I had the funds to do it as well as a reputation for getting things done. But I rejected the idea, for I could not see myself becoming a journal editor. I had seen many good philosophers end up becoming journal administrators, and what I wanted to do in my life was philosophy.

After the NEH Institute was over, there were several attempts in the Southwest to arrange something that would look like a journal, but nothing seemed to work out. In time, however, Gregory Pappas made a proposal to Texas A&M University for the creation of a journal that would include Latin American philosophy but would not be solely devoted to it. The university was receptive because of the pressure of Hispanics/Latinos in Texas.

The journal would be entitled *Inter-American Journal of Philosophy*, and it would include American philosophy (this was Pappas's main field) and also Latin American philosophy. This was a welcome breakthrough, and to a certain point it was better that the journal was not exclusively devoted to Latin American philosophy, for it was not clear that there would be enough scholarly literature to publish if there were further restrictions in the title. But the outcome for Latin Americanists was that they now had a place to publish.

It was around this time that Susana Nuccetelli proposed that she and I produce a *Blackwell's Companion to Latin American Philosophy*, which I discussed earlier. As noted then, I had thought of that too but rejected the idea. Still, with Nuccetelli's help, maybe the work would not have been overwhelming. My problem was that I had just finished publishing the *Companion to Philosophy in the Middle Ages* and that had been a tour de force, with more than 150 articles covering the entire period. I think my partner, Timothy Noon, and I did a good job, but it cost me much pain because many of the contributors did not deliver after they had committed to write for the publication. And then there were the sloppy writers whose pieces I had to correct myself line by line. So when Nuccetelli proposed that we edit a *Blackwell's Companion* on Latin American philosophy, I turned her down, although I suggested some names for the project and I served as a consultant when problems arose.

The NEH Institute, the publication of the *Companion*, and the founding of the *Inter-American Journal of Philosophy* were major advances in the field of Latin American philosophy in the United States and definitely helped establish it as a viable one. This was a good foundation and I felt satisfied for having done my bit. Other events would follow. One commonality of these last events was that the participants were Mexican American. This group has been very productive and has a much needed historical sense, for Mexico is a major country of Latin America and has a long philosophical history going back to the sixteenth century. This has helped establish a group of Mexican Americans working on Latin American and particularly Mexican philosophy, such as Roberto Sánchez, Carlos Sánchez, and Manuel Vargas, to mention three of the most active.

22

Return to Philosophy through Its History (1990–2000)

Although I have a great love for the history of philosophy and could easily have spent my entire life doing nothing else, I have never considered myself exclusively, or even primarily, a historian of philosophy. I have always thought of myself as a philosopher and of the work I do, even when it is guided by historical goals, as philosophical work.

Indeed, from the very beginning my full dedication has been to philosophy. However, anybody that looks at my CV for the first ten years of my professional life, say between 1966 and 1976, will surely think of me primarily as a historian, and a historian with a capital "H," because most of the work I did during those years involved painstaking historical labor, such as the research I did on individuation in the early Middle Ages, or the translation and commentary on Suárez's works—although to tell the truth, none of it was painful. Yes, I had to work hard, but the challenges of understanding the past and simultaneously understanding some perennial philosophical questions were always deeply interesting and satisfying.

Can one find pleasure looking through old manuscripts, figuring out the meaning of passages written in dead languages, and uncovering texts that no one has seen or analyzed for centuries? Yes, because historical work is detective work and detective work is always fascinating in that it satisfies our curiosity as humans. Our past, whether philosophical or not, is a mystery that requires hard work to be uncovered, and once undertaken, that work can become an addiction. The challenge of solving mysteries is a perennial enticement to humans.

But it is true that my record looks like that of a historian, both when one considers the work in medieval philosophy and the work on

Latin American philosophy. The list of publications is greater than the list produced by many well-known historians. Still, not all publications are historical. One of the first articles I wrote was not historical and concerned the notion of artistic forgeries. Moreover, throughout the years I published a constant stream of articles that continued to increase even though they were not primarily historical. Indeed, the number and importance of what might be called systematic, rather than historical, publications were going to change toward the end of the 1980s.

In each decade of my professional life I have experienced a cosmic shift, almost an intellectual earthquake that has opened new directions in my work without requiring that I abandon earlier ones. This happened in the 1960s in Cuba, when my goals and interests changed from architecture and the sciences to philosophy in general and medieval philosophy in particular. It happened in the 1970s, when I discovered Latin American philosophy and I made room for the exploration of a field I knew nothing about. It occurred again in the 1980s, when I turned a good part of my efforts toward two new fields that I was to explore systematically rather than historically: metaphysics and historiography. This pattern was repeated in the 1990s, when I moved toward interpretation and meta-metaphysics. It appeared again in the first decade of the twenty-first century, when I directed my efforts to Hispanic/Latino identity, the nature of racial and ethnic groups, and the understanding of interpretation in the context of art and literature.

Let me turn now to the focus on metaphysics and historiography because these constitute the foundation of my thought. Although the brunt of these was not historical, both were in part the result of the historical work I had been doing and the way I had approached it. In the book on individuation in the early Middle Ages I introduced a systematic methodology at the beginning that would facilitate the understanding of past philosophers and their comparison with each other and ourselves.

A result of that effort was that I was forced to think systematically about the topics on which I was working historically. And these topics were eminently metaphysical. Consider the topics I had explored historically, such as individuation, universals, good and evil, the transcendentals (being, unity, goodness, and truth), the interpretation of texts, and the nature of authorship, among many others.

All of these are metaphysical, so that without intending to do so, I had become a budding metaphysician. All that remained was that I begin to write about metaphysics without the intent to understand the historical past but rather to solve metaphysical conundrums. The case with historiography also came about because of the work I had been doing, in that I had spent a great deal of time worrying about the understanding of the past, that is, doing history of philosophy.

In time it became clear that I needed to address the very practice in which I had been engaged for years and determine how to do history of philosophy well. It was essential to my conceptual needs that I address fundamental issues in historiography—I needed to examine critically the possibility and justification of history.

Note that "history" can be understood in two senses: first, the series of events that constitutes the past, and second, the knowledge and narrative of those events. It is the second understanding of history that worried me. Are we able to know history in the first sense? Can we bridge the gap between the United States, for example, and the past? And if it is possible, to what extent, and what method do we need to succeed?

This was the challenge I faced, for I could continue my work as a historian without knowing the meaning and validity of what I had been doing for years. Were the historical works I had written an accurate description of the past or were they merely fancy myths I had created? In short, the idea of a historian becoming a philosopher sounds preposterous to both a historian and a philosopher, and frequently causes many to dismiss them.

Each of my books is the result of trying to develop and answer questions and explore ideas in a chapter of a previous book that needs expansion and development. For example, the systematic chapter on individuality and individuation that preceded the historical discussion became the conceptual map of a book-long systematic discussion of individuality and individuation in *Individuality*. At this point it became clear why I had some trouble finding a publisher: the methodology did not fit neatly into any of the cubicles that had been used by my predecessors. First, because it was not historical in one of the generally accepted ways. Second, because it cut across different philosophical traditions while not quite belonging to one of them, be it analytic, scholastic, continental, and so on. Third, because it presented a comprehensive discussion of its topic, going contrary to the favored piecemeal approach.

To make matters even worse, it proposed new answers to the problems it raised, arguing that most discussions of these issues were muddled both in contemporary philosophy and in the history of philosophy. Finally, following one of my dearest principles, the book was written in plain English—as plain as I could make it both for the sake of clarity and to make it possible to cut across different philosophical traditions that use different jargons while hiding biases and presuppositions.

But the book did get published and it was read by a good number of relevant philosophers. For me the book was important not because it gave me a kind of name in philosophical circles where I did not have one before, but because it answered questions that had bothered me, questions I felt I needed to answer. Again, I began with a careful distinction among different understandings of the basic concepts that play roles in the problems it explored, followed by the distinction among several questions that one needs to ask about these concepts.

Indeed, much of the confusion in philosophy concerning the notions of individual and individuation, for example, arises because these terms are understood differently by different authors, vitiating any further discussion. *The poison of unclarity*, which is often regarded as *the virtue of depth*, is something I have never accepted willingly. Of course, I owed this to my training in medieval and scholastic philosophy, and more than anybody else to Suárez's uncompromising honesty and precision. In fact, I have repeatedly said that I learned to do philosophy by translating Suárez. He was a master of dividing an issue as a first step in the process of solving a philosophical problem, and a virtuoso when it came to devising arguments and objections against widely accepted philosophical opinions.

Of course, it is not surprising that he had read everything when it came to scholastic philosophy and had been heavily influenced by both Thomas Aquinas and William of Ockham. Owens was right when he said that everything could be found in Suárez. The best way to learn medieval and scholastic philosophy is to begin with Suárez and then work backward. This is what I did with individuation, and it was extraordinarily useful.

I owe an explicit interest in historiography to Peter Hare. In the late 1980s he organized a conference in Buffalo with the catchy title "Doing Philosophy Historically." Its aim was to explore ways of using the history of philosophy in philosophy and to determine which methods of doing so were good and which were bad. At the conference I presented a paper entitled "Philosophy and Its History," which in time turned into a plan for the book I subsequently wrote.

Of course, it made good sense for me to explore this topic. I had been working on the history of philosophy from the time I decided to become a philosopher and I had done some very serious historiographical work. But was the work I had been doing any good? What was its purpose and how was it related to doing philosophy? The resulting book is still the thickest volume devoted to the theoretical underpinnings of philosophical historiography available, and I flatter myself by still believing that it is the most systematic and the one that offers the most sensible and complete theory about philosophical historiography. It began with an ambitious introduction in which I argued that one way to bring about a rapprochement between the two schools of philosophy that dominate the field in the twentieth century, analytic and continental, is to engage the history of philosophy, for both have a history with many parts that coincide.

Does anyone want to disclaim Plato, Aristotle, and Kant as his or her philosophical ancestors? Besides, as Sellars put it so well in *Science and Metaphysics*: "The history of philosophy is the *lingua franca* which makes communication between philosophers, at least of different points of view, possible. Philosophy without the history of philosophy, if not empty or blind, it is at least dumb."

Following the introduction, I added chapters on an understanding of history, philosophy, and the history of philosophy; the relation between philosophy and its history; the justification and value of the history of philosophy; texts and their interpretation; uses and abuses of the history of philosophy; and the development of philosophical ideas. In each case I put forward major theses, often controversial, such as the ones presented in the first and fifth chapters. In the first I argued that historical claims include value judgments, a position disputed by those who argue that a completely disinterested approach to the history of philosophy is not only possible, but is the only one that should be properly used. I find this view unrealistic if one takes into consideration the history of the discipline and the fact that the mere choosing of a philosopher, a text, or a view to engage historically implies a point of view guided by an assessment of value.

In chapter 5, I presented what I call the Framework Approach. This is a method of doing history of philosophy that allows not only a contemporary understanding of the past but also makes possible the comparison of past philosophical views with other philosophical views, not only with contemporary views but also with other past historical views. The method or approach involves precisely the method I put into practice in *The Problem of Individuation in the Early Middle Ages*. It assumed that to do good history of philosophy one has to do it philosophically, because otherwise one would miss the philosophy in the history. The idea is to begin by formulating a philosophical problem, the various possible understandings of it, the various possible solutions to it, and the arguments for and against such solutions.

With this framework in hand, then, one can turn to particular texts and authors in order to see what they were trying to do, their successes and failures, as well as the lessons that a contemporary philosopher can gather from such a study. The history of philosophy is inevitable, but bad history of philosophy is all too often a reality. In order to understand the past we need to live it, and in the context of philosophy this means that the ideas in it must be alive for us.

It always surprises me that contemporary philosophers pay so little attention to the issues that can be raised concerning the relation of philosophy to its history. This seems to be a blind spot that extends not only to philosophy in the United States but in Latin America, Europe, and other parts of the world. The number of publications written on issues concerned with what I like to call "philosophical historiography" is very small. If we speak of books published in the last two decades, one can count their number published in English on one hand. And although the number of relevant articles is much larger, in comparison with most other philosophical fields, the number is still rather disappointing, and the articles tend to be concerned with a rather narrow range of topics.

This pattern is common throughout the twentieth century except perhaps for a flurry of activity that occurred around the mid-1980s when Charles Taylor and Richard Rorty were active, and when Peter Hare organized the aforementioned conference, which gathered the most salient group of philosophers to discuss this matter at the time.

It surprises me that philosophers generally pay little attention to these matters, first because in practice they regularly write about the work of other philosophers, whether living or dead. It is rare to find philosophers who do not do so. Indeed, it is almost a condition of getting published that one refer to, discuss, or criticize the work of other philosophers.

Moreover, it is not only in their publications that philosophers engage in the discussion of historical figures but also in the classroom, which is the locus of most of their activities as philosophers. A quick perusal of the majority of courses offered in undergraduate and graduate programs shows titles that suggest their content has to do with the history of philosophy, and even in courses that have topical titles that are not bent toward history, such as ethics or metaphysics, syllabi indicate that these nonhistorical topics are discussed in the context of texts from past philosophers that have become classic formulations of well-known philosophical positions.

The second source of my surprise is that on the rare occasions when philosophers mention philosophy and the history of philosophy in the same context, they generally draw a strong line between philosophy on the one hand and the history of philosophy on the other, and between philosophers and historians of philosophy.

Now, it is true that one can find differences between the approaches and methodologies used by philosophers who do not consider themselves to be historians, particularly when the historians are concerned with the development of good editions of works by past philosophers and with philosophers who are not engaged in that sort of activity. But not all historians of philosophy do textual work. The majority of them discuss the views of past philosophers and, when they do so, it is not always clear that they are doing something different from what those who do not consider themselves to be historians are doing.

The third cause of surprise is that the absence of interest in historiographical issues is not restricted to philosophers who do not consider themselves to be historians; it extends to those philosophers who do consider themselves to be historians of philosophy. My experience in graduate school in both Chicago and Toronto, the places where I received my graduate degrees, vouches for these judgments. In the 1960s, Chicago was among the top ten philosophy departments in the United States and its graduate program was regarded as the cutting edge of the field. The course offerings were both in philosophy and the history of philosophy—I remember a course on medieval philosophy, for example, and one on Kant, in addition to courses that were not considered to be historical, such as those on political philosophy and logic.

Considering this curriculum, one would have expected that there would have been some attempt among Chicago faculty and students to raise and answer some of the questions that explore the relations between philosophy and its history. But there was nothing of the kind.

Not a single course was offered, and not a single comment was made, in any of the courses I was taking at the time about historiographical issues. Perhaps this could be justified by arguing that the Chicago program was not particularly geared toward the history of philosophy, in spite of the presence of Richard McKeon in the faculty and the fact that other members of the faculty, such as Alan Gewirth, had publications on historical texts. However, this is not a satisfactory argument insofar as a nonhistorical bent would seem to require a discussion of the merits of teaching the many historical courses that were taught.

The situation was even more shocking in Toronto. At the time, the Pontifical Institute of Mediaeval Studies was considered the premier venue for the study of medieval philosophy in the world, and its founder, Etienne Gilson, was the kind of philosopher who not only wrote historical books on medieval philosophy, but also books that were considered to be nonhistorical. Yet again, not a single course was offered in Toronto that explored the issues raised by the history of philosophy in philosophy, and in the five years that I spent there I can't recall a single comment by a faculty member that dealt with historiographical issues.

The lack of concern with the relation between philosophy and its history seems particularly odd, because from the very beginning an interest in philosophy drew me to the study of its history, and the more I studied the history of philosophy, the more I was drawn to philosophy and philosophical historiography. Indeed, the reason I became a historian of philosophy was precisely because of my interest in philosophy, and the reason I became a philosopher was precisely because of my interest in the history of philosophy. This confirmed my belief that the divide between philosophy and the history of philosophy is, in fact, artificial.

So, yes, it is not right to say that the history of philosophy is necessary for philosophy insofar as one can engage in doing philosophy without engaging its history. For example, I can develop views about death that aim to be accurate, consistent, comprehensive, and supported by sound evidence, without prior knowledge of anyone else having done so.

Strictly speaking, the history of philosophy is not necessary for philosophy. Nonetheless, most philosophy is done as a result of a preceding history, for that history functions as a motive and testing ground for philosophical reflection. In the face of death we can ask questions and engage in reflections that end up in views that are classifiable as philosophy.

Nonetheless, most philosophy is prompted not only by pertinent phenomena such as death, but also by what others have said and thought about such phenomena. In other words, most philosophical reflection arises in a context where others have engaged in such reflection, whether those who are doing it acknowledge that what they are doing involves the history of philosophy or not.

In short, philosophy is generally done historically, and the history of philosophy requires doing philosophy not just because its object has to do with philosophy but also because one cannot understand the history of philosophical views without grasping their philosophical significance. Why, then, do many philosophers fail to recognize the role that the history of philosophy has in doing philosophy? And why do many historians of philosophy fail to recognize that they are doing philosophy when they are engaged in producing an account of its history?

One reason is the fear of being regarded as antiquarians. An antiquarian is someone who puts enormous value on antiquity, believing that an old philosophical view has some unique value because it is old. The rationale behind this perspective is not silly and cannot be easily dismissed in that the survival of ideas says much about their value. Ideas survive because they appeal in some way, such as that they have proved useful and enlightening.

For that reason, antiquarians believe that it is the job of the historian to safeguard the insights they reveal and to insulate them from biases and distortions that may have been added to them. The history of philosophy, so the argument goes, must be objective and pure, objective in that it reveals its object as it is, and pure in that it preserves it uncontaminated by accretions added to it through the ages. It is a mistake to view the philosophical past in terms of the present in that this requires such a past to cease to be what it actually was, becoming something else. And this, other philosophers believe, stands in the way of advancing the discipline and adapting it to new scientific discoveries. At the other extreme, some historians of philosophy reject engaging philosophy for fear of becoming anachronists, appearing to value originality for its own sake. A philosophical view is valuable in that it offers a new and fresh explanation of phenomena.

Conditions are always changing, and this requires that our views about the world also change. Reviving old ideas based on antiquated technologies and methods makes no sense unless they are adapted to the new circumstances, and then it is questionable whether they are really old ideas and not new ideas under the garb of old ones.

Just as happens in the field of science, philosophy must abandon past ideas even if they seem to have worked in the past. Philosophy should imitate science. Medicine today has no use for Hippocrates. We do not bleed people to cure them. Now we have drugs and procedures that are effective in fighting decease.

Likewise, philosophy should approach our new situation and forget the past. And if the past seems to offer something valuable to our contemporary concerns, we must begin by contextualizing it in the present so as to explore its relevance and usefulness. The history of philosophy is useful only if it is transformed to deal with our currents needs and concerns.

Paradoxically, both antiquarianism and anachronism may have a common root, namely, a historicist point of view. Historicism comes in two varieties. One is metaphysical and the other epistemic.

Metaphysical historicism is the view that historical facts are unique and irreproducible, because the conditions in which they take place are unique. Epistemic historicism derives from metaphysical historicism. Accepting that history is always unique, it argues that we cannot reproduce understandings of the world that have occurred at different times. Understanding the past is always misunderstanding it. Aristotle's understanding of substance is a unique event in history that would be impossible to reproduce in, say, my understanding of substance even if my aim were to reproduce Aristotle's understanding of it. This means also that the knowledge of substance I have can never match the one Aristotle had.

Both approaches are mistaken not because they misunderstand some of the difficulties posed by the relation between philosophy and its history, but because they drive a chasm between them. The sensible solution is not to follow their lead, but rather to understand the way that philosophy can play a role when we engage in doing history of philosophy, and the way that the history of philosophy can play a role when our goal is philosophical.

The essential factor in both is to keep two things in mind. The first is that our goal in both has to do with understanding, and second is that both philosophers and historians of philosophy carry with them a heavy baggage of assumptions and biases. The aim of both is to reach understanding and to eliminate as much as possible the baggage that they carry.

So, how can this be done? In my view by modifying the method that they use. I call the resulting method the "framework approach," although the framework for the historian is primarily conceptual and for the philosopher it is primarily historical. The fact that they are different and appear to originate in opposite procedures is the key not only to a deeper understanding of philosophy and its history, but also to avoiding the heavy baggage that each of them carries.

The framework approach that historians of philosophy need is conceptual. Good historical understanding should be based on good philosophical understanding. And how is this achieved? By developing a framework of concepts that can be used to understand the philosophical issue that prompted the inquiry.

One place that was attracted to my approach to philosophy and its history was the Institute for Philosophy in Liechtenstein. And they lost no time in trying to get me to accept an endowed chair and join them. This was a small institute, apparently well endowed by the country's prince. The location was extraordinary—at the top of the mountains in a hotel that had failed, it was close to heaven. The views from every angle were magnificent. In addition, they had a fine library, located in the town below, and a good number of European students. Their director, Joseph Seifert, was well known in Europe and a leader of the movement called phenomenological realism, and the Institute took students who paid tuition through the European Union.

Norma and I loved the place—for a vacation or a sabbatical it had no equal. But we both questioned the stay for an extended period of time. Besides, the position required a full-time presence and we were not sure about that. Of course, we wanted to explore it further before making any kind of arrangement. So I agreed to give a set of lectures there and take the opportunity to meet the students and staff more in depth. Seifert himself was a most charming host, in the Austrian style that is so captivating.

In addition to the lectures and some discussion of the details of the appointment, I asked about various issues, from Seifert's position and role at the institute to the financial situation of the entire enterprise. For me there was also the difficulty that this was more than anything else an Austrian operation, and I do not know German well enough to function effectively in this kind of environment. Naturally, everybody knew English well, but I was still uneasy. And I was concerned with the financial situation of the institute. The prince of Liechtenstein and his brother were major benefactors of the institute, so at a reception in my honor attended by the prince, I took the opportunity to raise with him some questions about the financial viability and future plans for the institute.

Unfortunately, my conclusion was that the institute was not in a sound financial situation. This meant, of course, that I could not give up my very sound position in Buffalo for a perilous one in Liechtenstein. It turned out that I was right, for the institute closed its doors in the hotel and moved to a house at the bottom of the mountain for lack of funds. I am not sure what has become of it, except for the fact that Seifert moved to Chile. For me a great result of this affair was that I met Daniel Novotny there and convinced him to apply to our program in Buffalo, where he wrote a brilliant PhD dissertation on beings of reason in the sixteenth century, and cooperated on some projects with me.

High school graduation day, with my mother, Leonila Gracia (Cuba 1960). Photograph courtesy of the author.

23

A Paradigm of Courage
(1971–1976)

From the time I entered the United States in 1961, I had made a life for myself independent of Cuba. I was alone in this country and had managed to move forward, both personally and in terms of a career. But this did not mean that I was out of touch with the very small pool of family members that still remained on the island, and particularly with my mother, who was left alone after the death of one of her sisters and felt desolate. To live under such circumstances required an enormous degree of courage, which my mother amply demonstrated.

Telephone conversations with her had become increasingly difficult and nothing of substance could be said in letters for fear of reprisals from the Castro regime. Indeed, as the Cuban Revolution continued to develop an increasingly intransigent and hard-core communist state, properties and assets were taken away from those who had owned them.

I heard about their difficulties and tribulations and their fears. I was particularly concerned with my mother. Her strength and her courage to remain optimistic about what looked like a bleak future was a profound example to me. It was difficult for me to understand how she could be so strong and help me in times when I felt lonely and exiled.

Mother's situation continued to deteriorate as time passed. By the late 1960s, she had been left with no resources except for Father's pension plus a few pesos a month to compensate for the loss of the rent from the apartment building the government had confiscated. She received nothing as compensation for the confiscation of our sugarcane plantation, the pharmacy in Havana, stocks and bonds, or the house in

Ciego de Avila (the town closer to what had been our plantation), the unfinished beach home, and other properties we had to abandon or that the government expropriated. What she received was barely sufficient for survival, but she managed by bartering and selling things: coffeepots, a set of dishes, linens, kitchen gadgets, tools, frames, pictures, lamps, books, jewels—anything that would fetch some money. My old school uniforms and clothing had long ago been recycled into clothing for my sister's children. Curtains had been used to make dresses for my mother, sister, grandmother, and aunts. The paraphernalia of my military school, swords, epaulets, medals, and hats, which my nephews used to play with, were also eventually sold or bartered.

By the late 1960s, Mother was running out of things to sell, and her needs and those of my sister Nena's family had increased dramatically. They were particularly hard hit when Nena and her family decided to ask for permission to emigrate to the United States, because the revolutionary government immediately fired her husband from his job and sent him, as was usual, to cut sugarcane in the provinces. This left Nena with no income and four children to feed. My mother was the only resource left in the family, and she also had to support my aging grandmother and her own sister, Maruca, who had moved in with Mother after her husband had died.

The situation was becoming desperate, but something came up that solved her financial plight. Although the Castro government was firmly entrenched and did not tolerate even the vaguest hint of dissent, there were Cubans both inside and outside Cuba who were betting on the fall of the government. Some of them had money stashed away, for which they had no use, so they began to speculate. They would buy properties that had been taken over by the government from their owners. This was all done on the black market, but satisfying all the requirements of Cuban law prior to the revolution. One of these people was interested in the sugarcane plantation and offered to buy it. The price was a small fraction of its value prior to 1959, the year Castro triumphed, but Mother felt that this was an opportunity that she could not pass up. Her situation did not allow it, and besides, she was convinced, as I was, that Castro was there to stay. Although Nena and her husband were opposed to this transaction, Mother insisted and eventually decided, wisely as we shall see, to proceed.

The transaction took some time. First the parties had to agree on a price, which included a substantial amount of pesos in cash and a number of jewels, including rings, gold bracelets, pendants, and other bibelots. Second, because I had inherited part of the plantation, I had to approve the transaction, which meant that some papers had to be sent to me to be signed and legalized in the United States before returning them to Mother so she could close the sale. The paperwork was complex, but eventually the needed documents were ready and the sale was carried out. Mother was elated; all her money worries were now over.

As was her custom, she gave 10 percent of the proceeds to her church. Then she distributed some money among my two aunts and my sister, Nena. Of what remained, she decided to put 35,000 pesos in a safe place, but it took her some thought to decide where. She did not want to put the money in the hole I had dug in one of the bathroom closet floors, where the silver and Father's handgun had been hidden for a while and where she had put the jewels that had been given as partial payment for the sugarcane plantation. The problem with this hiding spot was the humidity. Moreover, she did not want to put the money in any place where someone would think she would keep it. She spent most of her time at home, but she did go to church and occasionally to buy some things, and there was no security in her apartment. Finally, she thought of a place people would not think of. In her bedroom, in addition to her bedroom suite, she also kept a large sofa. So she made a hole in the cushions from below, pushed the money in through it, and then disguised the hole by sewing a piece of cloth over it first and then covering the entire back with another piece of cloth. That night she slept better than she had in years.

The money she had given Nena was sufficient to tide her and her family over for some years until they were allowed to leave Cuba, and the money Mother kept out of her hiding place was sufficient for her everyday needs. Echoing better times, she even used some of the money to replace some of the furniture that had become too shabby. And she contributed generously to her church and helped many people in need, apart from the original tithes she had given. She also used some of the money to get rid of my car just after Nena left for the United States.

My car had become a nightmare. The family sedan had been sold by Nena's husband after I left Cuba while such transactions were still allowed, and he began to use my car, which was newer and in better shape. But when my sister and her family left, Mother got the car back. The problem with having a car was that before Cubans were allowed to leave the island they had to turn in any cars they owned, and the cars had to be in working order. But my car had not had maintenance to speak of after Nena and her husband left in 1969, and Mother was trying to leave in 1976. The car would not start. It took all the expertise of a first-rate mechanic to get it started. Indeed, to get it to that point it was necessary to get some parts that were only available illegally, through bribes that had to be paid in various ways. When everything was done, the car barely moved, but a friend was able to drive it to the place where it was supposed to be handed over to the government, where it collapsed.

Some of the jewels that Mother had received as part of the payment for the sugarcane plantation had been used to defray the costs associated with the departure of Nena's family. It was not easy to get rid of valuable objects, because all sales were regarded as illegal. But thanks to the help of friends and the greed of corrupt government officials, everything worked out. We frequently complain about corruption, but sometimes corruption is a lifesaver.

After Nena's departure and our grandmother's death, Mother decided that it was time for her to leave Cuba. She got her papers together and, after many bureaucratic hurdles, finally came to the last stage, where approval of her departure was to take place. Naturally, we had sent her the cost of the airfare from Havana to Madrid. She had prepared everything carefully and presented herself to the appropriate government bureaucrat in charge of these matters.

After a long day of waiting, she was able to present her papers. Unfortunately, the person in charge told her that her departure could not be approved because she still owed the government 10,000 pesos from back taxes that Father had never paid. Imagine the shock. Mother could not understand this. Everything had been gone through carefully and was supposed to be in order. Still, there was nothing that could be done. The bureaucrat, with her sense of entitlement and authority, so common among those in power in Cuba, simply dismissed her. She said that she should return only if she had the 10,000 pesos in cash.

In spite of Mother's frustration, she felt that this was only a minor inconvenience, for she still had the 35,000 pesos she had stashed away in the sofa in her bedroom. Originally, she had intended to leave this money to her sister, but even if she had to pay 10,000 pesos, there would still be enough left for Maruca to live reasonably well until her death.

So Mother went home, turned the sofa over, ripped the cloth that covered the hole where the money was supposed to be, and looked inside.

Instead of the money, she found dust, small pieces of the money, and a nest of termites. The termites had eaten every peso; there was nothing left. Mother went into shock. What could she do? Where could she go to get the 10,000 pesos she needed?

Endless thoughts passed through her mind; she felt desolate, abandoned, lost. None of her children could lend her a hand, she hardly had any friends left, and this amount of money was just too large. As she was used to doing in the face of adversity, she fell on her knees and prayed.

Mother was a resourceful woman, she was strong, and she did not give up easily. She faced the facts and then devised a plan—just as my landlady Felina had done in Miami. She would sell everything she could, including a couple of pieces of jewelry she still had, and she would go around to everyone she knew and beg them to lend her the money with the promise that she would pay it back once she got out of Cuba. She went to everyone, all the members of our family, my uncles, particularly Carlos, who had been an associate of Father's, and anyone else she could think of.

With enormous effort she was able to put together 6,000 pesos. This was not enough, but her plan was to go back to the government office, present what she had, and beg for the love of God. (Of course, the appeal to God was not quite what would work with hard-core Marxists-Leninists.) She was all alone in the country, with no children or help, and she was old. She prayed that the officer would take pity on her and let her go. And if not, she was convinced God would perform a miracle.

In fear and trembling, she approached the fateful window where the documents were supposed to be presented and payments made. Her legs almost did not support her. She assured herself that God would help her in this moment of trial, but she really did not know the outcome. When she got to the window, the female clerk with whom she had dealt before was not there. A man had taken her place. Mother, not knowing what to do, kept quiet about the 10,000 pesos she had been told she needed and simply presented her papers and petition without mentioning that she had been there before. The man took a while to look through the papers. The silence was ominous and frightening. Mother could hardly stand, so weak was her certainty. And she used the little energy she had to appeal to Jesus. She was prepared to beg, cry, plead for mercy, and bring up her age. Eventually, the clerk said that everything was in order and stamped her papers, thus approving her request without asking for a single penny.

Walking out of that office Mother felt as if she had been delivered from a death sentence; it was a triumphal march. She could not believe what had just happened, but a renewed strength filled her. As was her custom she straightened herself, raised her head, and walked out as if she owned the place. She had won—although it was not her but God through her who had won. She was nothing without Him, but with Him she was all powerful and no abuse from corrupt petty bureaucrats or corrupt governments could prevail. And as she walked out she began to compose a poem, as she did every time she felt joy or pain.

Obviously, the previous officer was trying to cheat her. She had wanted the 10,000 pesos for herself for she had left no record in Mother's file that she owed anything. In my mother's view, God had safeguarded her. It was the miracle she had expected, a testimony to God's power and mercy. The trip home was glorious. The sun was shining, the birds were singing, and she saw everything in a new light. She would see her children again! When she got home, she returned all the money she had borrowed from family and friends and told them what had happened. She kept what was left from the sale of the jewels and just before leaving Cuba divided the money between her church and her sister.

My mother told me her story when she met me in the United States. As the religious person she was, she believed this was God's doing. I did not say anything, but I thought of the termites eating the money. Why did God allow them to do this deed and yet not allow the corrupt government official to cheat her? I did not ask her this because I knew what her answer would be: God's actions are mysterious. Clearly, for the faithful, faith trumps everything else.

Mother's arrival in the United States brought back many of my childhood memories of her. When I was small, I took great pride in Mother's appearance. I thought she was beautiful and she was always elegantly dressed. Although I did not know what elegant was, I surely noticed that she was dressed differently, and what seemed to me to be better, than other women. And she had flair, *salero*, as Spaniards call it. When she entered a room, everyone noticed. It was not the dress but the way she carried herself that caused this reaction—her back straight, her walk controlled, her demeanor that of a queen. But the dresses she bought helped too. She bought her clothing at the famous store El Encanto, which sold the latest Christian Dior designs in Havana.

My mother liked to go to Havana frequently. Although sometimes the entire family went at least a couple of times a year, she traveled to the city more often, with Nena who at the time was a teenager, sometimes staying for as long as a month. When the visits were shorter, I stayed at home with Aunt Maruca, my brother Ignacito, and Father. I missed her, and I vividly remember her returns. I recall one homecoming in particular. As usual, we had gone to the train station in Ciego de Avila to wait for her, and the train was late. I was anxious, angry that she had abandoned me for so long, and elated that she was coming back. Finally, the train made its way to the platform. A big, black steam locomotive, puffing, clanking, seemingly exhausted, like a great giant after a long run, ready to collapse.

The noise was overpowering, the whistles deafening. The behemoth finally stopped, and the porter brought out the portable stairs for passengers to disembark. Mother was one of the first. There she was. Her image is still vivid in my mind. Dressed in black, with a colorful orange collar of velvet decorated with black filigrees. I had never seen anything so fine. There was no one like her. She stood out like a diamond among coals, like a queen to be honored. This was my mother. I felt like the most important person in the world, proud because she was mine. And she singled me out. I was the first one she came to. Was there anything better than this?

Years later, after the Cuban Revolution had taken away everything we owned and Mother finally left Cuba, she spent a couple of months in Madrid, waiting for permission to enter the United States. She stayed in a *pensión*, where a high school friend of my wife went to visit her. Antonia, my wife's friend, reported that mother came out to see her dressed in very modest clothes, worn out by repeated use for over fifteen years in Cuba. Cubans had been suffering enormous deprivation since the revolution had triumphed, and in a country where food was scarce, all efforts were directed toward getting enough to eat, not clothing. Yet, in spite of the poor garments, Mother shined in her grace and demeanor. Antonia reported that the other pensioners affectionately referred to her as "my Queen." The saying goes that the clothes make the man, but I rather think that in Mother's case the woman made the clothes. When I heard Antonia's story, the memory of that meeting at the station years earlier unfolded again before my eyes, and I felt the same pride, deep and rewarding, because this incomparable woman happened to be my mother.

Epilogue

With a Diamond in My Mind

I began this memoir with a reference to a diamond I had hidden in one of the shoes I was wearing during my trip from Havana to West Palm Beach. The trip was of supreme importance because it was my only chance to escape from revolutionary Cuba, and the diamond was the only valuable possession I owned that I could sell in case of need. The diamond helped me face the fear of an uncertain future, and eventually I realized it had more than commercial value. Its true value was not only a matter of safety and security but of its power to reveal different aspects of my experience.

Thus, I conclude the book with a reference to the diamond in my mind, a diamond that is not a physical object but nonetheless continues to reveal unknown dimensions of my identity. Indeed, it could make the difference between life and death. Throughout history, persecuted refugees have often bribed their persecutors to make their escape possible. Entire groups of victims oppressed because of their religion, ethnicity, race, gender, or class, among other factors, have learned that a diamond is worth far more than its beauty. One of my friends tells me that a diamond facilitated the escape of a member of her family from Nazi Germany to neutral Switzerland during World War II.

Wearing a diamond in a ring may also make a difference in what others think of the one who wears it, for a diamond may represent wealth, taste, elegance, distinction, and pedigree, as well as just the opposite of these. A diamond is often used to signal difference from others in some ways, perhaps most often in that the wearer is engaged in a love relationship, having made promises and established bonds. In this sense, the diamond becomes a symbol of our relationships apart from the fact that it can open the possibility of buying basic necessities in moments of need and desperation.

The diamond that I carried in my shoe the day I left Cuba had many of these and other meanings and connotations. Apart from its value in times of necessity, it brought up memories of what Cuba had signified for me, of the woman who had worn it, my mother, and indirectly of the man who had given it to her, my father. It could represent the wound caused by their absence in my life as well as the risk I was taking should it be found by Cuban authorities on the day of my departure from the island. It was, then, a symbol of love and trust, of fear and peril, and the suffering that my mother and other compatriots who remained in Cuba would endure.

But there was an important distinction between its significance before I left Cuba and its significance after I had arrived in the United States. In terms of the latter, it could become a beacon of my future, the goals I would pursue, and the identity I would forge. And, of course, the diamond could refer to the treasures that my family had passed on to me, their values, generosity, sense of justice, love for each other, their education, and their wisdom. The diamond could represent everything that was valuable to me.

At first, it looked as if I were leaving Cuba a pauper, without anything of value. But in fact I was leaving loaded with riches that no one knew and that no one, including the Cuban authorities, could take away. The diamond in my shoe could serve a purpose that would be critical in some moment of desperation and need. I am talking about the love and education that my family had passed on to me and that survived in my thoughts and behavior. In short, and contrary to appearances, I was rich rather than poor, and my job in the future would consist of investing wisely the treasure I would safely guard.

The diamond, then, is symbolically central to the present narrative. It stands for the narrative itself and for the memories to which it also points in the facets that illuminate us. Its central location at the beginning and end of the narrative points not only to the past and the present, but also to the future. It brings me back to the time I spent in my native land and to my experiences after I left it, my life as a philosopher, and my search for the new life and identity I hoped to develop when I came to the United States.

This should not be surprising insofar as wisdom, the eternal goal of philosophers, and diamonds are both intrinsically desirable and justify the search for beauty, purity, incorruptibility, and truth. A diamond, like wisdom, is a valuable treasure that must be guarded carefully, as we do with our most appreciated treasures.

Thinking about a diamond and its properties has led me to understand the search for identity that has informed my life as a philosopher and as an immigrant in America. It has shown me that in moments of crisis, the contemplation of a single goal like a diamond, as Buddhist sages believe, can help strengthen one's resolve to continue the search in a more tangible way than in the abstractions that sometimes obscure the path forward.

Indeed, the few moments in which we reach immortality by understanding a universal truth resemble the moment in which we look at a diamond and marvel at its perfection, its multifaceted structure, and its inner strength. And when the diamond that we observe is still in the rough, in need of further refining, we can compare these moments to the times in which we realize that the search for identity and wisdom is hard, never ends, and rewards us with precious brief moments of immortality. At such moments the truth of a thought is precious. The diamond in my mind consists in fact, in a philosophy that integrates the values, principles, and truths learned over a lifetime and which, as my former student William Irwin pointed out, "helps develop the virtues of wisdom, patience, tolerance, and a thick skin," all of which make our lives dear and fruitful.

With Norma and grandchildren (*from left*) James Griffin, Clarisa Griffin, Sofia Taberski, and Eva Taberski. Photograph courtesy of the author.

Acknowledgments

I am grateful to my family, especially Norma, my wife of fifty-three years, for their support and encouragement as I worked to complete this project.

I am grateful to many friends, colleagues, and former students who read parts of this manuscript at various stages of completion. Their reactions, suggestions, criticisms, and encouragement were invaluable. I am deeply indebted to all of them, but particularly to the following: Rosemary Feal, William Irwin, Iván Jaksić, Carolyn Korsmeyer, José María Medina, Vicente Medina, Justin Murray, Amy Oliver, Gregory Pappas, Stephanie Rivera-Berruz, Paul Vincent Spade, and Manuel Vargas.

I am particularly grateful to Rebecca Colesworthy, acquisitions editor for SUNY Press, for her interest in this project, and to Debra Kolodczak, my digital media manager at the Capen Chair, for her assistance in preparing the materials and images used in this edition.

www.ingramcontent.com/pod-product-compliance
Lightning Source LLC
Chambersburg PA
CBHW030531230426
43665CB00010B/844